Critical Essays
on Alice Walker

Critical Essays on Alice Walker

Edited by
Ikenna Dieke

Contributions in Afro-American and African Studies, Number 189

GREENWOOD PRESS
Westport, Connecticut • London

Library of Congress Cataloging-in-Publication Data

Critical essays on Alice Walker / edited by Ikenna Dieke.
     p. cm.—(Contributions in Afro-American and African
studies, ISSN 0069–9624 ; no. 189)
   Includes bibliographical references (p.) and index.
   ISBN 0–313–30012–7 (alk. paper)
   1. Walker, Alice, 1944– —Criticism and interpretation.
2. Women and literature—United States—History—20th century.
3. Afro-Americans in literature. I. Dieke, Ikenna, 1949–
II. Series.
   PS3573.A425Z6   1999
   813′.54—dc21   98–37719

British Library Cataloguing in Publication Data is available.

Library of Congress Catalog Card Number: 98–37719
ISBN: 0–313–30012–7
ISSN: 0069–9624

First published in 1999

Greenwood Press, 88 Post Road West, Westport, CT 06881
An imprint of Greenwood Publishing Group, Inc.
www.greenwood.com

Printed in the United States of America

The paper used in this book complies with the
Permanent Paper Standard issued by the National
Information Standards Organization (Z39.48–1984).

10 9 8 7 6 5 4 3 2 1

To my wife, Josephine,
and my children, this book
is affectionately dedicated

Contents

Introduction: Alice Walker, A Woman Walking into Peril

Ikenna Dieke

Few twentieth-century American writers have left their imprint on several generations of readers as Alice Walker has. From the time she emerged on the literary scene in 1968 with the publication of her first volume of poetry, *Once*, to the present, Walker appears to have been imbued with an insistent, almost dour and sacrificial determination to tell the truth, a truth that has insistently and consistently evoked contradictory feelings in her readers. To some readers, a growing circle of detractors and die-hard traditionalists, many of them black cultural nationalists and Black Muslim brotherhood, her writing is nothing but a witch's brew, ever troublesome and woeful, threatening the essential foundation of traditional lore. For these readers, Walker remains, at bottom, a writer set apart from the cloddish world by her heightened capacity for feeling —a cloddish world, that is, all too willing to employ flatulent rhetoric, to utter imprecations and frenzied diatribes under its smouldering breath. To others, a coterie of encomiastic enthusiasts, friends, and admirers, her creative energy is nothing but a godsend, a sacramental vessel through which the redemption of women in general, and African American women in particular, is and will be forever consummated. And to still others, an old order of moral purists, Walker's writing, with its "decadent" thought and sensibility, is a brazen profaning of the old "sacred shrines" and the "gods" that dwell in them, and thus must be expunged from the public school curriculum. Let us examine in brief some of the grieved outcries of the first and third groups of readers.

For these readers, their anger and hostility toward Alice Walker rests largely on her third and most polemical novel, *The Color Purple* (1982), and its film adaptation by Hollywood filmmaking guru, Steven Spielberg (1985), a work they claim distorts black history, demeans black men, and leaves in its "savage" wake a most deleterious impression of blacks. From the irate Black Muslim brothers led by Louis Farrakhan's former national spokesperson, Dr. Khallid Muhammed, who filed past Walker at a 1987 Founders' Day ceremony at Spelman College, to the NAACP-supported protesters in Los Angeles picketing *The Color Purple* film's premiere, Walker appeared headed for calumny, even demonization of the worst kind. In print reviews of both novel and film, the same passionate intensity was frighteningly evident. For example, in a January 1986 review in the *New York Times*, E. R. Shipp summarizes why people are mad at Walker, particularly her "mephistophelian" collaboration with Spielberg. First, they charge Walker with gross historical distortion. Second, they fault her for misrepresenting blacks, especially black men in America, even to the point of denying them *agency*. And third, they accuse Walker of collusion with white oppressors in order to blame the victim—black people (A13).[1]

Other critics were equally vociferous, turned off, as it were, by the seeming ribaldry and impieties in Walker's writing. Courtland Milloy was particularly upset over what he saw as a calculated and insidious attempt by Hollywood film-makers, aided and abetted by Walker herself, to cast the black man in his most sexual incontinence and moral turpitude. He declared: "As far as I'm concerned, I don't have to see this movie to write about it" (B13).[2] In a somewhat strident *argumentum ad hominem* review of *The Color Purple* as film, Pauline Kael accused Walker of "rampant female chauvinism" (69). John Simon's rhetoric was even more opprobrious. To him, the Spielberg film was nothing but "an infantile abomination," and the novel itself an overvalorized tinsel literary work "unable [finally] to transcend the two humanly legitimate but artistically burdensome chips on its shoulders—feminism and Black militancy" (56). In a fit of vituperation, David Demby described *The Color Purple* as a "quick, heart-pounding read," a "candy passing itself off as soul food" (56). The movie version faired no better; Demby called it "a hate letter to Black men" (56). William Willimon was equally upset, insisting that the novel could "only have been created by a writer more interested in writing a polemic than a novel" (319). Spike Lee, commenting on the parallel ends of Walker's and Ntozake Shange's writings, suggested that perhaps the only reason *The Color Purple* was selected by Hollywood was precisely that it perpetuated the long-standing Euro-American imaging of black men as "one-dimensional animals," adding that "the quickest way for a Black playwright, novelist, or poet to get published has been to say that Black men are shit. If you say that, then you are definitely going to get media, your book published, your play done—Ntozake Shange, Alice Walker" (qtd. Glicksman 48).

And yet, judged by every conceivable set of dialectic canons, Walker's escutcheon remains mightily unscathed. Few people would deny that Alice Walker's singular achievement as a writer rests inarguably, and perhaps immutably, on her articulate capacity to inscribe black womanism, the discourse of which some of her vitriolic critics might have wished had remained an immanent token in the "transcendent" logos of a patriarchal and racist culture. She herself had said that her one overriding preoccupation was "the spiritual survival, the survival *whole* of my people. But beyond that, I am committed to exploring the oppressions, the insanities, the loyalties, and the triumphs of black women" (O'Brien 192). She once spoke candidly of her solidarity with a number of women writers, such as Bessie Head, Kate Chopin, the Brontë sisters—Charlotte and Emily—Simone de Beauvoir, Doris Lessing, and of course, Zora Neale Hurston, and others, and of her admiration for their courage and their vision, the vision to rise above their oppression by searching unceasingly for a kind of deliverance. For Walker the path to inscribing this womanism is like a dire strait fraught with danger and cultural demons. But it is a risk and a burden she is fully prepared to take and bear with courage and tenacity aforethought.

More than anything else, Walker sees herself as a lone exorcist battling the demons lurking in the hallways and mindways of institutional establishment, an establishment that, in all intents and purposes, has shoehorned women, especially black women, into a dark alley, resigned them to a fixed, reified, "profane" level of existence, and subsequently corralled them at the short end of a very long, ponderous stick.

Ursula K. LeGuin has said that

nothing is more personal, more unshareable, than pain; the worst thing about suffering is that you suffer alone. Yet those who have not suffered, or will not admit that they suffer, are those who are cut off in cold isolation from their fellow men. Pain, the loneliest experience, gives rise to sympathy, to love: the bridge between self and other, the means of communion. So with art. The artist who goes into himself most deeply—and it is a painful journey—is the artist who touches us most closely, speaks to us most clearly. (qtd. Schechter and Semeiks 446)

Lorraine Hansberry, writing on the very end of art, suggests that every serious artist is a didacticist par excellence and that all serious art is, in a foundational sense, social. And social art, she continues, is "that which agitates and that which prepares the mind for slumber. The writer is deceived who thinks that he has some other choice. The question is not whether one will make a social statement in one's work—but *what* the statement will say" (5).

One cannot think of an apter, more pertinent description of Walker's art than LeGuin's and Hansberry's statements already afford. Even Walker herself has said that "the gift of loneliness is sometimes a radical vision of society or one's people that has not previously been taken into account" (O'Brien 204). Thus Walker's art is an art borne of pain and bred in social specifying, emanating from an inexorable didactic impulse that lies brittle in the deep gorges of a wounded self—a self that is private, feminine, and social. And yet remarkably, it is the one element, the truly lively image, that draws us passionately to her. It is the treasure that we are blessed with in her first novel, *The Color Purple,* and even in her fifth, *Possessing the Secret of Joy.* Through her art, Walker, like the wise old man Carl, alias Mzee, in *Possessing,* reminds us of what all of us, regardless of race, gender, class, sexual or ideological orientation, have in common—the region of the mind/body that lies beyond the narrow, brightly lit domain of consciousness. It is to this domain that each of us must constantly return in order to understand, even if only vicariously, the wrong and injustice that lies at the very heart of female immanent existence.

Female circumstance, especially black female circumstance, with its "contrary instinct/contrariness of will" is the Alice Walker turf, a turf distilled in a number of familiar thematic motifs. One such motif is the regenerate self, the belief by Walker that it is possible for human beings to transform themselves. It is a belief rooted in the triune mythic drama of birth, death, and rebirth. Walker's writing is graced with characters who undergo inner development and maturation, and in the and in the process abandon their old attitudes and assumptions. Other characters simply leave their former empty, wretched existence and embrace an entirely new lease of life. Characters such as Grange Copeland in *The Third Life of Grange Copeland*, Truman Held in *Meridian,* Albert and Celie in *The Color Purple,* and Suwelo in *The Temple of My Familiar*, leave behind what seems like an outmoded existence or established patterns of orientation and behavior to embrace a new philosophy of life. At times, this regenerative spirit in Walker takes on a certain reincarnational meaning. Here the author plays with the idea that when a person dies, her soul returns momentarily to its primal, extraterrestrial origin prior to being dispatched back to earth to indwell another body, usually (though not necessarily) human. Lissie, in *The Temple of My Familiar*, is probably the most memorable character possessing this unique power to incarnate successively, lifetime after lifetime.

Another familiar motif of Walker, somewhat akin to the rebirth theme, is that of the questing self. At the root of most of Walker's writing is the penultimate sense that human life is a journey, a continuing process of growth and discovery. Quite often the journey takes place on a hard Walker road, the kind of journey on the hard, rocky road of life alluded to by J. R. R. Tolkien in *The Fellowship of the Ring*. Tolkien writes: "At least none can foretell what will come to pass, if we take this road or that road. But it seems to me now clear which is the road that we must take. Now at this last we must take a hard road, a road unforeseen. There lies our hope, if hope it be. To walk into peril." (qtd. Schechter and Semeiks 320). Walking into peril is exactly what most of Walker's characters and personae are doing as they each seek to navigate their own path of fulfillment, a crooked path gravid with dangers, possibilities, changes, personal adventures, triumphs—big and small—and, of course, occasional setbacks. Many of them seem endowed with special attributes. Some, like Celie, show remarkable courage in the face of adversity and abuse. Others, like Grange Copeland, Meridian, and Truman Held, embody strength and dedication. And yet others, like Lissie and Tashi, demonstrate imagination and resilience. Walker singularly imagines each one of them enacting her or his own monomyth as an authentic heroic self, without for a moment pretending that the path to each character's fulfillment or self-actualization/redemption could be anything less arduous. In fact, for some of them, self-redemption is troped in the cradles of personal suffering, and distilled peculiarly in the form of gaining mature wisdom, achieving a permanent sense of atonement, and returning "home" with a unique gift for one's loved ones.

A third familiar motif in Alice Walker's writing has to do with what Barbara Christian identifies as "a sense in which the 'forbidden' in the society is consistently approached by Walker as a possible route to truth" (40). Christian calls this particular characteristic Walker's "contrariness," insisting that it is a direct function of the author's readiness to impugn old, witless assumptions, to call to question outmoded social and cultural beliefs, and to rethink those beliefs in light of her own life encounters and circumstances. In another essay, I have suggested that this kind of radical disposition is consistent with Walker's consuming attempt to understand herself, which in turn is predicated upon, even imbricated, within a kind of personalist idealism, an idealism that lies beyond axiological or moral categories (Dieke 8–9). It is an idealism that celebrates autonomy as a fundamental individual right. It is an idealism of the self that Mihaly Csikszentmilhalyi has identified as "the autotelic self—a self that has selfcontained goals" (207). It is a self that fiercely asserts and guards the validity and integrity of her own experience, a validity and integrity that requires no other validation except that the self be wholly content.

The fourth motif of Walker, somewhat antonymous to the third, relates to the subject we have touched on earlier—the ubiquity of pain in Walker's writing. Quite often this pain results from the lyric cry of a sundered, stunted black feminine self. Walker has, since her debut as a writer, been concerned, even discomforted, by the systematic stifling of the creative impulse of black people, especially black women artists. According to Mary Helen Washington, this concern has led Walker to attempt to construct the black woman's history—"the woman suspended, artist thwarted and hindered in her desires to create, living through two centuries when her main role was to be a cheap source of cheap labor in the American society" (41). Black poet June Jordan has called these black women "black-eyed Susans—flowers of the blood-soaked American soil" (qtd. Washington 40).[3]

A fifth motif in Walker's writing concerns the narratology of the subliminal ego in creative process. In this regard, Walker assumes the role of the avant-garde artist willing to experiment, to flirt with the domain of the objective psyche far below the threshold of conscious awareness. It is a creative act that produced the collage technique of her second novel, *Meridian*, the psychoanalytic structure of *Possessing the Secret of Joy*, and the ubiquity of the aboriginal (i.e., archetypal) self in *The Temple of My Familiar*. Washington has said that "though Walker does not neglect to deal with the external realities of poverty, exploitation, and discrimination, her stories, novels, and poems most often focus on the intimate reaches of the inner lives of her characters; the landscape of her stories is the spiritual realm where the soul yearns for what it does not have" (38). We recall an interview granted by Walker to John O'Brien in which she confessed her fascination with a novel, *The Concubine*, written by a prominent African novelist from Nigeria, Elechi Amadi. Walker believes that Amadi is a unique writer because in his works he explores the subconscious dimensions of the corporate life of his people, their *collective unconscious.*[4]

The sixth and final motif in Walker's writing is the emphasis on the unity and interconnectedness of all life—human, vegetable, animal—what we identify as the holistic (as opposed to the mechanistic) view of life. There is always in Walker's art an abiding faith, in fact—a yearning for such a view, a yearning that assumes a myriad of elemental forms. These include, but are not limited to, the quest for what Walker herself has called "the human touch," a kind of sympathetic human community; the sacramental value of the past, the continuum between ancient and modern; ancestorism, which Robert Farris Thompson in *African Art in Motion* defines as "the belief that the closest harmony with the ancient way is the highest of experiences, the force that enables a man to rise to his destiny" (qtd. Witt

462); the belief in rebirth and reincarnation, "which unites living vitality with orientation toward the ancestral" (qtd. Witt 462); animism, the belief in the spiritual vitality of the natural world; ecofeminism, the belief in the nurturing balance or interdependent relations between humans, animals, and the ecosystem; and finally, female bonding, or what has been stylized as the "sistern mystique"—black sisterhood to the rescue with security, affability, and protection.[5]

Walker's struggle to contest patriarchy and racism and black male failings has, within its painful rhetoric, as she herself has said, "survival whole." The motif of survival whole in turn subserves a private proverbial phrase—"Pygmalion in reverse." The phrase itself was once employed by Walker to describe Brownfield, Mem's almost diabolical and pathological husband in *The Third Life of Grange Copeland*.[6] Pygmalion was the king of Cyprus, and a celebrated sculptor. Thoroughly disgusted with the debauchery of females, he developed an aversion for women and resolved never to marry. He bestowed his affection upon a beautiful marble statue of a lovely girl, fell in love with the statue, and prayed to Aphrodite to give it life. Aphrodite changed the statue into a woman, Galatea, whom Pygmalion married (Zimmerman 224).

Like Pygmalion, Brownfield sets out to cut and mold an object of his sexual and violent desires, his own love slave—Mem. Like the statue of Pygmalion, Mem has become not really a wife—a lifelong partner—but instead a sculptured mimicry of self, something set before Brownfield's warped mind so as to be apprehended solely in reified relations. Walker puts it this way: "Everything about her he changed, not to suit him, for she had suited him when they were married. He changed her to something he did not want, could not want, and that made it easier for him to treat her in the way he felt she deserved. A fellow with an ugly wife can ignore her, he reasoned. It helped when he had to beat her too" (*The Third Life of Grange Copeland* 57).

Thus for Walker, the phrase "Pygmalion in reverse" has become a carefully tailored, private metaphor, an intensional trope for describing two parallel and/or divided processes in gender relations. The first process involves the archaic male propensity to construct women in agnate cultural terms. In this connection, women become the unessential, immanent objects to be controlled and manipulated at will by "transcending" men. The second and the more important process involves the exercise of the contrary will of women to overthrow or subvert this traditional perception, to break the knotted "jinx" put on women by patriarchal culture. In a larger sense, the will is to undermine the traditional representation of reality or ways of knowing inimical to womanist instincts. In brief, "Pygmalion in reverse" is a sententious expression of Walker's revisionary temper, a temper largely imbricated in feminine ego as apostate, an ego, though faithless to male allegiance, that remains faithful to breaking the mold of the woman as the mule of the world.

The phrase is also in direct opposition to the proscriptive ideology of those whom Richard Wesley has called "the guardians of the Black image" (90). For these putative guardians, there is an unspoken pact or covenant among black writers regardless of gender or ideological persuasion. The terms of this covenant, explains Mel Watkins, are that black writers must never bare "aspects of inner-community life that might reinforce damaging racial stereotypes already proffered by racist antagonists" (36). Watkins declares: "Those Black women writers who have chosen Black men as a target have set themselves outside a tradition that is nearly as old as Black American literature itself. They have, in effect, put themselves at odds with what seems to be an unspoken but almost universally accepted covenant among Black writers" (36).

But the covenant Watkins speaks about may be more of a myth than reality, and may in fact be a tawdry pretext for perpetuating black male domination. So by coining the phrase "Pygmalion in reverse," Walker is clearly signaling her opposition to what Jacqueline Bobo characterizes as Watkins's "avuncular pronouncements" (338). It is an opposition to the call to tread the same old beaten path. But like Frost, Walker would rather diverge to the path not taken; her desire would rather be guided by what she herself has called "contrariness of will" (Bobo 340), a contrariness of will that Barbara Christian regards as inhering in "a philosophical orientation," a heretical act of courage, "and radical revisioning that challenges traditional definitions and acts for the common good" (qtd. Bobo 341). This contrariness of will is exactly what Henry Louis Gates has in mind when he discusses Walker's radical imagination, an imagination that seeks to "step outside the white hermeneutical circle" (258) and that employs (as in *The Color Purple*) the speakerly language in ironic context (255). Thus the essays that follow represent a concerted effort to delineate Alice Walker's contrary will in all its strategic manifestations.

In a provocative retread, Abend-David suggests that Linda Abbandonato's reading of *The Color Purple* as a text which attacks the bourgeois mentality that Samuel Richardson's *Clarissa* endorses is flawed. His basic contention is that in many respects the two texts espouse the same conviction, insisting that Walker's achievement in coupling social resistance and moral self-sufficiency with the prospect of practical success and self-satisfaction represents a throwback, of sorts, to *Clarissa*. But while not advocating a totalizing critical canon, Abend-David, however, makes an intelligent case for reading contemporary works such as *The Color Purple* within the broadest possible context/intertext of prior works that are germane to women's experience in general.

David Cowart suggests that Walker's "Everyday Use" is a study in dis-simulation involving a sassy but calculating young protagonist who, though quick to upbraid others for their "unenlightened" approach to heritage, remains largely outside the orbit or orchestration of its relational sentiments. Using Henry Louis Gates's theory of the Signifying Monkey, Cowart concludes that "Everyday Use" is Walker's signifying on the pretensions and pieties of die-hard Africanists and black nationalists as well as the dominant culture's attempts to thwart African American yearnings.

Catherine A. Colton reads *The Color Purple* as a rhetorical work grounded in the African American voodoo and conjure tradition. Her thesis is that language is employed by Walker as an instrument of discovery, the discovery of what means to be fully human and feminine in the sense of having the capacity for personal freedom and initiative.

Like Cowart, Margaret D. Bauer also examines the implications of how a minority person, especially a woman, faced with the despotic benevolence of the dominant culture, constructs an authentic identity. In an illuminating comparison of Walker's "Diary of an African Nun," Dunbar-Nelson's "Sister Josepha," and Native American writer Louise Erdrich's "Saint Marie," Bauer argues that quite often the minority woman in a largely agnate and Eurocentric world is left with limited choices for self-fulfillment and self-definition, most of which, regrettably, in any case, are no more than Hobson's choices at best.

E. Ellen Barker suggests the one way, perhaps the most compelling means, through which women, especially black women, can begin to free themselves from the torturing confines of agnate culture that Bauer discusses. Female bonding—that special interractive isodynamics among women. Focusing on the Celie-Shug mentor relationship in *The Color Purple*, Barker argues that the realm of possibility and the hopeful vision that the novel celebrates is directly related, in fact engendered, by the exercise of the womanist instinct, sympathetic womanist relatedness.

Both Thielmann and Kelly examine the place of men in Walker's writing. While Thielmann expresses concern that a positive portrayal of men in Walker's latter novels, *The Temple of My Familiar* and *Possessing the Secret of Joy,* because it represents something startlingly contrary to expectation and because it may signal a caving in on the part of Walker to male demands rather than the demands of her art, may in fact end up compromising the "woman question," Kelly is confident that the flame of the "woman question" will never be extinguished because womanist perspective will always guarantee for Walker the survival and wholeness of an entire people and provide a sane alternative to a culture that valorizes hierarchical and invidious distinctions, sadistic strength, duplicity, and perilous meanness.

While Thielmann and Kelly ponder the rights, privileges, and perils of gender, Jeffrey Lamar Coleman reaches out for the human and deontological dimensions of Walker's revolutionary poetry. Convinced that, for the most part, Walker's poetry is a political act of personal and collective redemption, Coleman then contends that the interconnection between cultural consciousness and social change rests on deconstructing contemporary feminist histriography with the aim of securing for human beings, especially women, their fundamental civil and human rights.

Marc—A Christophe, using the existentialist discourse of Simone de Beauvoir in *The Second Sex*, reads *The Color Purple* as a work that formulates a dialectic dyad, a manichean conception of self in consciousness. On the one hand is the transcendent, dominant ego—the male; on the other, opposed to it, is the immanent, unessential consciousness—the female. The net result is that the former is seen as the defining subject, the latter as the defined, reified object. This is the basic antinomian conception in feminist existentialism. Christophe suggests that *The Color Purple,* however, moves beyond this antinomy by having the woman Celie refuse her Otherness and immanence and insist on participating in her own naming, thus ensuring her triumph over sexism and social determinism.

Felipe Smith is concerned about how Alice Walker's art is shaped by an immanent purpose, insisting that the one impression that emerges from reading Walker is that of a literary-cum-artistic process as something conceived as determined by the utility and/or design of the author herself. Smith says that for Walker the end of art is salvation and redemption; in other words, salvation as the affect of artistic and womanist agency. And this soteriological canon seems to be the afferent force of Walker's creative imagination. Smith concludes by saying that Walker's complex intertextual strategy of redemptive and soteriological art involves her two most cherished literary forebears—Jean Toomer and Zora Neale Hurston.

The relationship between the redemptive and regenerative process and quilt-making in Alice Walker is the focus of both Priscilla Leder's and Judy Elsley's essays. Convinced that *The Color Purple* is a great all-American quilt, Leder argues that Walker both appropriates and deconstructs American literary traditions in an attempt to visualize a harmonious and interdependent community. For her part, Elsley suggests that quilt-making in Walker's *The Color Purple* is a trope for Walker's deconstructive temper and for understanding the paradox that in order to find the self one would have to lose the self. In the final analysis, Elsley maintains, quilt-making is therapeutic, because it is interwoven with the whole elemental process of restoration and wholeness so central to the novel's realm of valorizing signification.

Ruth D. Weston joins issues with the assertion that Alice Walker is linked to Walt Whitman because both in their poetry presumably celebrate a sense of the self. While concurring that Walker's song of the self is as much an indulgent celebration as Whitman's, Weston, however, insists that the vision of reality that gave rise to such commemoration is different for each writer. Where Whitman envisions a utopian commonweal of gender equality, argues Weston, Walker, on the other hand, begins by contemplating a dissonance, at the center of which is the unsettling irony of an undervalued and violated female self. So in a sense, Weston is suggesting that, contrary to the insistent view of many critics, Walker's poetry is, by and large, by reason of gender, race, epoch, and/or received tradition, a revision of Whitman's.

Ikenna Dieke reads Walker's fourth novel, *The Temple of My Familiar*, essentially as an incarnation of ecological idealism. Dieke claims that in the novel, Walker, relying on African traditional worldview, transcends binary opposition and constructs a complex holistic triad of time, nature, and self "in which humans, animals and the whole ecological order coexist in a unique dynamic of pancosmic symbiosis."

The odyssey that is this collection ends on a relatively lighter note with two essays: Priscilla L. Walton's and Ikenna Dieke's. Against the overwhelming critical concensus that *The Color Purple* remains at bottom a bleak novel, Walton posits that, in the final analysis, "the ideal 'womanist' world in which it culminates is joyous and celebratory—a condition of the comic." Dieke examines Walker's "earthling subjectivity" in her poetry. His conclusion is that the essential elements of Walker's earthling imagination include a flair for the commonplace, an impassioned celebration of nature, an intense exploration of the self, and the use of restrained verbal and satirical wit, all of that a revisionary throwback to the low mimetic mode of eighteenth-century English and American literature.

Alice Walker's art is like an exorcist ritual of communion, with terror as its damnation and wholeness its saving grace. It sounds more like an ecumenical service or high mass, with Walker as chief priestess or celebrant, or as she has previously described herself, *medium*, and the readers as concelebrants. In a conjurer's incantatory act of defiance, she leads her congregation (readers) on a fateful journey or dark night of the soul, each one, in propria persona, bearing her own insignia of pain, beyond the marbled archway (female pedestal), each one exorcising the demons that lurk deep in her/his heart, and cleaning up our Augean stables inhabited by a powerful "evil" jinni incarnate in oppressive patriarchy and other forms and varieties of agnate culture that seem to have usurped the female ambit. At the end, though, the demons are banished and peace descends. And out of the torturing inferno, the woman or womanist ego emerges, whole and fulfilled. Walker's art asserts inexorably her own unique peremptory claim to the notion of fulfillment and knowledge of the black woman's turf, ego, and circumstance.

In the John O'Brien interview of 1973, Alice Walker had expressed the hope that

someday a generation of men and women will arise who will forgive me for such wrong as I do not agree I do, and will read my work because it is a true account of my feelings, my perception, and my imagination, and because it will reveal something to them of their own selves. They will also be free to toss it—and me—out of a high window. They can do what they like. (203)

It is equally the sincere hope of the editor and contributors of this collection that after the dust has settled and the ululations of critics and detractors have quietened down, those of us who still believe in the unimpeded, free reign of the imagination will continue to savor the gift that is Alice Malsenior Walker and to lift our voices in an impassioned concelebration of her remarkable prehensility.

I would like to express my sincere appreciation to each and everyone remotely and/or immediately connected with the fruitful outcome of this book. They include all the essayists whose timely response to the advertised national call for papers made it possible for the project to hit the ground running; the other contributors whose fine essays had appeared previously in refereed journals; Ahmadou Bocar N'Diade   a doctoral candidate in anthropology, University of Arizona— for being such an indispensable graduate associate; the staff at the Humanities Computing and Technology Center, University of Arizona, for their help with scanning significant portions of the manuscript; Jessie Fryer, administrative assistant in the Department of Educational Psychology, University of Arizona, for an excellent typing job; Mary Ann Laverty of Hampton University and Margaret Bristow of Benedict College, for generously sharing some of their seasoning thoughts about black women writing in general and Alice Walker in particular; Shirley McDowell, former administrative assistant in the African American Studies Program, University of Arizona, for her indispensable logistical support; all the staff at Greenwood Publishing Group who contributed immensely to the production of this book, especially Elisabetta Linton, Assistant Humanities

Editor, Leanne Jisonna, Assistant Manager of Editorial Administration, Heidi L. Straight, Production Editor, and Jackie Remlinger, copyeditor.

Finally, I wish to thank most especially my family, my wife and children, for their most wonderful support, prayers, and sacrifice, without which this project might not have come to fruition.

NOTES

1. The information about the Los Angeles picketers, the Spelman College incident, as well as the E. R. Shipp review was all culled from Cheryl B. Butler, "*The Color Purple* Controversy: Black Woman Spectatorship" *Wide Angle* 13.3 & 4 (July–October 1991): 63–64.

2. Milloy so hated the film that he snapped: "Here is the holiday season, when families are out looking for something to do together, and Hollywood brings us a story that has a black man raping his daughter and selling the children to an adoption agency" (B13).

3. This statement is also quoted in Mary Helen Washington, "An Essay on Alice Walker," p. 40.

4. In fact, in the same interview, Walker spoke of a handful of other African writers she hoped would influence her. Among them are Okot p'tek, Camara Laye, Bessie Head, and so forth. Walker was convinced that these writers did not appear to be afraid of fantasy, of myth and mystery. She declared: "Their work deepens one's comprehension of life by going beyond the bounds of realism. They are like musicians: at one with their cultures and their historical subconscious" (O'Brien 200).

5. According to Cheryl B. Butler, "sistern" is the Black English vernacular version of the term sisterhood (69).

6. See Donna Haisty Winchell, *Alice Walker.* New York: Twayne, 1992 (49) for more details of how Brownfield serves as revised Pygmalion for Walker.

WORKS CITED

Bloom, Harold, ed. *Alice Walker.* New York: Chelsea House. 1989.

Bobo, Jacqueline. "Sifting through the Controversy: Reading *The Color Purple.*" *Callaloo* 12.2 (Spring 1989): 332–42.

Butler, Cheryl B. "*The Color Purple* Controversy: Black Woman Spectatorship." *Wide Angle* 13.3 & 4 (July–Oct. 1991): 62–69.

Christian, Barbara. "The Black Woman Artist as Wayward." In *Alice Walker.* Ed. Harold Bloom. New York: Chelsea House, 1989. 39–58.

Csikszentmilhalyi, Mihaly. "The Autotelic Self." *Reading Critically, Writing Well.* Ed. Rise B. Axelrod and Charles R. Cooper. 3rd ed. New York: St. Martin's Press, 1993. 207–10.

Demby, David. "Purple People-Eater." *New Yorker,* 13 Jan. 1986: 56.

Dieke, Ikenna. "Alice Walker: Poesy and the Earthling Psyche." Published in this collection.

Gates, Henry Louis, Jr. *The Signifying Monkey: A Theory of Afro-American Criticism.* New York: Oxford University Press, 1988.

Glicksman, Marlaine. "Lee Way." *Film Comment* (Oct. 1986): 48.

Hansberry, Lorraine. "The Negro Writer and His Roots: Toward a New Romanticism." *The Black Scholar* (Mar.–Apr. 1981).

Kael, Pauline. "Current Cinema: Sacred Monsters." *The New Yorker,* 30 Dec. 1985: 69.

Milloy, Courtland. "A 'Purple' Rage Over a Rip-off." *The Washington Post*, 24 Dec. 1985: B13.

O'Brien, John, ed. *Interviews with Black Writers*. New York: Liveright, 1973.

Schechter, Harold, and Jonna Gormely Semeiks. *Patterns in Popular Culture*. New York: Harper & Row, 1980.

Shipp, E. R. "Blacks in Heated Debate Over 'The Color Purple.'" *New York Times*, Jan. 1986: A13.

Simon, John. "Black and White in Purple." *National Review*, 14 Feb. 1986: 56.

Walker, Alice. "In Search of Our Mothers' Gardens." *Ms.*, May 1974: 66–69.

_____. *The Third Life of Grange Copeland*. New York: Harcourt Brace Jovanovich, 1970; New York: Pocket Books, 1988.

Washington, Mary Helen. "An Essay on Alice Walker." In *Alice Walker: Critical Perspectives Past and Present*. Ed. Henry Louis Gates, Jr. New York: Amistad, 1993. 37–49.

Watkins, Mel. "Sexism, Racism and Black Women Writers." *The New York Times Book Review*, 15 June 1986: 36.

Wesley, Richard. "The Color Purple Debate: Reading between the Lines." *Ms.*, Sept. 1986: 90.

Willimon, William H. "Seeing Red over *The Color Purple*." *Christian Century*, 2 Apr. 1986: 319.

Winchell, Donna Haisty. *Alice Walker*. New York: Twayne, 1992.

Witt, Mary Frese., et al., eds. *The Humanities*. 2nd ed. Vol. 1. Lexington, Mass.: D.C. Heath, 1985.

Zimmerman, J. E. *Dictionary of Classical Mythology*. New York: Harper & Row, 1964.

The Occupational Hazard: The Loss of Historical Context in Twentieth-Century Feminist Readings, and a New Reading of the Heroine's Story in Alice Walker's *The Color Purple*

Dror Abend-David

By entitling her article "Feminist Criticism in the Wilderness," Elaine Showalter presents feminist criticism—which she renames "gynocritics" (335)—as a unique phenomenon which sprang in the empty desert of theory about women. While Showalter's notion of the "wilderness" may point out the fact that feminist theories of literature are the product of the last decade, it may be dangerous to interpret her metaphor of "an empirical orphan in the theoretical storm" (331) as a statement about female history, ignoring earlier discussions of feminism such as those of turn-of-the-century Virginia Woolf, and late-nineteenth-century Mary Wollstone-craft, Maria Mulock, Florence Nightingale, and Sara Stickney Ellis. Showalter certainly distinguishes between the past of feminist criticism and that of women's history, actually referring to some of the discussions just mentioned in her article, particularly to Woolf. Nevertheless, the "wilderness" is a dangerous term which, in her title, as well as in that of Geoffrey Hartman's *Criticism in the Wilderness*, draws on the old Puritan concept of the American wilderness, a domain free of past histories and traditions and, consequently, one that is flexible to new ideologies, theories, and orders.

But as history teaches us—and American history in particular—the idea of wilderness is very often an illusion which ignores the prior inhabitants of a domain, only to be forced to acknowledge them at a later stage. Therefore, without ignoring the significance of feminist theories in the last twenty years nor of Showalter's summaries of such theories, it is likely that feminist readings of contemporary texts that ignore the "prior inhabitants" of female history and thought run the risk of misjudging the achievements of such texts, awarding them with credit of their precursors.

While feminist readings of pre-twentieth-century texts are necessarily aware of the fact that every work that is written either by a woman or about a woman enhances the possibility that women have spent as much time on this planet as men, it is the occupational hazard of contemporary readings, such as the one discussed in this essay, that they may rely heavily on the notion of a feminist, feminine, and female wilderness, and, in fact, not be twentieth century interpretations at all. They are, like any denial of the past, a repetition of pre-twentieth-century reflections, assertions, and social commentary.

It is precisely because feminist theory did not emerge out of the wilderness that Linda Abbandonato's article, "A View from 'Elsewhere': Subversive Sexuality and the Rewriting of the Heroine's Story in *The Color Purple*," is interesting (1106-15). In her feminist reading of Alice Walker's *The Color Purple*, Abbandonato demonstrates what she sees as the achievement of a modern feminist novel, not only in relation to contemporary theory, but also in comparison to Samuel Richardson's eighteenth-century novel *Clarissa*, which, like *The Color Purple*, is an epistolary novel that deals with the hardships of a young woman within the patriarchal system. Abbandonato's article may be particularly interesting because the genre of the novel, as Juliet Mitchell tells us in "Femininity, Narrative, and Psychoanalysis," and may very well be the link in the developing chain of female consciousness over the last two hundred years. The history of the novel, according to Mitchell, is one aspect of female history, a history that was mainly created by female writers "in the process of becoming a woman (or man) as today we understand that identity" (430). In deconstructing this aspect of history, as Mitchell reminds her readers at the end of her article, "we can only construct other histories. What are we in the process of becoming?" (430). One attempt to answer this question can be carried through the dissertation of Sandra Waters Holt, entitled "A Rhetorical Analysis of Three Feminist Themes Found in the Novels of Toni Morrison, Alice Walker, and Gloria Naylor." Holt awards the novel the same historical significance as Mitchell, claiming that "novelists can be rhetors and that their works have wide persuasive appeal" (3224A). Holt sees the novels of the mentioned writers as critical narratives that comment on issues of feminism as well as African American identity. But, while Holt reaffirms Mitchell's presentation of the novel as a significant part in the development of feminist history, without making the connection to its past manifestations—the prior inhabitants of the genre—she cannot identify the nature of such a development. Certainly, only a discussion that allows for a wide chronological perspective of texts, such as the one that is found in the article by Abbandonato, can give some idea of the theoretical, ideological, and political development of the image of women as it is presented in the novel.

But Abbandonato does not seem to spend enough time in evaluating *Clarissa*, using it only as an essential antithesis to the rhetorical achievements of *The Color Purple*. Using the theories of Hélène Cixous in her article "Sorties" and the term 'Elsewhere'—an independent realm of female consciousness—quoted in her article in reference to Teresa de Lauretis, Abbandonato presents *The Color Purple* as a revolutionary novel within the wilderness of patriarchal thought. *The Color Purple*, she claims, is not only a Cixourian alteration of the traditional male-dominated myth, but also the insertion of female-oriented themes from the domain of de Lauretis's "Elsewhere"—a domain that is unadulterated by male domination. It is a "conscious rewriting of canonical male texts" (Abbandonato 1106), texts for which *Clarissa* is the perfect example, being the product of traditional male authorship. "Richardson himself perfectly symbolizes white patriarchy: the founding father of the novel; he tells the woman's story, authorizing her on his terms, eroticizing her suffering, representing her masochism as virtue and her dying as the emblem of womanly purity" (Abbandonato 1107).

While Mitchell refers to the novel as the historical—and in her own words, hysterical (427)—product of female writing, to judge a novel by the sex of its author, as Abbandonato seems to be doing in regards to *Clarissa*, is not only to ignore the possible merits of a work but, more importantly, to misread the "Heroine's Story." For, as this essay will finally argue, Abbandonato fails to recognize an important merit of *The Color Purple*, one that is the antithesis of the prior image of women in this genre. Yet, for the time being, it is necessary to examine some of Abbandonato's assertions about the achievement of *The Color Purple* in comparison with *Clarissa*. Indeed, Abbandonato's comparison of the two texts, which she sees as the comparison between the epitome of feminist writing and the prototype of chauvinist literature, awards *The Color Purple* every possible merit that contemporary feminism can award a text, reading it as a critique of the patriarchal system, the denial of the commodity value of women, an insistence on female self-sufficiency, the preference of sexual deviation, and even as the construction of an alternative language for women (1106–12). While most of these interpretations are true in regard to *The Color Purple*, it may be interesting to see whether any of these qualities can already be attributed to an old "male dominated" novel such as *Clarissa*.

Fortunately, there is also an article that employs a different reading of *Clarissa*. Under the title "Comedy, Tragedy, and Feminism: The Novels of Richardson and Fielding" (13–26), Margaret Lenta is able to see the significance of Richardson's work within the context of his own time, claiming that "there can be no doubt that Richardson's novels are important for the new sense of women's inner lives which they gave their readers" (13). She adds, "In the cases of both Richardson and Fielding, we can certainly see that like most eighteenth-century writers they were intensely interested in women and the new possibilities of all kinds which the social changes of the age were offering them" (14). Lenta is careful, of course, to notice that Richardson is certainly not a "feminist" according to a twentieth-century definition. Nevertheless, her reading of Richardson—with many references to *Clarissa*—can be helpful in establishing certain ideas as to what was available already two hundred years ago in terms of female consciousness.[1] Incidentally, Lenta's article reveals that she is even mild in her evaluation of Richardson, as she quotes the zealous assertion of Katharine M. Rogers that Richardson was a radical feminist. In fact, Lenta is writing in order to defend Fielding, who, next to Richardson, is considered a chauvinist (Lenta 13).

Abbandonato's initial assertion is that "*Clarissa* fully endorses the bourgeois mentality that *The Color Purple* attacks" (1107). Lenta agrees that "none of Richardson's writings suggest that society could be anything other than patriarchal." Nevertheless, she points toward Richardson's interest in "woman's inner urge toward self-sufficiency, of which chastity is the symbol," as well as his notion that Clarissa is, undoubtedly, "best fitted to direct herself" morally, as well as practically, when her patriarchal environment is misdirecting her affairs (17–18). This notion of moral, practical, and even sexual autonomy within the patriarchal system certainly "conflicts with the contention of eighteenth-century society that women should be dependent on men in every respect" (Lenta 17–18). It seems, then, that *Clarissa* does not "fully endorse" her environment, but, within the boundaries of that environment, has certainly some criticism to offer, perhaps even a few suggestions for change. "How much rather, I think, should I choose to be wedded to my shroud than to any man on earth," says Clarissa in what can hardly be considered an endorsement of the male-oriented tyranny to which she is subjected (Richardson 190).

Another ideological triumph that Abbandonato relates to *The Color Purple* is the denunciation of the commodity value of women, as "women refuse to be co-opted into a system of compulsory heterosexuality, refuse in effect to become objects of exchange between men" (1110). Yet, if there is one literary character that fully understands, and criticizes, the marketing of young women in the "marriage game," it is Clarissa, who, in her letter to Miss Howe, explicates the full pecuniary scheme of her intended marriage to Mr. Solmes. "If I will suffer myself to be prevailed upon, how happy (as they lay out) shall we all be! Such presents am I to have, such jewels. Mr. Solmes' fortunes are so great, and his proposals so very advantageous (no relation whom he values)" (24). In her refusal to become the currency in the transaction between the Harlowes and the Solmeses, Clarissa shows not only a deep understanding of the monetary ends of marriage, but also an active objection to be used for such purposes. Beyond her refusal to marry Solmes, Lenta adds that Clarissa's rejection of Lovelace after she had been raped by him is an even greater assertion of her rights over her body and soul: Clarissa's refusal to marry him afterwards [after the rape] is her counterassertion that "he has not possessed her, that she remains essentially intact, and that if she were to marry him it would be tantamount to agreeing that he had the right to possession of her, however his generosity might afterwards lead him to vary the terms" (18).

It seems, then, that in regard to the financial understanding of male-female alliance, *Clarissa* is a very conscious text. The heroine's relations are carefully examined in terms of possession, financial gain, and titles of nobility—all of which are the incentives to the support or objection of her family in regards to possible engagements. Moreover, these pecuniary considerations are employed not only in appreciation of the financial welfare Clarissa may gain by marriage, but also—and even more so—in selfish appreciation of the possible profit of her relatives from her intended union with either Mr. Solmes or Lovelace. Her refusal to marry is, therefore, a challenge to one of the most significant principles of the patriarchal system: the undisputed control of the male over the benefits of marriage, and, consequently, his total ownership of the body of his wife, daughter, sister, or mother.

Even the idea of self-sufficiency, which serves as fertile ground for feminist interpretation in *The Color Purple*, is viewed incorrectly in Abbandonato's comparison between the two texts. In no way does Abbandonato relate to the self-sufficiency of the heroine, Celie, in the terms of her acquired skills as a seamstress, or in those of her inheritance of her father's house, both of which stand as legitimate symbols of practical female independence. In fact, Celie's success in becoming her own master, totally self-dependent, and—perhaps most important—happy, is one aspect in which she is superior to Clarissa. Unlike Richardson, Walker is able to proclaim not only the moral superiority of her heroine, but also the chance that she may prevail. However, Abbandonato is so impressed by the sexual significance of *The Color Purple* that, through the supposedly ultracontemporary idea of lesbian relationships, she drives towards the exact same definition of self-sufficiency that one can find in *Clarissa*: spiritual autonomy that is not dependent on the male partner for either love or sexual enjoyment. Abbandonato's discussion of "the radical political implication of the shift from vagina to clitoris that the lesbian relationship involves" (1112) reminds one of Showalter's discussion of "Bio-Criticism" (336). But even if one ignores Showalter's objection to the dangerously essential nature of such critique as well as her claim that it is just a Freudian over-association of women with sex at the expense of the "egoistic/ambitious," professional fantasy that is most often associated with male writing (337, 342)—one still wonders whether the achievement of the relationship between Celie and Shug is that of protesting against the common media image of human sexuality, as Abbandonato claims in one paragraph of her article (337). As for the sexual independence that is gained through this relationship, it is certainly one that is not greater than Clarissa's, whose choice of celibacy is, as Lenta points out, not only an assertion of her right over her body, but also a symbol of self-sufficiency (17). Perhaps one of the strongest points in *Clarissa* is the moral self-sufficiency of a young eighteenth-century woman who is so independent of the judgments of her society that even after she is raped and, in the eyes of her contemporaries, defiled and humiliated, she rejects the possibility of summoning her rapist into court, for, in her own eyes, she remains morally and sensibly intact. "The injury I have received from him is in deed of the highest nature. Yet, I bless God, it has not tainted my mind; it has not hurt my morals" (437).

Therefore, if through her discovery of lesbian sex Celie arrives at the rejection of men-oriented values, the most significant of which is her "reconceptualization of God as a Patriarch" (Abbandonato 1112), she paraphrases only slightly on Clarissa's assertion of her right to criticize the judgments and values of society from her morally sufficient position of sexual independence. This is not to say that Celie's "reconceptualization" of God is not an important notion in the text. Still, the significance is not so much in the qualities that God is denied as in the qualities that God is finally awarded.

Even the most striking difference between the two texts, their antithetical uses of language, is not the great feminist achievement of *The Color Purple*. Abbandonato sees in Celie's dialect an alternative to logocentric expression by which "Alice Walker confronted the challenge of constructing an alternative language (for women)" (1108). There are a few directions that one can take in claiming that Walker did not intend the dialect of her heroine as an alternative language for women. One can observe, for instance, that male characters in *The Color Purple* use the same "alternative language" to express themselves. But, to apply some common sense to the matter, it is likely that if any one wanted to invent a new language for women, s/he would have made an effort to award them with a language that is in no way limited, incoherent, or—as a tool for communication—inferior in comparison with that of men. After all, Celie does not choose her forms of expression, and her language is the result of white, male oppression rather than an expression of her independence. While Abbandonato is right in claiming that any attempt to force Celie into using a language that is not her own will be in the service of a logocentric, thought-limiting, and sexually frustrating structure (1109), one has to be a misogynist in order to claim that all women should imitate her speech. In comparison with *Clarissa* it may only be necessary to add that, since Clarissa's language is as fluent and credible as Celie's, both forms of speech seem to serve their users perfectly. Celie's statement, quoted by Abbandonato, that "only a fool would want you to talk in a way that feel peculiar to your mind" (Walker 194), points towards the obvious observation that neither of the two heroines should adopt the language of the other.

In the previous paragraphs, several of Walker's achievements in *The Color Purple* are examined in comparison with those of *Clarissa*: her critique of the patriarchal system, her denial of the commodity value of women, and her creation of female self-sufficiency in the terms of sexual and moral independence from male domination. Except for Abbandonato's notion with regard to the linguistic triumph of *The Color Purple*, none of the qualities are denied. Still, through the comparison with a prior text, the critique of a preexisting patriarchal system— its financially prejudiced, socially overbearing, and sexually frustrating qualities intact—is presented as a worn-out attitude that is as old as *Clarissa*. While *The Color Purple* gives a wonderful redemonstration of the evils of male-oriented society, this can hardly be the text's achievement in the projection of female imagery. Moreover, while Abbandonato promises in her article to expose the novel as "A View from Elsewhere"—a gaze towards the unadulterated domain of female consciousness—she cannot deliver on this promise as long as she stresses the ideological achievements of criticizing, protesting, and denying the undesirable characteristics of male society—none of which can be considered new discoveries. Hopefully, establishing what is not new ideology in the novel may help in determining what is. While Lenta tells her readers that "none of Richardson's writings, and especially not *Clarissa*, suggest that society [and marriage] could be any thing other than patriarchal" (19), it seems rather obvious that Walker assumes that society can be changed. The concentration, then, should be on what society may change into rather than what it must change from. As already mentioned in relation to Celie's reconceptualization of the patriarchal nature of God, the key to this change—the "Elsewhere" element in the novel—is not so much in the qualities that are denied or criticized in the novel, but more in the qualities that are endorsed.

In establishing what these new and exciting qualities are, it may be helpful to consider the settings of the novel. For, as one considers the time, the place, and the situation in *The Color Purple*, certain doubts concerning the settings of the novel seem inevitable: Why does Walker place her novel in a time prior to the Civil Rights Movement, the Feminist Movement, or, in fact, any organizations, laws, or ideologies that can support Celie in her strife?   Indeed, the radical feminist realizations of Celie seem anachronistic when they are placed within a 1920s environment, which, for most African American women, yielded more incentive for plain economic struggle than for the search of personal freedom and erotic happiness. But perhaps Walker's choice is precisely that of a time that lacks pre-established feminist ideologies that claim worldwide remedies for women. Unlike Clarissa, who is proposed by Richardson as "an Exemplar of her Sex" (xix–xx), Celie's triumph is a personal one which, if it is to be a symbol for others, can only be followed in terms of one's personal search for identity, an identity that is not necessarily purple, or rooted in the needlework business, or even lesbian. One is likely to support the notion of the heroine's personal construction of her identity if s/he considers the ideological statement of *Meridian* as text in which Walker demonstrates a firm dislike of mass movements and "professional" ideologists. Certainly, in consideration of Meridian's disappointment with ready-made ideologies, it is easy to understand why Walker sets *The Color Purple* in an environment that is forty years earlier than that of *Meridian*—a time in which female self-expression is more likely to be defined individually. Indeed, for different female characters in the novel, such as Celie, Nettie, Shug, Sofia, and "Squeak", there are different definitions of life, love, and sexuality. Perhaps the most symbolic of this ideological plurality is, again, Celie's definition of God, which, throughout the novel, becomes less and less expected. Although the idea that God may not be a white male is hardly Walker's invention, it may be more interesting to notice that Celie does not replace one image of God by another, but leaves the possibility of creating one's own god, one that is not related to society, friends, or even to her lover, Shug, who awards Celie with the possibility of finding God but does not dictate any one image of it. Similarly, the ideological achievement of *The Color Purple* is not, as Abbandonato may suggest, in denouncing a male-dominated society, but in describing the possibilities in the absence of such domination.

It may be worthwhile now to return to the open question at the end of Mitchell's article, inquiring what would be the further development of the images of women in the novel after the denial of old male-dominated images of the past. It seems that beyond its own protest against the same old images, *The Color Purple* also contains a partial answer in regards to the future: that further development of the images of women in the novel will not be male dominated, but it will not be female dominated either. It will be, like Celie's own God, a matter of interpretation. Cixous seems to phrase it best when predicting "a phantasmatical mingling of men, of males, of messieurs, of monarchs, princes, orphans, flowers, mothers, breasts, gravitates around a marvelous 'sun of energy' love, which bombards and disintegrates these ephemeral amorous singularities so that they may recompose themselves in other bodies for new passions." (293).[2]

In fact, this utopian imagery of Cixous seems to capture the precise development of *The Color Purple*, in which characters not only disintegrate out of their predetermined stereotypical images, but are also able to recompose their own individuality. Yet, in order to recognize this important merit in the text, the reading of *Clarissa* just described is required. For certainly Clarissa demonstrates an impeccable ability to disintegrate, but it is Celie's unique ability to recompose—or rather, to rewrite—herself, that is the great achievement of *The Color Purple*. Indeed, while feminist theory is one of the great achievements of twentieth-century scholarship, the loss of historical context is its occupational hazard, one that results from our condescending image of the prior, nontheoretical discourse of women. Awareness of such hazard may be helpful not only in avoiding a repetition of voices from the past, but also in discovering the innovations in contemporary texts.

NOTES

This essay is dedicated to Drs. Deborah Guth and Karen Alkalay-Gut, who helped the author in his research, and to his wife, Ilana Abend-David, who first brought to the author's attention the similarities between *The Color Purple* and *Clarissa*.

1. Certainly the author of this article is aware that Samuel Richardson was a man. Nevertheless, when Richardson writes of women, and certainly when he is read by women, he necessarily enters the realm of female consciousness.

2. There is a reference here to the work of Jean Genet, French novelist and playwright.

WORKS CITED

Abbandonato, Linda. "A View from 'Elsewhere': Subversive Sexuality and the Rewriting of the Heroine's Story in *The Color Purple*." *PMLA* 106.5 (October 1991): 1106–15.

Cixous, Hélène. "Sorties." In *Modern Criticism and Theory*. Ed. David Lodge. Singapore: Longman, 1992. 287–93.

Holt, Sandra Waters. "A Rhetorical Analysis of Three Feminist Themes Found in the Novels of Toni Morrison, Alice Walker, and Gloria Naylor." *Dissertation Abstracts International* 50.10 (April 1990): 3224A.

Lenta, Margaret. "Comedy, Tragedy and Feminism: The Novels of Richardson and Fielding." *English Studies in Africa* 26.1 (1983): 13–26.

Mitchell, Juliet. "Femininity, Narrative and Psychoanalysis." In *Modern Criticism and Theory*. Ed. David Lodge. 426–30.

Richardson, Samuel. *Clarissa*. Boston: Houghton Mifflin, 1962.

Showalter, Elaine. "Feminist Criticism in the Wilderness." In *Modern Criticism and Theory*. Ed. David Lodge. 331–53.

Walker, Alice. *The Color Purple*. New York: Washington Square Press, 1982.

Heritage and Deracination in Walker's "Everyday Use"

David Cowart

"Everyday Use," a story included in Alice Walker's 1973 collection *In Love and Trouble*, addresses itself to the dilemma of African Americans who, in striving to escape prejudice and poverty, risk a terrible deracination, a sundering from all that has sustained and defined them. The story concerns a young woman who, in the course of a visit to the rural home she thinks she has outgrown, attempts unsuccessfully to divert some fine old quilts, earmarked for the dowry of a sister, into her own hands. This character has changed her given name, "Dee Johnson," to the superficially more impressive "Wangero Leewanika Kemanjo"—and thereby created difficulties for the narrator (her mother), who recognizes the inappropriateness of the old name but cannot quite commit herself to the new. She tries to have it both ways, referring to her daughter now by one name, now by the other, now by parenthetically hybridized combinations of both. The critic, sharing Mrs. Johnson's confusion, may learn from her example to avoid awkwardness by calling the character more or less exclusively by one name. I have opted here for "Wangero"—without, I hope, missing the real significance of the confusion. Indeed, in this confusion one begins to see how the fashionable politics espoused by the central character of Walker's story becomes the foil to an authorial vision of the African American community, past and present, and its struggle for liberation.

Walker contrives to make the situation of Wangero, the visitor, analogous to the cultural position of the minority writer who, disinclined to express the fate of the oppressed in the language and literary structures of the oppressor, seeks a more authentic idiom and theme. Such a writer, Walker says, must not become a literary Wangero. Only by remaining in touch with a proximate history and an immediate cultural reality can one lay a claim to the quilts—or hope to produce the authentic art they represent. Self-chastened, Walker presents her own art—the piecing of linguistic and literary intertexts—as quilt-making with words, an art as imbued with the African American past as the literal quilt-making of the grandmother for whom Wangero was originally named.

The quilts that Wangero covets link her generation to prior generations, and thus they represent the larger African American past. The quilts contain scraps of dresses worn by the grandmother and even the great grandmother, as well as a piece of the uniform worn by the great grandfather who served in the Union Army in the War Between the States. The visitor rightly recognizes the quilts as part of a fragile heritage, but she fails to see the extent to which she herself has traduced that heritage. Chief among the little gestures that collectively add up to a profound betrayal is the changing of her name. Mrs. Johnson thinks she could trace the name Dee in their family "back beyond the Civil War" (54), but Wangero persists in seeing the name as little more than the galling reminder that African Americans have been denied authentic names. "I couldn't bear it any longer, being named after the people who oppress me" (53). She now styles and dresses herself according to the dictates of a faddish Africanism and thereby demonstrates a cultural Catch-22: an American who attempts to become an African succeeds only in becoming a phony. In her name, her clothes, her hair, her sunglasses, her patronizing speech, and her black Muslim companion, Wangero proclaims a deplorable degree of alienation from her rural origins and family. The story's irony is not subtle: the visitor who reproaches others for an ignorance of their own heritage (a word that probably does not figure in the lexicon of either her mother or her sister) is herself almost completely disconnected from a nurturing tradition.

Wangero has realized the dream of the oppressed: she has escaped the ghetto. Why, then, is she accorded so little maternal or authorial respect? The reason lies in her progressive repudiation of the very heritage she claims to revere. I say progressive because Walker makes clear that Wangero's flirtation with Africa is only the latest in a series of attempts to achieve racial and cultural autonomy, attempts that prove misguided insofar as they promote an erosion of all that is most real—and valuable—in African American experience. Wangero's mental traveling, moreover, replicates that of an entire generation. Her choices follow the trends in African American cultural definition from the simple integrationist imperative that followed *Brown v. Board of Education* (1954) to the collective outrage of the "long hot summer" of 1967 and the rise of an Islamic alternative to the Christianity that black America had hitherto embraced. Proceeding pari passu with this evolution was the rediscovery of an African past,[1] a past more remote—and putatively more authentic—than that of the preceding two hundred years. The epoch-making decade of the 1960s was bracketed by two sensational defections to Africa. In 1961 the ninety-three-year-old W.E.B. Du Bois, having been denied a passport and investigated by the House Un-American Activities Committee, moved to Ghana and renounced his American citizenship. In 1968 Eldridge Cleaver—less distinguished and less principled than Du Bois but one of the culture heroes of his day—made a similar gesture when he left the United States on an odyssey that would eventually take him, too, to a new home on the African continent. Midway between these two dates, in 1964, Walker herself traveled to Africa, and one imagines her character Wangero among the enthusiastic readers of the enormously popular *Roots* (1976), in which Alex Haley memorably describes the researches that eventually led him to the African village from which his ancestor, Kunta Kinte, had been abducted by slavers.

In other words, the Africa-smitten Wangero one meets in the opening pages of the story is a precipitate of the cultural struggles of a generation—struggles adumbrated in the stages of this character's education. She had left home to attend school in Augusta, where apparently she immersed herself in the liberating culture she would first urge on her bewildered mother and sister, then denounce as oppressive. Now, with her black Muslim boyfriend or husband in tow (her mother hears his name as "Hakim-a-barber"), she has progressed to an idea of nationality radically at odds with all that has hitherto defined the racial identity of African Americans.

Though Walker depicts "Hakim-a-barber" as something of a fool, a person who has embraced a culture as alien as anything imposed on black people by white America, her quarrel is not with Islam, for she hints (through the perceptions of Wangero's mother) that a nearby Muslim commune is an admirable, even heroic, institution. But the neighboring Muslims have immersed themselves in agrarian practicality. They are unlikely to view relics of the rural life as collectors' items. Their sense of purpose, their identity, seems to contain no element of pose. Wangero and her companion, on the other hand, are all pose.

Wangero despises her sister, her mother, and the church that helped to educate her. Her quest is ultimately selfish, and Walker focuses the reader's growing dislike for the heroine in her indifference to Maggie, the pathetic sister she seems prepared to ignore in a kind of moral triage. Maggie represents the multitude of black women who must suffer while the occasional lucky "sister" escapes the ghetto. Scarred, graceless, "not bright" (50), and uneducated, Maggie is a living reproach to a survivor like her sister. Maggie is the aggregate underclass that has been left behind as a handful of Wangeros achieve their independence—an underclass scarred in the collective disasters Walker symbolizes neatly in the burning of the original Johnson home. Wangero had welcomed that conflagration. Her mother remembers the "look of concentration on her face as she watched the last dingy gray board of the house fall in toward the red-hot brick chimney. Why don't you do a dance around the ashes? I'd wanted to ask her. She had hated the house that much" (49–50). Wangero did not set the fire, but she delighted in its obliteration of the house that represented everything she sought to escape. When, predictably, the house reappears as before, she may have understood that fire alone cannot abolish a ghetto. This burned house, however, represents more than a failed attempt to eradicate poverty. It subsumes a whole African American history of violence, from slavery (one thinks of Maggie's scars multiplied among the escaped or emancipated slaves in Morrison's *Beloved*) through the ghetto-torching riots of 1964, 1965, 1967, and 1968 ("Burn, Baby, Burn!") to the pervasive inner-city violence of subsequent decades. The fire, that is, is the African American past, a conflagration from which assorted survivors stumble forward, covered like Maggie with scars of the body or like Wangero with scars of the soul.

Assimilation, torching the ghetto, Islam, the Africanist vision—Walker treats these alternatives with respect, even as she satirizes her character's uncritical embracing of one after another of them. The author knows that each represents an attempt to restore a sense of identity terribly impaired by the wrongs visited on black people in the new world. Wangero, however, fails properly to appreciate the black community's transformation of these wrongs into moral capital. She does not see the integrity of African American cultural institutions that evolved as the creative and powerful response to the general oppression. In simpler terms, she is ashamed of a mother and a sister who, notwithstanding their humble circumstances, exemplify character bred in adversity.

"It all comes back to houses," Walker remarks in her essay on Flannery O'Connor (*In Search* 58). Freud associates houses with women, and this story of three women is also the story of three houses, one that burned, one that shelters two of the fire's survivors, and one, never directly described, that is to be the repository of various articles of this family's past, its heritage. This last house, owned by and symbolic of Wangero, embodies also the cultural problem Walker seeks to address in her story. How, she asks, can one escape the margins without a catastrophic deracination? Is the freedom Wangero achieves somehow at odds with proper valuation of the immediate cultural matrix out of which she comes? Can she, like Dickens's Pip, embrace a grand heritage only by betraying the simpler heritage necessary to emotional and psychological wholeness?

Wangero claims to value heritage, and Walker is surely sympathetic to someone who seems to recognize, however clumsily, the need to preserve the often fragile artifacts of the African American past. But Walker exposes Wangero's preservationism as hopelessly selfish and misguided. Though the author elsewhere laments the paucity of photographs in the African American historical record (*Living by the Word* 63), she evinces little patience with Wangero's desire to photograph mother and cow in front of the house. Wangero's desire is to have a record of how far she has come. No doubt she will view as "quaint" these images of a rural past. She wants the photographs—and presently the churn lid, the dasher, and the quilts—for purposes of display, reminders that she no longer has to live in such a house, care for such a cow, have daily intercourse with such a mother and sister. She "makes the mistake," says Donna Haisty Winchell, "of believing that one's heritage is something that one puts on display if and when such a display is fashionable" (81). Wangero seems to think the African American past can be rescued only by being commodified. She wants to make the lid of the butter churn into a centerpiece for her table. She wants to hang quilts on the wall. She wants, in short, to do what white people do with the cunning and quaint implements and products of the past. Wangero fails to see the mote in her own eye when she reproaches her mother and her sister for a failure to value their heritage—she, who wants only to preserve that heritage as the negative index to her own sophistication.

One wonders if Wangero's house, unlike the houses of her childhood, will have a lawn. Doubtless she has never paused to think about the humble yard of her mother's house as anything more than another shabby badge of poverty. But like the more obviously significant quilts, this yard—a description of which opens the story—is another symbol of the cultural something produced out of nothing by people lacking everything:

A yard like this is more comfortable than most people know. It is not just a yard. It is like an extended living room. When the hard clay is swept clean as a floor and the fine sand around the edges lined with tiny, irregular grooves, anyone can come and sit and look up into the elm tree and wait for the breezes that never come inside the house. (47)

A paragon of meaningful simplicity, this yard. The grooved borders even put one in mind of the artfully raked sand in a Japanese *hira-niwa* garden (indeed, the breezes sound like a plural visitation of *kamikaze,* the "divine wind"). In Japan, such a garden affords emotional balm and spiritual serenity to those who tend or contemplate it, and Walker implies similar restorative properties in the uncluttered plainness of the narrator's yard. Mrs. Johnson mentions neither grass, nor shrubs, nor (surprisingly for Walker) flowers. In its stark vacuity the yard evokes the minimalist lives of poor people; yet the author describes that emptiness in terms suggestive of spiritual wealth.[2]

If conversely Wangero is described in language evocative of spiritual poverty or confusion, the reader does not completely despise her, for even as it satirizes her pretensions, "Everyday Use" hints at an affinity between its author and its central character.[3] "Walker's *writing,*" says Marianne Hirsch, "constitutes a form of distance" (207) from the real-life mother and home on which she bases the story. The story can be read, in fact, as a cautionary tale the author tells herself: a parable, so to speak, about the perils of writing one's impoverished past from the vantage of one's privileged present. The deracination of Wangero, that is, can represent the fate of anyone who, like the author, goes from sharecropper's daughter to literary sophisticate. I refer here to an autobiographical dimension that proves interestingly unstable, for Walker's self-depiction as Wangero actually displaces an intended self-depiction as Maggie. That Walker would represent herself in the backward, disfigured Maggie strains credulity only if one forgets that the author was herself a disfigured child, an eye having been shot out with a B.B. gun. In a 1973 interview, moreover, Walker makes clear the autobiographical genesis of a poem ("For My Sister Molly Who in the Fifties" in *Revolutionary Petunias)* in which an ignorant and unglamorous girl discovers that her "brilliant" older sister, home for a visit, is ashamed of their uncouth family (*In Search* 269–70). "Everyday Use" is the prose version of that poem.

But how many of Walker's post–*Color Purple* readers recognize its gifted author in the Maggie of the earlier story? Indeed, as Walker's literary reputation grows, her readers may with increasing frequency identify the apparently successful and prosperous sister of "Everyday Use" as some kind of distorted reflection of the author, an exercise in autobiographical self-criticism of the type that, on a larger scale, generates a Stephen Dedalus, a Paul Morel, or a Hugh Selwyn Mauberley. (Toni Morrison, I have always thought, projects a male version of herself in Milkman Dead, the *Song of Solomon* character with whom she shares a birthday—and Wright, Ellison, and Baldwin all critique themselves in their protagonists.) Projections of this type constitute the examined life of the artist, at once an exorcism of unworthy versions of the self and a rhetorically effective shielding of the vulnerable ego, whose pretensions might otherwise be dismissed by captious readers.

Walker, then, actually doubles the self-mocking portrait of the artist, projecting herself as both the benighted Maggie and the sophisticated but shallow Wangero. She does so, I think, because she recognizes and wants to respond to the distorting pressures brought to bear on African American identity and the discourse that, over time, reflects or shapes it. In a sense, Walker's life as a writer has been devoted to preserving a proximate past in the form of its language (or, as will be seen, languages). In her essay "Coming in from the Cold," she discusses her desire to preserve the language of "the old people," her forebears—even when cultural displacements cause it to ring false. Thus she points out that words like "mammy" and "pickaninny" (long since appropriated in the construction of racial stereotypes) actually figured in the speech of earlier African Americans.[4] These words, and the language of which they are part, constitute an irreplaceable record of otherwise unrecorded lives, generations denied the "visual documentation of painting and photography" (*Living by the Word* 63). By transmitting the words of the ancestors "in the context that is or was natural to them, we do not perpetuate stereotypes, but, rather expose them. And, more important, we help the ancestors in ourselves and others continue to exist. If we kill off the *sound* of our ancestors, the major portion of us, all that is past, that is history, that is human being is lost, and we become historically and spiritually thin, a mere shadow of who we were, on the earth" (*Living by the Word* 62).

In short, to preserve the sound, the artist must preserve the words. To preserve the words, the artist must preserve the meanings and the sense of linguistic difference. Thus the great challenge of Walker's career (met most memorably in *The Color Purple*) has been to write a language at once true to "the old people" and viable in the marketplace of mainstream American ideas. Thus, too, like the poets of every literary renascence, Walker engages in a necessary program of linguistic reclamation. Like Wordsworth, she aspires to recover "the language actually spoken by men"—and women. Like the Frost of "The Pasture," she clears the leaves of linguistic debasement and cooptation away from the Pierian source of linguistic purity and good art. Like the Toomer or Hurston she admires, she insists on recapturing the authentic African American voice—whether in dialect, as they do, or in standard English, as in "Everyday Use" and the other stories in *In Love and Trouble*.

But things are never this simple. When Wangero greets her mother in Lugandan ("Wa-su- zo-Tean-o!"—52),[5] she affirms her repudiation of English, the language of slavery. By implication, she indicts the practice of authors—Joyce, for example, or Walker herself—who decline to abandon that language at the bidding of political visionaries. Thus Walker remains enmeshed in problems of cultural access and linguistic authenticity, for writers at the American margins have long struggled with a paradox basic to their artistic identities: their language and their craft are inextricably intertwined with the hegemonic Anglo-Saxon culture that has systematically denied them their own voice, their own autonomy, their own identity.

Black writers, their very tongues colonized, find themselves torn between the language they grew up speaking and some more authentic language or cultural orientation. How, demand artists like the American James Baldwin or the Caribbean George Lamming, can they ever achieve a voice of their own, a cultural authenticity, when they remain in linguistic bondage? Such writers fashion work that exists in a precarious and almost parasitic relation to a dominant and more or less unfriendly cultural and linguistic mainstream. They create what has been called a "minor literature."

Deleuze and Guattari, who refer briefly to "what blacks in America today are able to do with the English language," say that in "minor literatures everything is political" and that "everything takes on a collective value" (17). They argue, too, that the minor writer—notably Kafka—often effects revolutionary advances in literary sensibility. But I remain doubtful that such an argument is really needed to explain the ability of marginal writers to produce substantial work across a broad spectrum. I would argue that in the hands of a sufficiently resourceful literary practitioner, language can always be made to subvert hegemonic structures. Walker casts her lot with writers who remain confident of the boundlessness of literary affect achievable in English—writers like the Nobel laureates Derek Walcott and Toni Morrison, who seem effortlessly to transcend the kind of anxieties Deleuze and Guattari would wish on them. These writers believe that culture is naturally enough eclectic, and that a language as rich as English, not to mention the manifold cultures that speak or are spoken by it, provides plenty of latitude for new voices, however subversive. They seem to view the possibilities of literary art as affording sufficient latitude to circumvent linguistic colonization. They prefer to see the resources of the English language and its canonical literature, as well as the larger cultural resources of the West, as theirs for the appropriating. Thus in *Beloved,* as Ellen Pifer has argued, Morrison rewrites *Huckleberry Finn* (511), and thus in *Omeros* Walcott reimagines several millenia of colonial history and culture to shape a vision that remains wholly of its Caribbean time and place. Thus, too, Walker loses nothing when she opts not to write in dialect—or Lugandan.

Walker refuses, then, to write "protest literature," in which the shallow is passed off as the profoundest truth. She credits Tolstoy with showing her the practical wisdom of partaking in the socio-political process in order to delve into the essential nature of individual disposition. In "Everyday Use" Walker explores with great subtlety the demands—often conflicting—of ideology and art. She contemplates the culturally distorting pressures brought to bear on another kind of language, another vehicle whereby African American experience is embodied and transmitted. This other language—the quilts—exhibits a special integrity resembling that of the language in which the author writes her story. As this story engages the theme of heritage, it resolves the dilemma inherent in ideologically self-conscious art (how simultaneously to be politically engaged and free of a limiting topicality) by inviting a connection between writing and quilt-making, a connection between types of textuality that prove complementary.

"In contemporary writing," Elaine Showalter observes, "the quilt stands for a vanished past experience to which we have a troubled and ambivalent cultural relationship" (228). Certainly the quilts over which Wangero and her mother quarrel represent a heritage vastly more personal and immediate than the intellectual and deracinated daughter can see; indeed, they represent a heritage she has already discarded, for she no longer shares a name with those whose lives, in scraps of cast-off clothing, the quilts transmute. Moreover, Wangero herself has not learned to quilt—the art will die if women like Maggie do not keep it up. Yet as Barbara Christian observes, a "heritage must continually be renewed rather than fixed in the past" (87). Thus for Maggie and her mother the idea of heritage is perpetually subordinate to the fact of a living tradition, a tradition in which one generation remains in touch with its predecessors by means of homely skills—quilt-making and butter-churning, among others—that get passed on. The quilts remain appropriate for "everyday use" so long as the art of their manufacture remains alive. They can be quite utilitarian, and indeed, they are supposed to be a practical dowry for Maggie.

Of course the quilts, like this story, are beautiful and merit preservation. Walker seems to intimate, however, even in her own literary art, a belief in the idea of a living, intertextual tradition, a passing on of values as well as skills that ought only occasionally to issue in canonization or any of the other processes whereby something intended for "everyday use" ends up framed, on a wall, on a shelf, in a library or museum. Indeed, as Faith Pullin notes with regard to the quilts, "the mother is the true African here, since the concept of art for art's sake is foreign to Africa—all objects are for use. Dee has taken over a very Western attitude towards art and its material value" (185). Walker, by the same token, seems to conceive of her own art as part of a dynamic process in which utility (domestic, political) meets and bonds with an aesthetic ideal. Her story/quilt is intended as much for immediate consumption—that is, reading—by the brothers and sisters of these sisters as for sacralization on some library shelf or college syllabus.

Thus Walker, though she mocks Wangero's idea of heritage, nevertheless aspires to project herself as sensitive artist of the African American experience, and she does so by inviting recognition of a further parallel between the contested quilts and her own fictive art. Quilts are the "texts" (the word means *weave*) of American rural life. Moreover, they are palpably "intertextual," inasmuch as they contain literal scraps of past lives. Engaged in her own version of quilt-making, Walker weaves in stories like this one a simple yet richly heteroglossic text on patterns set by a literary tradition extending into communities black and white, American and international. The interested reader may detect in Walker's work the intertextual presence of a number of writers she names as influences in the 1973 interview mentioned previously: Tolstoy, Turgenev, Gorky, Gogol, Camara Laye, García Márquez, Flannery O'Connor, Elechi Ahmadi, Bessie Head, Jean Toomer, and especially Zora Neale Hurston (*In Search* 257 260). Like any other writer, any other user of language, Walker "pieces" her literary quilts out of all that she has previously read or heard. Perhaps it is with Maggie after all that the author exhibits the most comprehensive affinity.

African American writing, according to Henry Louis Gates, enjoys its own distinctive brand of intertextuality, and I should like to conclude this discussion by glancing at a couple of the ways in which "Everyday Use" exemplifies the theory developed by Gates in *The Signifying Monkey*. Borrowing a term from the vernacular, Gates argues that texts by African American writers "Signify" on prior texts: they play with their predecessors in a perpetual and parodic evolution of meanings congenial to a people whose latitude for direct expression has been historically hedged about by innumerable sanctions. Gates explains Signifyin(g) with reference to Bakhtin's idea of a "double-voiced" discourse, in which one hears simultaneously the present text and the text being augmented or ironically revised. Not that Signifyin(g) need always be at the expense of its intertext: in one of the analytic set pieces of his book, as it happens, Gates reads Walker's *The Color Purple* as what he calls "unmotivated" (that is, non-disparaging) Signifying on texts by Rebecca Cox Jackson and Zora Neale Hurston.

In "Everyday Use" one encounters Signifyin(g) in both its street sense and its literary sense. "To rename is to revise," says Gates, "and to revise is to Signify" (xxiii). Thus Wangero thinks she is Signifyin(g) on white culture when she revises her name, but inadvertently she plays false with her own familial culture, as her mother's remarks about the history of the name Dee allow the reader to see. Indeed, if the mother were not so thoroughly innocent, one would suspect her of Signifying on her daughter's misguided aspirations. The master manipulator of the intertexts is of course Walker herself as she Signifies on Africanist pretension, calling into question the terms with which a number of her contemporaries are repudiating the language and culture of what Wangero calls "the oppressor."

Though Gates more or less exclusively considers how African Americans Signify on the discourse of other African Americans, his theory also lends itself to sorting out relations between the shapers of a "minor literature" and the mainstream or majority writers encountered on the road to a problematic literary autonomy. Gates himself dismisses as "reductive" (59) the idea that the Signifying Monkey's adversarial relationship with that ubiquitous authority figure, the powerful but unsubtle Lion, can be understood as symbolically representative of power relations between black and white. But I would argue that insofar as those relations are literary, they prove interesting and complex. The critic interested in them ought only to keep in mind Gates's assertion that when "black writers revise texts in the Western tradition, they do so 'authentically,' with a black difference, a compelling sense of difference based on the black vernacular" (xxii). Surely, then, one can legitimately consider the possibility that Walker plays the Signifying Monkey to a white literary Lion more or less literally in her own Georgia back yard. To come to cases: what is the relationship between Walker's story and the respected and influential body of short fiction about the rural South written by Flannery O'Connor?

As noted previously, Walker considers O'Connor an influence, and Margaret D. Bauer, who has remarked some of the parallels in the work of these two artists, tends to see their relationship as healthily non-agonistic (149–150).[6] But anyone who dips into the essay on O'Connor that appears in *In Search of Our Mothers' Gardens* will be struck by the ambivalence of the younger author's feelings about the elder. While admitting that she has long admired her writing, she at the same time gauges feelings of fury and bitterness when she visits O'Connor's house outside Milledgeville, Georgia. Thus one should not be surprised to discover something other than simple homage in "Everyday Use," the little comedy of superficial sophistication and rural manners in which Walker replicates and plays with the many such fictions of O'Connor.

O'Connor contrasts intellectual pretension with certain transcendent realities: Original Sin, Grace, prospects for redemption. Walker, meanwhile, assesses ideas of cultural identity within a community only a few minutes drive from the home in which O'Connor spent her last years. O'Connor relentlessly exposes liberal pieties—notably regarding race—as humanistic idols that obscure the spiritual realities central to her vision. Writing at the height of Civil Rights agitation, she delights in characters like Asbury in "The Enduring Chill" or Julian in "Everything that Rises Must Converge"—characters who have embraced the new ideas about race only to be exposed for their concurrent spiritual folly. I have been arguing all along that Walker, too, satirizes the heady rhetoric of late 60s black consciousness, deconstructing its pieties (especially the rediscovery of Africa) and asserting neglected values. At the same time, however, she revises—Signifies on—the O'Connor diagesis, which allows so little real value to black aspiration. Thus Walker parodies the iconoclastic tricks that O'Connor uses over and over again. As Wangero meets in Maggie the self she wants to deny, Walker Signifies on O'Connor's fondness for characters that psychologically double each other. Walker Signifies, too, on the O'Connor moment of divine insight, for Mrs. Johnson's decision to reaffirm the gift of the quilts to Maggie comes as heaven-sent enlightenment. Mrs. Johnson, however, enjoys a positive moment of revelation—unlike Mrs. May in "Greenleaf," Mrs. Turpin in "Revelation," or the Grandmother in "A Good Man is Hard to Find." When, finally, Walker represents Wangero's intellectual posturing as shallow beside the simple integrity of her mother and sister, she plays with the standard O'Connor plot of the alienated and superficially intellectual young person (Hulga, in "Good Country People," is the definitive example) who fails conspicuously to justify the contempt in which she or he holds a crass, materialistic, and painfully unimaginative female parent. Walker tropes even the O'Connor meanness. Where O'Connor allows at best that the petty complacency and other failings of the mothers in "The Comforts of Home" and "The Enduring Chill" are venial flaws beside the arrogance, the intellectual posturing, and the spiritual blindness of their children, Walker declines to qualify her sympathy and admiration for Maggie and Mrs. Johnson.

One of the ironies here is that both Walker and O'Connor are themselves intellectuals struggling to make their way in a world of competitive ideas and talents—not to mention competing ideologies. Each critiques herself through mocking self-projection, and each stakes out an ideological position at odds with prevailing thought. O'Connor addresses herself to the spiritual folly of a godless age, Walker to a kind of social shortsightedness. The measure of Walker's success may be that one comes to care as much about the question she poses—"Who shall inherit the quilts?"—as about the nominally grander question posed by O'Connor:

"Who shall inherit the Kingdom of Heaven?"

In "Everyday Use," then, Walker addresses herself to the problems of African Americans who risk deracination in their quest for personal authenticity. At the same time she makes the drama of Wangero and Maggie emblematic of the politically charged choices available in minor/minority writing. With wit and indirection, she probes the problem of post-colonial writers who, as they struggle with a cultural imperative to repudiate the language and the institutions of the colonizer, simultaneously labor under the necessity—born in part of a desire to address an audience that includes the colonizer and his inheritors—of expressing themselves in that language and deferring to those institutions. In her problematic repudiation of oppressor culture, Wangero represents, among other things, the marginalized individual who fails to see this dilemma as false. She seems willing to lose her soul to be free of the baleful influences that she thinks have shaped it.

Walker hints that the false dilemma behind Wangero's blindness afflicts the narrowly political writer as well. The alternative to the dilemma is the same in both instances: a living tradition that preserves a true heritage even as it appropriates what it needs from the dominant culture it may be engaged in subverting. African Americans, Walker says, can take pride in the living tradition of folk art, seen here in the example of the quilts, and they can learn from a literary art like her own, a literary art committed at once to political responsibility and to the means—through simple appropriation of linguistic tools—of its own permanence.

NOTES

1. A rediscovery that is itself evidence of a limited cultural horizon; Pan-Africanism had in fact been around since the turn of the century. Readers who know Walker's novels will recognize in this thematic element one of the foundational gestures of a career-long effort to construct or discover an idea of Africa that would not violate the geographical and historical reality. It is a struggle shared by all who seek to recover a suppressed history. The poet Derek Walcott speaks for many when he asks, "How can I turn from Africa and live?" Thus Walker spins a romantic fantasy about the Olinka in *The Color Purple*, imagines an Afro-feminist mythology of Africa in *The Temple of My Familiar*, and strives to achieve utter, unsparing candor regarding Africa's most abhorrent cultural practice—female circumcision—in *Possessing the Secret of Joy*. Africa is a complex place in the psyche of Alice Walker. If in this essay I suggest that it is a less complex place in the psyche of Wangero, I would not like to be seen as arguing that her creator is insensitive to the hunger to know Africa.

2. For the ingenious suggestion that the yard, in its tended state, becomes "ritual ground prepared for the arrival of a goddess" (311), see the article on this story by Houston Baker and Charlotte Pierce-Baker.

3. Alice Hall Petry documents "autobiographical dimensions" (19) in a number of Walker stories, notably those in *You Can't Keep a Good Woman Down* (1981). Petry sees only a kind of narcissism in Walker's autobiographical characters. I argue here that "Everyday Use" is exceptional in the sophistication with which it exploits the self-regarding impulse.

4. She also claims that these words are of African origin, but in fact "pickaninny"

derives from the vocabulary of Portuguese slavers, whose wares included children, *pequeninos.*

    5. I am indebted to my colleague, Carol Myers Scotton, for identifying the language.

    6. Bauer sees some especially intriguing similarities between O'Connor's *Wise Blood* and Walker's "Entertaining God" (another of the stories in *In Love and Trouble*). She also notes some similarities of "plot line and character type" (150) between "Everyday Use" and O'Connor's short fiction.

WORKS CITED

Baker, Houston, and Charlotte Pierce-Baker. "Patches: Quilts and Community in Alice Walker's 'Everyday Use.'" *Alice Walker: Critical Perspectives Past and Present.* Ed. Henry Louis Gates and K. A. Appiah. New York: Amistad, 1993. 309–316.

Bauer, Margaret D. "Alice Walker: Another Southern Writer Criticizing Codes Not Put to 'Everyday Use.'" *Studies in Short Fiction* 29 (1992): 143–151.

Christian, Barbara. *Black Feminist Criticism: Perspectives on Black Women Writers.* New York: Pergamon, 1985.

Deleuze, Gilles, and Felix Guattari. *Kafka: Toward a Minor Literature.* Minneapolis: University of Minnesota Press, 1986.

Gates, Henry Louis. *The Signifying Monkey: A Theory of Afro-American Literary Criticism.* New York: Oxford University Press, 1988.

Hirsch, Marianne. "Clytemnestra's Anger: Writing (Out) the Mother's Anger." *Alice Walker.* Ed. Harold Bloom. New York: Chelsea House, 1989. 195–213.

Petry, Alice Hall. "Alice Walker: The Achievement of the Short Fiction." *Modern Language Studies* 19 (Winter 1989): 12–27.

Pifer, Ellen. "Toni Morrison's *Beloved*: Twain's Mississippi Recollected and Rewritten." Ed. Francois Piquet. Paris: Didier, 1993. 511–514.

Pullin, Faith. "Landscapes of Reality: The Fiction of Contemporary Afro-American Women. *Black Fiction: New Studies in the Afro-American Novel since 1945.* Ed. A. Robert Lee. New York: Barnes and Noble, 1980. 173–203.

Showalter, Elaine. "Piecing and Writing." *The Poetics of Gender.* Ed. Nancy K. Miller. New York: Columbia University Press, 1986. 222–247.

Walker, Alice. *In Love and Trouble: Stories of Black Women.* New York: Harcourt Brace Jovanovich, 1973.

_____. *In Search of Our Mothers' Gardens.* San Diego: Harcourt Brace Jovanovich, 1983.

_____. *Living by the Word: Selected Writings 1973 1987.* San Diego: Harcourt Brace Jovanovich, 1988.

_____. *Revolutionary Petunias and Other Poems.* New York: Harcourt Brace Jovanovich, 1973.

Winchell, Donna Haisty. *Alice Walker.* Boston: Twayne, 1990.

Alice Walker's Womanist Magic: The Conjure Woman as Rhetor

Catherine A. Colton

The Color Purple has been a much-discussed novel since its publication in 1982. In this essay, I will examine it as a rhetorical work, that is, as an illustration of language aimed to effect change in the minds of readers and/or in the world. Drawing in part on the African American traditions of voodoo and conjure and their reliance on the power of language to invoke change, Alice Walker creates Celie, conjure woman and rhetor par excellence. Celie's story raises consciousness, opens up new possibilities for building communities, and argues for a womanist version of justice. These are all acts of rhetoric.

Voodoo is a religious system born of the contact between the religion Africans brought as slaves to Haiti and the Roman Catholicism that their masters attempted to impose. Since these Africans came from different countries and cultures, their religious beliefs varied; when brought together in Haiti, however, those elements held in common were highlighted in the adapted religion (Courlander 26). Key elements of African religions are beliefs in a spirit-infused natural world, reverence for spirits of ancestors, and a perceived unity between the spiritual and physical worlds. Magic—inhering in people's ability to make good or ill use of their connections with the spiritual world—is a part of this religion. The practice of voodoo was a way for displaced Africans in Haiti to maintain some of their own traditions, develop a sense of community, and organize a network between slaves on different plantations. In 1804, Haiti achieved its independence from France. Laguerre writes that "while voodoo was not the only factor in the success of this revolution, it was partially confidence in Voodoo *loas* [spirits], the political instructions of their followers and the unifying effect of this belief" that led to political independence (66).

In the United States, the religious/magical traditions of voodoo and conjuring were also used to preserve and pass down African cultural beliefs and traditions, to resist oppressors, and to maintain order in the community. Historian John Blassingame writes:

Because of their superstitions and beliefs in fortune tellers, witches, magic and conjurers, many of the slaves constructed a psychological defense against total dependence on and submission to their masters. Whatever his power, the master was a puny man compared to the supernatural. Often the most powerful and significant individual on the plantation was the conjurer. (qtd. in Baker 79)

In 1935, Zora Neale Hurston published her ethnographic study *Mules and Men*, chronicling her experiences with voodoo doctors in New Orleans. The book describes rituals illustrating both the positive and malevolent aspects of voodoo. While Nigel Thomas warns against confusing conjure and voodoo, describing the first as a "deadly art" and the second a "religion" that aims toward spiritual wholeness (40), others, including Hurston and Baker, see conjure as being part of voodoo. Like any form of power, conjure can be employed for either good or bad purposes, depending on the motives of the person using it.

Traditionally, this power is closely tied to the transformative power of language. The voodoo genesis myth, as Hurston relates it, holds that "six days of magic spells and mighty words and the world with its elements above and below was made" (229). Moses was the first person, according to legend, to learn God's "power-compelling words" and write them into a book. John Mbiti writes that to Africans "there is mystical power in words. The words of the medicine-man work through the medicine he gives, and it is this, perhaps more than the actual herb, which is thought to cause the cure or prevent misfortunes" (192). This understanding of the magical nature of language has a long tradition in Western cultures as well. Drawing in part upon the theory of Kenneth Burke, William Covino writes that

performing magic has always involved issuing a "coercive command"; insofar as such commands are intrinsic to language, and really do make and re-make reality, we "do magic" when we "do rhetoric," and vice-versa. For the Greek orator, the Renaissance magus, the Romantic poet, and the variety of present-day institutional authorities who invoke a cosmology of sanctioned forces in every act of official discourse, language alters the social situation. ("Magic And/As Rhetoric" 355)

Voodoo in the United States has also been closely tied to the power of women. Houston Baker asserts that it has a "strikingly womanist power" (81) and Luisah Teish, whose book reclaims voodoo for women as a means of empowerment, writes that it is a "science of the oppressed, a repository of woman knowledge" (171). This is most powerfully rendered in the figure of the conjure woman. Marie Leveau, conjure woman and mother of voodoo in the United States, has her power through possession by the gods. One of her disciples, an informant of Zora Hurston, explains how Leveau worked:

She go to her great Altar and seek until she become the same as the spirit, then she come out into the room where she listens to them that come to ask
Marie Leveau is not a woman when she answer the one who ask. No. She is a god, yes. Whatever she say, it will come so. (qtd. in Hurston 243)

She conjured a curse which reads in part:

To The Man God: O great One, I have been sorely tried by my enemies and have been blasphemed and lied against. My good thoughts and my honest actions have been turned to bad actions and dishonest ideas. My home has been disrespected, my children have been cursed and ill-treated. My dear ones have been backbitten and their virtue questioned. O Man God, I beg that this that I ask for my enemies shall come to pass. (Hurston 245)

Alice Walker, for whom Zora Neale Hurston was a model, uses Hurston's ethnographic material in her work and continues the conjure tradition in literature. In one of Walker's early stories, "The Revenge of Hannah Kemhuff," Marie Leveau's curse is central. Hannah Kemhuff comes to the root worker/conjure woman, Tante Rosie, and her assistant seeking revenge on Sarah Holley, a white woman who many years before had denied Hannah and her family government aid when they needed it. Hannah's husband subsequently left her, her children sickened and died, and she became an alcoholic. The power of voodoo to lift up the powerless is suggested in Hannah's bearing upon receiving Tante Rosie's assurance that "within a year's time the earth will be rid of the woman. Mrs. Kemhuff turned and left, bearing herself grandly out of the room. It was as if she had regained her youth; her shawls were like a stately toga, her white hair seemed to sparkle" (70).

The psychological effects of the conjure are evident in Mrs. Holley as well. After praying the Leveau prayer with Mrs. Kemhuff, Tante Rosie's assistant asks Mrs. Holley for some of her fingernail clippings, hair, urine, feces and clothes that she's worn in the last year. Though Mrs. Holley refuses, professing not to believe in such "heathen nigger paganism" (76), she is dead within a few months. After the visit from the conjure woman's assistant, she locks herself in her room, avoiding everyone, eating her fingernails, collecting all stray hairs from her comb, and storing her waste in barrels and plastic bags in her closet. "The mouth that had grinned behind the hands grinned no more" (80). The justice that Mrs. Kemhuff had waited for God to perform for so long comes about through the conjure woman,[1] and voodoo works "as a weapon against oppression" (Walker, "Interview" 266). In 1982, Walker wrote "Only Justice Can Stop a Curse," an essay in which she again employs the curse-prayer of Marie Leveau in order to bring about justice in the world, a veritable sense of justice in which every living organism will partake.

Depending upon one's perspective, the magic of conjure women can, in Covino's terms, function as either "generative" (expanding possibility) or "arrest-ing" (reducing or foreclosing possibility) (*Magic, Rhetoric, and Literacy* 8–9); Hannah Kemhuff enjoys the former possibility, while Sarah Holley suffers the latter. For Walker, what determines whether the magic is either generative or arresting is the issue of justice. In *The Color Purple*, Walker dramatizes the claim that "only justice can stop a curse." Once again, the tradition of a previously powerless woman conjuring up a curse to empower herself, gain revenge on an oppressor, and bring about justice is played out. Further, in the context of hundreds of years of African and African American traditions of conjuring and of at least a hundred years of an African American literary tradition of conjuring, Alice Walker serves as the "medium" (as she terms herself in the postscript) for Celie, conjuring *The Color*

Purple into existence.

The Color Purple is the story of Celie, a powerless woman until her friendship with Shug Avery, blues singer and lover of her husband, who is first friend, then lover to Celie, helping her to develop a sense of self-love and a new sense of God. After many years of marriage, Celie finally determines to leave "Mister" and her curse is delivered on the occasion of informing him of this decision. Prior to engaging in conjure, Celie, like Hannah Kemhuff, transfers her faith from God to the conjure woman, with one very important difference. For Celie, the conjure woman is within herself. This shift is made possible by her new understanding of spirituality. Celie's description of the scene in which she curses Mister appears in the two letters immediately following the one in which she voices her new understanding of God. She finally loses her faith in God when she finds out that her natural father had been lynched, resulting in her mother's nervous breakdown, and that the man she knew as her father—the man who had raped her—was really a step-father. She writes to God: "My daddy lynch. My mama crazy. My children not my sister and brother. Pa not pa. You must be sleep" (183). She informs Shug of her decision to write her letters to her sister Nettie rather than to God, justifying it by saying: "[T]he God I been praying and writing to is a man. And act just like all the other mens I know. Trifling, forgitful and lowdown" (199). This is a radical departure from the Celie who earlier in her life had tried to explain to Sofia her lack of angry feelings:

I can't even remember the last time I felt mad. Couldn't be mad at my daddy cause he my daddy. Bible say, Honor father and mother no matter what. Sometime Mr._____ git on me pretty hard. I have to talk to Old Maker. But he my husband. I shrug my shoulders. mis life be over, I say. Heaven last all ways. (43–4)

Shug offers Celie a very different understanding of God:

I believe God is everything, say Shug. My first step from the old white man was trees. Then air. Then birds. Then other people. But one day when I was sitting quiet and feeling like a motherless child, which I was, it come to me: that feeling of being part of everything, not separate at all. I knew that if I cut a tree, my arm would bleed. (202–3)

This sense of connection and the interrelatedness of everything in the natural world is crucial to the African understanding of conjure. Annette Van Dyke writes that "it is the responsibility of individuals to use carefully th[e] power of words to activate selectively the power in everything using their understanding of relationships" (44). It would appear to follow then that the better one's understanding of relationships in the world, the more powerful one's word would be to effect a magical change. It is precisely with Celie's new understanding of the interrelatedness of everything in the world that she is empowered finally to speak up for herself, usurping Mister's verbal and physical power over her.

When Shug tells Mister that Celie is leaving to go to Memphis with her, he responds, "Over my dead body" (206) and asks Celie what's wrong with her. For the first time, she talks back to him: "You a lowdown dog is what's wrong, I say.

It's time to leave you and enter into the Creation. And your dead body just the welcome mat I need" (207). Mister can only respond by sputtering: "But ButButButBut. Sound like some kind of motor" (207). His ability to verbalize is deteriorating while Celie's power is increasing. The climactic moment exhibiting Celie's newfound power of the word is when she curses Mister. She now understands the relationship between male power and patriarchal religion. She writes:

Man corrupt everything, say Shug. He on your box of grits, in your head, and all over the radio. He try to make you think he everywhere. Soon as you think he everywhere, you think he God. But he ain't. Whenever you trying to pray, and man plop himself on the other end of it, tell him to git lost, say Shug. Conjure up flowers, wind, water, a big rock. But this hard work, let me tell you. He been there so long, he don't want to budge. Us fight. I hardly pray at all. Every time I conjure up a rock, I throw it. (204)

As soon as she is able to "git man off her eyeball," as Shug recommends, Celie is able to conjure up more than just a rock. She is able to conjure up words—words that can "activate the power" of her new interconnected, more African world-view—and throw them at Mister. They prove to be much more powerful than any rock.

    Celie's curse is narrated in a letter to her sister Nettie. The transcription is a triple-voiced discourse, with her words, Mister's responses, and Celie's reflections on her delivery all interwoven. Her curse is both similar to and dissimilar from that of other conjure women in African American tradition. Like Marie Laveau, Celie is "possessed" by some outside force while delivering her "message." Unlike the curse of Marie Laveau and so many others, this one is delivered straight to its intended victim by his accuser. Celie becomes her own conjure woman. She writes:

Any more letters come? I ast. He say, What? You heard me, I say. Any more letters from Nettie come? If they did, he say, I wouldn't give 'em to you. I curse you, I say. What that mean? he say. I say, Until you do right by me, everything you touch will crumble. He laugh. Who you think you is? he say. You can't curse nobody. Look at you. You black, you pore, you ugly, you a woman. Goddam, he say, you nothing at all. Until you do right by me, I say, everything you even dream about will fail. I give it to him straight, just like it come to me. And it seem to come to me from the trees. Whoever heard of such a thing, say Mr._____ I probably didn't whup your ass enough. Every lick you hit me you will suffer twice, I say. Then I say, You better stop talking because all I'm telling you ain't coming just from me. Look like when I open my mouth the air rush in and shape words. Shit, he say. I should have lock you up. Just let you out to work. The jail you plan for me is the one in which you will rot, I say. Shug come over to where us talking. She take one look at my face and say Celie! Then she turn to Mr. Stop Albert, she say. Don't say no more. You just going to make it harder on yourself. I'll fix her wagon! say Mr._____, and spring toward me. A dust devil flew up on the porch between us, fill my mouth with dirt. The dirt say, Anything you do to me, already done to you. Then I feel Shug shake me. Celie, she say. And I come to myself. I'm pore, I'm black. I may be ugly and can't cook, a voice say to I'm pore, I'm black. I may be ugly and can't cook, voice say to everything listening. But I'm here. Amen, say Shug. Amen, amen. (*The Color Purple* 75)

This curse is custom-made by Celie for Mister. When Mister does not "do right" by Celie in continuing to name her in a negative fashion, she reiterates her beginning statement "until you do right by me." When Mister refers to beating her, the next phase of her curse doubles those blows on to him. When he says that he should have locked her up, Celie's curse features a jail for Mister. This responsive nature of the curse not only illustrates its originality and playful creativity, but also represents what is, according to Karlyn Kohrs Campbell, a typical feature of women's rhetoric. Women orators, according to Campbell, respond to their audiences and attempt to get them involved (13). Celie's curse is also her first public speaking engagement and presents her as a rhetorical figure as well as a conjure woman.

The structure of the curse also exemplifies the call and response tradition predominant in African American churches. As Keith Byerman writes, "Black folk forms generally have a call-and-response structure that relates performer and audience" (3). In that respect, Celie is a performer, with Mister as her audience. She is in control of the "scene," possibly for the first time in her life. The curse rewrites the call-and-response, as Celie, a formerly powerless African American woman, assumes the role of the minister—the mediator between the congregation and God. The "god" in this scene is the spirit or spirits in nature: "it seem to come to me from the trees" and "look like when I open my mouth the air rush in and shape the words." Even the "dirty" aspects of nature are endowed with spirit as the "dust devil" rises up to fill Celie's mouth with dirt. The spirits are multiple, not one, and they are the more African-centered spirits of nature rather than the white male god of Christianity.

Regarding another literary curse, that of Miss Jane Pittman, Byerman writes that "the word and not the act is effective. The ability to call up not spirits but the truth of history is the power of the powerless" (142). In her curse, Celie for the first time is proclaiming her history—that of a woman who has been cut off from her sister, beaten and verbally abused by the man she is cursing. She replaces the "truth" of patriarchal religion—her prior understanding of the need to put up with Mister because he is her husband and heaven will eventually save her from the abuse—with that of her own history.

Illustrating Luisah Teish's definition of magic as "the art of using the forces of nature in the manipulation of symbols to manifest a desired change in people and things" (207), Celie invokes trees, wind, and dust to bring about a change in Mister. This change is marked; after her curse, Mister deteriorates.

Mr.—— live like a pig. Shut up in the house so much it stunk. Wouldn't let nobody in until finally Harpo force his way in. Mr._____ too weak to fight back. Plus, too far gone to care. He couldn't sleep. At night he thought he heard bats outside the door. Other things rattling in the chimney. But the worse part was having to listen to his own heart. (231)

It is not until he returns to Celie the letters from her sister that he had kept from her for years that he starts to improve. As Walker writes in her 1982 essay, "Only justice can stop a curse," and as Mae Henderson points out, this justice is not only justice and empowerment for Celie, but for Mister as well: "as conjure woman, Celie not only has the power to free herself from unjust oppression, but also the potential to release Albert from the burden of his own oppressiveness" (75). The curse is ultimately "generative" magic, for both Celie and Albert.

Celie's freedom from oppression and Albert's freedom from being oppressive are set in the context of a wider utopia that occupies the end of the novel. Celie, Nettie, and Celie's children are reunited; Celie's pants business (located in the store and house she inherited upon her stepfather's death) is successful, granting her both creative expression and economic independence; Albert has reformed himself into a sensitive man who cares for Celie and helps her with the sewing for her business; Celie and Albert have become friends; Harpo and Sofia are living together as husband and wife again. Celie closes her final letter by writing that "us so happy. Matter of fact, I think this the youngest us ever felt" (295).

In connection with this sort of utopia, Walker offers several definitions of "womanist" at the beginning of *In Search of Our Mothers' Gardens: Womanist Prose*, one of which includes the long-starved woman-to-woman same-sex love. To close *The Color Purple*, Walker conjures up a womanist vision of how she would like the world to be. As Annette Van Dyke writes of Walker's novels, they (including *The Color Purple*) "allow us visions of the possible" (42).

Alice Walker has often been criticized for this ending of *The Color Purple*. Robert Towers writes that "Alice Walker still has a lot to learn about plotting and structuring what is clearly intended to be a realistic novel" (qtd. in Hite 103). I would counter, along with Molly Hite, that perhaps Walker did not intend for it to be a realistic novel—or at least not realistic in a traditional understanding of that word. Hite suggests that when people say that something is "unrealistic" or that things don't happen that way "in reality," what they are really saying is "that things have never happened this way before" (107). That can almost certainly be said about the ending of *The Color Purple*. It probably is "unrealistic" for an abusive husband not only to stop being abusive, but to relinquish his stereotypical "masculine" role, take up sewing, become a compassionate listener, and accept the lesbian relationship between his wife and his former lover. It probably is "unrealistic" for a woman whose children—the products of rape—were taken from her in infancy to be reunited with them as adults and for everyone in the situation to be happy about it. It probably is "unrealistic" for a community of people consisting of adults involved in several "love triangles," children who are the products of a variety of those unions, heterosexuals and homosexuals, men and women, to live, work, and cooperate together as the characters of *The Color Purple* do at the end.

But is the point of the novel to depict a situation that is realistic? Relationships between women and between women and men are rewritten at the end of this novel. Rather than realistic in the traditional sense of that word, I would argue that the end of the novel is instead a product of Alice Walker's magic. It is a rhetorical move, intended to be effective in bringing about change. It presents what *should* be in "reality."

While "many reviewers" criticize Walker for being too imagina-tive—criticize the last third of the book because "the narrator-protagonist Celie and her friends are propelled toward a fairy-tale happy ending with more velocity than credibility" (Hite 103), others recognize the powerful possibilities of such a "fairytale" or "mythic" ending. Mary Daly offers *The Color Purple* as one of three examples of a Fairy Tale, as it is defined in her *Wickedary*: "an Archaic story that transports the Hearer into Fairy Time," which is defined, in part, as "Time that moves Counterclockwise and is accessible to those who ask Counterclock Whys" (123), questions taking the questioners beyond the boundaries of the patriarchal world. Thus, Walker's story is empowering, for it enables the reader to transcend the patriarchy's boundaries for awhile, in order to begin questioning its vision of the world. While the story itself might be "unrealistic," it can serve, in the terms set out by Daly, to bring readers into a more critical relationship with the "real world."

Jane Campbell writes about the use of myth in African American historical fiction, claiming it as "a radical act, inviting the audience to subvert the racist mythology that thwarts and defeats Afro-America and to replace it with a new mythology rooted in the black perspective" (x). For Walker, such an act is even more radical: in addition to subverting racist ideology, she also subverts sexist and heterosexist ideologies, replacing them with "a new mythology" rooted in a womanist perspective. For Campbell, myth and history are not mutually exclusive: "romance weds myth, the ideal world, with history, the world of actual events" (161). African American writers do this "so that readers can re-envision the past and, thus, the future" (155). Therefore, use of these "unrealistic"elements in the story does not disqualify it from being considered historical. Again, as noted above, such use of myth can bring the reader into a different relationship with history, leading her or him to "reenvision" the world. It involves an effective use of elements of myth and fairy tale to rewrite history.

Alice Walker herself understands history in an unusual way. In "Writing *The Color Purple*," Walker calls the book a historical novel and tells the story of how the novel was first conceived. She and her sister were discussing a love triangle about which both of them knew, when Walker's sister related how one of the women asked the other for a pair of her "drawers." This small detail helped the pieces of the Celie/Shug/Albert story that Walker was mentally composing fall into place. She insists that history, at an intense personal level, enacts not the mania of territorial acquisitiveness nor the birth, exploits, and death of great personages, but rather the warmth and intimacy of reciprocal womanist love. The novel, then, is historical, dealing with one group of people's personal histories, rather than with world history.

Walker also acknowledges that the novel transcends history. Celie was modeled after Walker's great-grandmother, who at age twelve was raped by her slave master and Walker's great-grandfather. Walker purposely rewrote her great-grandmother's story: "I liberated her from her own history. I wanted her to be happy" (qtd. in Henderson 67). Thus, the novel is historical as well as realistic, while at the same time rewriting history and suggesting new boundaries for what might be "realistic." This is done through conjuration and to rhetorical purpose—to effect change. As Walker writes, "[I]f and when Celie rises to her rightful earned place in society across the planet, the world will be a different place" (qtd. in Van Dyke 77).

Such conjuration would not be possible, of course, without language. Once again, as with the voodoo creation myth, voodoo/magic is a function of the power of language. In *The Color Purple*, it is specifically women's language which is so powerful. Hite writes that in *The Color Purple* "it is evident that female voices have the power to dismantle hierarchical oppositions that ultimately oppress everyone and to create a new order in which time-worn theories about male and female 'natures' vanish because they are useless for describing the qualities of people" (117). To Alice Walker, the choice of language is extremely important. In response to criticism of Celie's language and that used to describe the scenes of rape, she writes:

If I had written of Celie's rape from the point of view of the rapist or that of the voyeur, very few people—other than feminists—would have been offended. We have been brainwashed to identify with the person who receives pleasure, no matter how perverted. It is language more than anything else that reveals and validates one's existence, and if the language we actually speak is denied us then it is inevitable that the form we are permitted to assume historically will be one of caricature, reflecting someone else's literary or social fantasy. ("Celie's Voice" 71-72)

This, too, involves rhetorical choices on Walker's part, as she considers the exact use of language that will both have an effect on the largest possible part of her audience and most faithfully represent the type of person her protagonist is. Baker writes that "the secret of the conjurer's trade is imagination" (99), and initially, Walker's creation of a "new order" is done in the imagination. Through her writing, Walker creates a space in readers' minds for an alternative reality. This is a rhetorical act. Rhetorical theorist Chaim Perelman writes that creating "presence" is an important aspect of the rhetorician's task:

Choosing to single out certain things for presentation in a speech draws the attention of the audience to them and thereby gives them a *presence* that prevents them from being neglected. Recourse to the effects of language and to their capacity to evoke establishes the transition between rhetoric as the art of persuasion and as the technique of literary expression. (35)

By making present to her readers a vision of redrawn human relationships, Walker reverses Perelman's move, going from literary expression to persuasion. A function of the end of Walker's novel is to persuade readers that the community depicted therein is a desirable alternative to the ones drawn in the earlier parts of the novel.

The seeming incongruity between this community and the way these people lived earlier in the book is what seems to be too much for some critics. Yet it all does follow logically within the context of a critique of patriarchy. What separates the women in the novel from other women are patriarchal values. What prevents men and women in the novel from interacting in constructive ways are also patriarchal values. The novel's conclusion asks the question, What would happen if these patriarchal values were replaced with womanist values? There are two situations, among others, that highlight especially well the replacement of one set of values with another.

Shug and Celie's relationship developed gradually, and it is only after they have discovered the stack of letters Albert had been keeping from Celie that Shug finally separates herself fully from him. She begins to reflect upon the way in which she had previously allowed her love for a man to get in the way of her relationship with women. The patriarchal value of women existing solely for men was, for many years, the one by which Shug operated. It is not until this point that she is finally able to relinquish that and fully adopt the womanist value of women loving women. In a confessional scene, following the discovery of the letters, Shug relates to Celie the story of her relationship with Albert and consequent separation from other women:

I was so surprise when I heard [Albert] was going to marry Annie Julia, she say. Too surprise to be hurt. I didn't believe it. Poor Annie Julia, Shug say. She never had a chance. I was so mean, and so wild, Lord. I used to go round saying, I don't care who he married to, I'm gonna fuck him. And I did, too. I went to school with Annie Julia, Shug say. She was pretty, man. And sweet too. Hell, say Shug, I liked her myself. Why I hurt her so? And when I come here, say Shug, I treated you so mean. And all because Albert married you. And I didn't even want him for a husband. (125–7)

Shug is able to realize that her exclusive focus on her relationship with a man put a wedge between her and potential women friends. Women siding with men over women is one of the values of patriarchy. With the replacement of this value with womanist values, Shug is able to develop and maintain strong relationships with women, and in the end, with Albert as well.

Both Shug's new relationship with Albert, and even more amazingly, Celie's new relationship with Albert are made possible by Albert's relinquishment of patriarchal values as well. After breaking Celie's curse by returning her sister's letters, Mister begins a transformation. Celie writes that "look like he trying to make something out of himself. I don't mean just that he work and he clean up after himself and he appreciate some of the things God was playful enough to make. I mean when you talk to him now he really listen" (267). He takes up sewing to help Celie with her pants business, having told her, "When I was growing up, I use to try to sew along with mama cause that's what she was always doing. But everybody laughed at me. But you know, I liked it." Celie responds, "Well, nobody gon laugh at you now" (279). Nobody will laugh at Albert now because the characters now live in a world governed by womanist values rather than patriarchal ones.

Such a value reversal is, of course, not going to go by uncommented on by the forces of patriarchy. Walker has drawn numerous criticisms for her portrayals of men in the book. One comes from George Stade, who writes sarcastically of the novel: "Celie, in short, redeems these men by giving them the courage to be women, by releasing the woman already in them. But masculinity is unredeemable; masculinity is radical evil, irreducible, the causeless cause of all that's wrong in the world" (266). Mister and Harpo he describes as "womanish men" (263). This, to Stade, is an insult, though it can only be so to those for whom being a woman is a negative thing. Contrary to what Stade and others argue, "masculinity" is not absent from Walker's utopia, it is just not present exclusively in male characters. Sofia, Celie, and Shug all embody some of those characteristics traditionally called "masculine," while Mister and Harpo embody some of those traits traditionally called "feminine." What *The Color Purple* finally concludes is that gender roles and stereotypes are meaningless. Celie and Albert realize this in the course of a conversation they have about Shug:

Mr._____ ast me the other day what it is I love so much bout Shug. He say he love her style. He say to tell the truth, Shug act more manly than most men. I mean she upright, honest. Speak her mind and the devil take the hindmost, he say. You know Shug will fight, he say. Just like Sofia. She bound to live her life and be herself no matter what.
    Mr._____ think all this is stuff men do. But Harpo not like this, I tell him. You not like this. What Shug got is womanly it seem like to me. Specially since she and Sofia the ones got it.
    Sofia and Shug not like men, he say, but they not like women either.
    You mean they not like you or me.
    They hold they own, he say. And it's different. (276)

This acceptance of difference—that of roles, talents, viewpoints, and sexual orientation—is part of the ideology Walker is attempting to persuade readers to adopt.

In *The Color Purple*, Alice Walker uses traditional African American magic to conjure up a rhetorical argument/vision of how the world should be, from a womanist perspective. Her vision is an uncompromising one that does not have room for interpretations of "justice" that are not completely liberating for African American women. It is rhetorically successful in several ways. First, the novel's utopian vision opens up a space in which people who are persuaded to its justice can imagine new possibilities and become empowered to work toward such changes. Second, it raises consciousness about issues faced by women, both African American and other women, and presents a model of resistance. And third, though its vision is such that some people will never be persuaded to subscribe to any portion of it, the novel has been fruitful by generating debate in academic journals and classrooms. In all of these respects, Walker's conjuring/rhetoric has entered the dialogue about what makes for truth and justice in our increasingly ambiguous moral world, and has effected change in the minds of its readers.

NOTE

1. As Trudier Harris points out, "an important aspect of this change in [Mrs. Kemhuff's] appearance is that Hannah has transferred her faith from God to the conjure woman" (5).

WORKS CITED

Baker, Houston A., Jr. "Workings of the Spirit: Conjure and the Space of Black Women's Creativity." In *Workings of the Spirit: The Poetics of Afro-American Women's Writing*. Chicago: University of Chicago Press, 1991.

Byerman, Keith. *Fingering the Jagged Grain: Tradition and Form in Recent Black Fiction*. Athens, Ga.: University of Georgia Press, 1985.

Campbell, Jane. *Mythic Black Fiction: The Transformation of History*. Knoxville: University of Tennessee Press, 1986.

Campbell, Karlyn Kohrs. *Man Cannot Speak for Her*. Vol. 1. Westport, Conn.: Greenwood Press, 1989.

Courlander, Harold. *A Treasury of Afro-American Folklore*. New York: Crown, 1976.

Covino, William A. "Magic And/As Rhetoric: Outlines of a History of Phantasy." *Journal of Advanced Composition* 12.2 (1992): 349–58.

_____. *Magic, Rhetoric, and Literacy: An Eccentric History of the Composing Imagination*. Albany: State University of New York Press, 1994.

Daly, Mary, and Jane Caputi. *Wickedary*. Boston: Beacon Press, 1987.

Harris, Trudier. "Folklore in the Fiction of Alice Walker: A Perpetuation of Historical and Literary Traditions." *Black American Literature Forum* 11 (Spring 1977): 3–8.

Henderson, Mae. "*The Color Purple*: Revisions and Redefinitions." In *Alice Walker*. Ed. Harold Bloom. New York: Chelsea House, 1989. 67–80.

Hite, Molly. "Romance, Marginality, and Matrilineage: *The Color Purple*." *The Other Side of the Story: Structures and Strategies of Contemporary Feminist Narrative*. Ithaca: Cornell University Press, 1989. 103–126.

Hurston, Zora Neale. *Mules and Men: Negro Folktales and Voodoo Practices in the South*. New York: Harper & Row, 1935.

Laguerre, Michel S. *Voodoo and Politics in Haiti*. New York: St. Martin's Press, 1989.

Mbiti, John S. *African Religions and Philosophy*. 2nd edition. Oxford: Heinemann, 1990.

Perelman, Chaim. *The Realm of Rhetoric*. Trans. William Kluback. Notre Dame: University of Notre Dame Press, 1982.

Stade, George. "Womanist Fiction and Male Characters." *Partisan Review* 52.3 (1985): 264–70.

Teish, Luisah. *Jambalaya: The Natural Woman's Book of Personal Charms and Practical Rituals*. San Francisco: Harper, 1985.

Thomas, H. Nigel. *From Folklore to Fiction: A Study of Folk Heroes and Rituals in the Black American Novel*. New York: Greenwood Press, 1988.

Van Dyke, Annette. *The Search for a Woman-Centered Spirituality*. New York: New York nyc University Press, 1992.

Walker, Alice. *The Color Purple*. New York: Pocket, 1982.

_____. "Finding Celie's Voice." *Ms.*, December 1985.

_____. "The Revenge of Hannah Kemhuff." In *In Love & Trouble*. San Diego: Harcourt Brace Jovanovich, 1973. 60–80.

When a Convent Seems the Only Viable Choice: Questionable Callings in Stories by Alice Dunbar-Nelson, Alice Walker, and Louise Erdrich

Margaret D. Bauer

> Get thee to a nunnery.
> —Shakespeare, *Hamlet*

In her 1899 collection of short stories, *The Goodness of St. Rocque and Other Stories*, Alice Dunbar-Nelson included the story "Sister Josepha," one of very few of her writings that deals with particularly African American concerns. In the second half of the twentieth century, one of Dunbar-Nelson's literary "granddaughters," Alice Walker, included a remarkably similar story, "Diary of an African Nun," in her collection of short stories *In Love and Trouble*. Recognition of the parallels between these two stories highlights the subtleties of each. For example, while Dunbar-Nelson can only allude—and very vaguely—to the mixed blood that contributes to the dilemma of her protagonist, for she might otherwise offend her white readers by suggesting blame, Walker distances her protagonist's dilemma from her American readers by setting her story in Africa. In spite of writing almost a century later, Walker knew that race relations in America had not changed significantly. Indeed, she wrote this story at the end of the Civil Rights Movement, a period of American history even more turbulent than the post-Reconstruction period in which Dunbar-Nelson wrote. On the other hand, Walker does apparently perceive herself as freer than Dunbar-Nelson was to examine closely the origin of her protagonist's conflict. In her story, Dunbar-Nelson merely presents a vague depiction of one woman's conflict of identity that led to her decision to become a nun. In Walker's, the author delves deeper into her character's consciousness as the African nun examines the effects of the encroaching European influence on her life, limited now by her decision to become a nun, and upon her people, who are being coerced into abandoning their own religions in favor of Christianity, the dominant religion of the Western world.

Turning from these two stories to Native American writer Louise Erdrich's "Saint Marie," one can see that this autonomous chapter of the composite novel *Love*

Medicine deals with the same issues regarding a kind of compulsory conversion to Christianity developed in the earlier two stories. In contrast to Dunbar-Nelson, Erdrich tells her story from the perspective of a character who, like Walker's African nun, analyzes the source of her "calling." In contrast to Walker, however, Erdrich does not soften her criticism of the treatment of her people through distancing her story or her character's conflict from this country.

"Sister Josepha" opens with a sympathetic description of a fatigued nun falling asleep as she says her rosary during vespers, after which she utters a more heartfelt prayer to the "cher Seigneur".[1] "[I]t is wicked and sinful, I know, but I am so tired. I can't be happy and sing any more. It doesn't seem right for le bon Dieu to have me all cooped up here with nothing to see but stray visitors, and always the same old work" (156). The narrator then provides the reader with a brief history of this "rebellious" nun, who was left at a New Orleans convent fifteen years before. All that is known about her is the name Camille. According to the narrator's description of Camille as a little girl "who ruled the children and dominated the more timid sisters in charge" (158), one might think she has the strength of character to overcome her orphaned state. However, the narration of events that occurred during Camille's fifteenth year reveals that she has significantly more to deal with than being without family. The narrator precedes the revelation of what occurred with the subtle description of Camille's "glorious *tropical* beauty of the type that matures early" (158, emphasis added), "tropical" being a significant word choice in its suggestion of Camille's Creole—that is, part African—heritage. The narrator reports then that a couple who were visiting the convent "were fascinated by [Camille] and asked the Mother Superior to give the girl into their keeping" (158).

Camille stole a glance at her would-be guardians, and decided instantly, impulsively, finally. The woman suited her; but the man! It was doubtless intuition of the quick, vivacious sort which belonged *to her blood* that served her. Untutored in worldly knowledge, she could not divine the meaning of the pronounced leers and admiration of her physical charms which gleamed in the man's face, but she knew it made her feel creepy, and stoutly refused to go. (159, emphasis added)[2]

Upon being questioned later by the Mother Superior as to why she refused the offer, Camille responds, "[T]hat man looked at me so funny, I felt all cold chills down my back" (161). It is at this moment that she expresses a desire to become a nun: "Oh, dear Mother, I love the convent and the sisters so, I just want to stay and be a sister too, may I?" (161). The narrator then immediately adds, "And thus it was that Camille took the white veil at sixteen years" (161), thereby emphasiz-ing—though without further comment—the true nature of Camille's "calling." The convent would protect her from men who would look at her as that one had. The intuitive reader knows that an orphaned girl of mixed blood would have little protection outside its walls in late-nineteenth-century New Orleans. Appropriately, then, she takes the name of Josepha, thus naming herself after the saint who is prayed to regarding issues of shelter. The reader will recall that, according to the New Testament, Mary's husband Joseph found shelter for his wife as the time came for her to give birth to Jesus, and that, before marrying Mary, he agreed to raise this child who he knew was not his son. One can see how Joseph would be a benevolent father figure to an orphan, given his acceptance of the role of Jesus' earthly father.

The narrative returns to the present with the remark, "Now that the period of novitiate was over, it was just beginning to dawn upon [Camille, now Sister Josepha] that she had made a mistake" (161)—not just in joining the convent, but apparently also in refusing the couple's offer. She does not at this point consider the possible implications of that offer, thinking only of how "tired" she is, how "dull" her life is, and that she is still "so young" (162). Again, her new name, while probably referring to Saint Joseph as noted above, may also refer to the Joseph with the many-colored coat in the Old Testament and thereby reveals, perhaps, particularly if she chose the name herself as novitiates are sometimes allowed to do, Camille's fantasies that she, too, might have emerged triumphant after being sold into a kind of slavery. The association is supported by the narrator's reporting just before Camille meets with the couple that she is envied by the other girls. Of course, though Joseph did rise above his slavery and become the right hand of the pharaoh to whom his brothers had sold him, it was also he who summoned his brothers and their families into Egypt where their descendants were eventually enslaved, thus reflecting a seemingly unending cycle of oppression from which it is not so easy to escape.

Although the reader cannot be certain that Dunbar-Nelson had this Biblical Joseph in mind (as well as, or rather than, Saint Joseph) when choosing a name for her nun, it is interesting to speculate upon the subtle reminder in this biblical allusion of the responsibility of some African blacks for the enslavement of others in America, having sold out members of their own race for the white man's treasures, just as Joseph's own brothers sold him into slavery. This notion anticipates the forthcoming discussion of Walker's similarly subtle criticism of Africans—and perhaps African Americans—for selling out their religion and culture for those of the white man, as well as Erdrich's similar criticism of some Native Americans in her story.

The next major event in Sister Josepha's life occurs during a festival Mass when she looks up from her torturous ruminating on all the splendor that she witnesses before her (and from which her vocation separates her) to find a young man gazing sympathetically at her. She makes up her mind a short time later to "escape to flee into the world, to merge in the great city where recognition was impossible, and, working her way like the rest of humanity, perchance encounter the eyes again" (168–69). The narrator remarks, "Penniless, garbed, and shaven though she would be, other difficulties never presented themselves to her. She would rely on the mercies of the world to help her escape from this torturing life of inertia" (169). The reader, however, knows more about the "merciful" nature—or lack thereof—of the world to which Sister Josepha would escape, a place where a woman of color without protection would be at the "mercy" of many who would exploit her. Indeed, this harsh truth is soon confirmed within the story when Sister Josepha overhears other nuns speaking of her:

"She is not well, poor child," said Francesca. "I fear the life is too confining." "It is best for her," was the reply. "You know, sister, how hard it would be for her in the world, with no name but Camille, no friends, and her beauty; and then——" (170)

Dunbar-Nelson does not allow them to continue, perhaps to avoid displeasing her reader with direct references to the mistreatment of people of color that occurs in the community outside of the convent. Her narrator remarks that Sister Josepha is so overcome by what she hears that the rest of the conversation is drowned out by the beating of her heart. The reader, however, can fill in the rest with common knowledge about the times, the few hints that have been given as to Sister Josepha's racial heritage, and her thoughts after eavesdropping:

No name but Camille, that was true; no nationality, for she could never tell from whom or whence she came; no friends, and a beauty that not even an ungainly bonnet and shaven head could hide. In a flash she realised the deception of the life she would lead, and the cruel self-torture of wonder at her own identity. Already, as if in anticipation of the world's questionings, she was asking herself, "Who am I? What am I?" (171)

The "deception" referred to above may allude to a life "passing" as white. Certainly the final question——"What am I?"——suggests her recognition, in spite of not knowing her exact nationality or parental origin, that she is "black" according to the one-drop rule supported in this region of the country. As such, her defenselessness as a woman without familial protection is aggravated: society would offer a black woman little protection in lieu of family. As a result of her moment of insight, the next morning at Mass Sister Josepha repents for her sinful desires, and after Mass, rather than slipping away as she had planned, she "followed the rest, and vanished behind the heavy door" (172).

As already noted, the similarities between this story and Alice Walker's "The Diary of an African Nun" are remarkable: Walker's unnamed nun also laments the oppressiveness of her life as a nun; she, too, utters her distaste in prayer; the spiritual nature of her "calling" is equally suspect; and in spite of the different time period in which the story was written and, presumably, takes place, her story's ending is only slightly more optimistic.

Walker's story is structured as its title implies: it is written as a diary kept by an African nun. In the first entry, the reader can find reminders of Sister Josepha's encounter with the couple who wished to adopt her in Dunbar-Nelson's story. Walker's nun begins her diary explaining that the mission she lives and teaches in serves, too, as a hotel for travelers, and she reports upon the various reactions travelers have to her. Some, like the couple who visits the convent in Dunbar-Nelson's story, are struck by her beauty; some, like the leering man in Dunbar-Nelson's story, "are coolly passionate and smile at [her] lecherously" (113). These people's objectification of her introduces the nun's central conflict: to no one——including, apparently, her new "husband"/ God,——is she an individual, with aspirations and desires of her own.

Walker begins her criticism of the missionary influence upon Africa by directing it toward the religion that allows the missionaries themselves to feel self-righteous about their intrusion upon Africans. In particular, she critiques the lifelessness of Catholicism, contrasting it with the passion of African fertility rituals. At the start of her diary, the young nun identifies herself as "a wife of Christ" and immediately alludes to the absence of passion in her "marriage" as she identifies Christ as "a *celibate* martyr and saint" (114, emphasis added). Her animosity further reveals itself as she explains that she "was born in this township, a village 'civilized' by American missionaries," the quotation marks she puts around "civilized" revealing her sarcasm.

Except for the diary structure and first-person perspective, this nun's story follows the pattern of Dunbar-Nelson's narration. After having the speaker situate herself in the present, Walker allows her to turn back to explain how it was that she became a nun. Her "calling," too, is suspect: as a naive child she was fascinated by "the nuns and priests who taught at [her] school. They seemed so productive and full of intense, regal life. [She] wanted to be like them" (114). Upon becoming a nun, however, she learned, first of all, that "they could not have children" (114), reflecting the "barren" nature of their religion to which the nun has the most trouble reconciling herself. Like Sister Josepha, then, she prays to the God of her new religion expressing her dissatisfaction with her life, focusing in particular upon the lack of passion in it, and consequently complaining about being neglected by her "husband":

How long must I sit by my window before I lure you down from the sky?
Pale lover who never knew the dance and could not do it.
I bear your colors, I am in your livery, I belong to you.
Will you not come down and take me!
Or are you even less passionate than your father who took but could not show his face?
(115, author's italics).

Within this first prayer, she remarks upon Jesus' presumed virginity—he "never knew the dance" that takes place between the lovers she watches from her window at night—again alluding to the passionlessness of Christianity reiterative in the same prayer to God who impregnates the Virgin Mary in the absence of a sexual union with her.

Later, she considers a prayer in which she would point out to the European God the difference between his religion, which covers her (literally and figuratively) in cold whiteness, and that of her passionate and fertile native people:

Dearly Beloved, let me tell you about the mountains and the spring. The mountains that we see around us are black, it is the snow that gives them their icy whiteness. In the spring, the hot black soil melts the crust of snow on the mountains, and the water as it runs down the sheets of fiery rock burns and cleanses the naked bodies that come to wash in it. It is when the snows melt that the people here plant their crops; the soil of the mountains is rich, and its produce plentiful and good. (117)

The nun reveals with her metaphor that she is longing for her white habit to melt away like the snow, thus releasing the passion and fertility underneath. At night she has watched, her people dancing themselves into a frenzy that climaxes with sexual union and at dawn heard "The acclaiming cries of babies" (116), and now, it is the Africans whom she envies and wishes to join. And yet her life is ironically devoted to converting these natives to the religion that now imprisons her.

The story approaches its close, not with the African nun running down from the convent into the midst of an orgy, but with her recognition that she will continue in her chosen vocation, because, paradoxically, she decides that this barren religion is the only hope of survival for her people: "To assure life for my people in this world I must be among the lying ones and teach them how to die. I will turn their dances into prayers to an empty sky, and their lovers into dead men [i.e., Jesus], and their babies into unsung chants that choke their throats each spring" (118). Chester J. Fontenot explains that the nun "sees Christianity as a sort of material salvation for her people," for she realizes that "the African people must function in a Christian world. Hence, Christianity becomes a way of teaching her people a conscious lie to further their own ends—survival" (193–94).

The diary ends abruptly with the notion that her people's unique culture will die—"the drums will soon, one day, be silent" (118)—as they are "civilized" into "carbon copies" of the European missionaries. Walker then adds a closing sentence, from a third-person voice, in which it is suggested that the nun's private writing may ultimately not only be for the ventilation of her criticisms of and complaints against Christianity: "In this way will the wife of a loveless, barren, hopeless Western marriage *broadcast* the joys of an enlightened religion to an imitative people" (118, emphasis added). Walker seems to be saying here that this diary, or at least the sentiments within it, will one day be presented to the nun's native people—that is, that the nun will eventually rebel and express her views publicly. Thus, on the one hand, her resignation to continue with her "duties" to the Church reminds the reader of Dunbar-Nelson's Sister Josepha's return to the convent, while on the other, one senses more possibility for future rebellion by Walker's nun. This is not surprising when one considers that Sister Josepha's life as a nun seemed to be debilitating only to herself, while Walker's nun is "corrupting" her own people by fulfilling her unsavory duty of converting them to Christianity.

At the end of his article on Walker's piece, Chester Fontenot illustrates how the story can be read as an allegory "of the Black intellectual or middle-class who find themselves caught between two worlds" (196). Given this reading, Fontenot might agree that Walker has thus distanced her story from some fairly explosive issues by setting it in Africa. Walker is, in fact, so successful in distancing her story that at least one reader completely missed the racial issues in the story. After the story first appeared in *Freedomways*, a Reverend Donald J. O'Leary wrote the magazine complaining about Walker's criticism of the vow of celibacy of Catholic nuns and priests (70–71). In his letter, Reverend O'Leary makes no mention of sociopolitical concerns in the story—which Walker, however, does address in her response ("Alice" 72–73). In spite of her willingness to address the racial issues in her response, the initial distancing suggests that this contemporary author was apparently as much concerned about offending her readers—black and white—as Dunbar-Nelson seems to have been about dealing with racial issues almost a century before. Not only might white readers be offended by Walker's criticism of supposedly benevolent missionary work in Africa, but so might Christian black readers. Her black readers might also be somewhat insulted by Walker's subtle criticism of the blacks in her story. One notes in the last line of the story, quoted above, that she calls them an "imitative people," suggesting criticism of their too-easy acceptance of the metaphorical glass beads—including Christianity—brought by the European invaders as well as their quickness to abandon their own culture in return for the material and technological wealth of the Western world. She may be depicting in her story the situation between natives and missionaries in Africa, but the events are also directly parallel to the events in the stories in the second part of Jean Toomer's *Cane*, in which Toomer criticizes the African Americans who moved to the city and assimilated into the dominant Euro-American culture there.

Louise Erdrich, who may be to Native American literature what Alice Walker is to African American literature, opens "Saint Marie" with her protagonist's pronouncements that she would not stand for being ignored or viewed as inferior: "I was going up there on the hill with the black robe women. They were not any lighter than me. I was going up there to pray as good as they could. Because I don't have that much Indian blood" (40). Her reference to her light skin and mixed blood recalls Dunbar-Nelson's vague suggestion that Sister Josepha might survive unmolested in the outside world by passing as white and her allusions to Sister Josepha's mixed blood in her descriptions of her physical appearance. In direct contrast to Sister Josepha, Marie will deny her heritage in order to be allowed to live inside of the convent rather than to escape it, and in further contrast, she believes it is her whiteness that makes her attractive. She later makes the remark, "I looked good. And I looked white," implying a connection between the two assessments of her appearance (45), whereas in Dunbar-Nelson's story, Sister Josepha's dark beauty is emphasized. The major point of contrast between the two stories is that Marie ultimately summons the strength to leave the convent, even if it means returning to a world that views her as inferior because of her race.

In "Saint Marie," Erdrich explores more deeply than do Dunbar-Nelson and Walker the issue of coerced conversion. Like Sister Josepha and the African nun, Marie's "calling" is not of a spiritual nature but, rather, a result of her position in the world outside of the convent. The pattern of narration is the same as in the two earlier stories. Erdrich opens with Marie's present situation—a young girl presenting herself at a convent in order to be tested to see if she is novitiate-material—then narrates the events that inspired her goal. More pointedly than Walker's nun, Erdrich's protagonist notes the significant contrast between her life of isolation and poverty at home and her perception of the nuns' seemingly luxurious life in the convent. Like the African nun, Marie is telling her own story, but from the perspective of some time later. Also like the African nun, she is bitter, as is clear from her tone in the following passage:

I had the mail-order Catholic soul you get in a girl raised out in the bush, whose only thought is getting into town. For Sunday Mass is the only time my father brought his children in except for school, when we were harnessed. Our soul went cheap. We were so anxious to get there we would have walked in on our hands and knees. We just craved going to the store, slinging bottle caps in the dust, making fool eyes at each other. And of course we went to church. (41)

Whereas the African nun's bitterness rose up against Catholicism for its neglect of her personal passions and desires, Marie's bitterness seems directed against the religion's exploitation of her people's poverty.[3] Only at the end of her story does the African nun express her awareness of the ultimate tragic consequences of the missionaries' presence upon her people—that is, that they will eventually lose their own culture. Distanced as she is by the time of the *telling* of her experiences from the personal desires that drove her at the time of her experience, Marie can see beyond herself and therefore suggest to the reader from the start how her people were taken advantage of.

While attending church allowed Marie and her siblings to escape the tedium and deprivation of their home life, at the nuns' school they were taught that their lives at home were inferior because they were being inhabited, as they were, according to a Sister Leopolda in particular, by the Dark One. This nun's appellation for Satan has racial connotations in that it alludes to the darker skin color of her Native American pupils. As "Indians" they were naturally consorts of Satan, Sister Leopolda believed. It was her duty, then, to drive Satan out of her students by whatever means necessary, including corporal punishment and their conversion to Christianity. She would "white-wash" them by teaching them to desert their own cultural ways and take up the manners and mores of the dominant culture.

Interestingly, the reader of Erdrich's sequel to *Love Medicine*, the novel *Tracks*, knows that Sister Leopolda has already been successful at such "whitewashing"—with herself. She is actually Pauline Puyat, a mixed-blood Chippewa. In fact, she is Marie's mother, and though she neglected her child when she was a baby, she apparently wishes now (at the time of the events Marie narrates in "Saint Marie") for her daughter to follow in her footsteps. In spite of her success at passing for white, Pauline/Sister Leopolda is still torn between the two cultures, much as is Walker's African nun. Just as the African nun tries to merge the passion of the African rituals with her relationship with Jesus as she asks him to "come down and take" her (115), Pauline merges the Satan of Judeo-Christian tradition with the Chippewa lake monster Matchimonito in *Tracks*. Also similar to thediscussion of Walker's character's reason for remaining a nun is Nancy J. Peterson's explanation of Pauline's motivation in the novel: "The white Christian capitalists will win the cultural-epistemological war, in Pauline's view, and she will side with the victor" (989).[4] It is important to note here that Pauline's misplaced loyalty, the novel shows, results in part from her alienation from the Chippewas because of her mixed blood. Thus, besides her exposition of the treatment of Native Americans by the dominant culture, Erdrich also reveals the role that the Native American plays in his or her own oppression—much as Walker criticizes the "imitative" tendencies of blacks at the end of "Diary of an African Nun" and as Dunbar-Nelson more subtly reminds us of Africans selling Africans into slavery in

"Sister Josepha."

Not surprisingly, the majority of Erdrich's work is directed toward exposing the strong influence of European America upon her people, rather than the partial responsibility of a few Native Americans for the culture's gradual demise. In "Saint Marie," the author explores, again more pointedly than does Walker, the suspicious nature of the supposedly charitable missionary work of the Catholic Church among Native Americans in the 1930s.[5] From her vantage point of a time presumably in her adulthood, Marie reports that she eventually learned that "the Sacred Heart Convent was a catchall place for nuns that don't get along elsewhere. Nuns that complain too much or lose their mind" (42). The reader realizes that if the Church were truly concerned with the souls of these people, they would more likely have sent their best teachers and preachers of their faith. Sending instead their malcontents and misfits reveals the Church's view of these "souls" as inferior, not worth wasting the best people on.

As already suggested, Marie has the strength of character to defeat her adversary—the nun/her mother (though she does not know their relation), Sister Leopolda, who almost succeeded in making her view herself as naturally depraved, indeed, as nearly subhuman—and leave the convent, returning to her own people where, as later chapters in *Love Medicine* reveal, she chooses an "Indian" to be her husband and drives him to become a leader of their people. In further support of her own culture, she takes in orphaned Native American children, perhaps thereby saving them from being sent to institutions like the convent that would try to get them to forget their culture.[6] Unlike Sister Josepha, Marie will not hide behind a habit, safe from those who mistreat her people—though of course Sister Josepha, having been left at the convent at such a young age, did not have a sense that she was part of a culture she could embrace or that there was a community outside of the convent which would embrace her.[7] Unlike the African nun, Marie tells the story of her experience of mental and physical abuse while in the hands of this Catholic nun—and not to a diary. The tone of the narration is that of someone telling her story to a listener. Furthermore, Marie does not resign herself to a "can't beat them, so join them" attitude by concluding, as the African nun does (at the end of her diary at least), that her people would be better off, whatever the cost to the cultural vitality, accepting the Church's view of them as inferior until they exorcise their "darkness."

Marie's insight at the end of this chapter of her life is also more useful than the insight reached by the other two characters at the ends of their stories. Sister Josepha learns that she is limited to two "career choices" in late-nineteenth-century New Orleans: concubine or nun. The African nun decides that converting to a "dead" religion is the only hope of survival since the majority of the world's power worships its God. Marie, however, recognizes the common humanity of all people, whatever their race. Sister Leopolda is not her superior, but neither is she superior to Sister Leopolda. At the moment when she has Sister Leopolda at her mercy, "there was no heart in it. No joy when she bent to touch the floor" (56). Rather, there "was dust. Dust my lips. Dust the dirty spoons on the ends of my feet. There is no limit to this dust!" (56). She is humbled, but not to the point of feeling limited like Sister Josepha or resigning herself to death-in-life like the African nun. She heads down the hill and leads her people toward achieving pride in themselves and their culture.

NOTES

1. Having her protagonist address God with this mixture of French and Spanish is one of the subtle ways in which Dunbar-Nelson reveals her character's Creole heritage.

2. Again, Dunbar-Nelson only subtly alludes to race by crediting Camille's "blood" as a particular kind, having particular sensitivities.

3. Andrew O. Wiget explains in his discussion of the story's cultural and historical background that "Indian reservations in the 1930s were notorious for their poverty, their high mortality rate, their chronic unemployment" (854).

4. Another comparison between the behavior of the two women satirizes the Christian belief in sacrifice and martyrdom: Walker's African nun comments upon how she must "always bathe [her]self in cold water even in winter" (114). In trying to prove herself worthy of Christ, Pauline tortures herself unmercifully. Two of the less abusive—but most revealing because ridiculous—ways are that she restricts the number of times a day she can relieve herself and wears her shoes on the wrong feet.

5. As Andrew Wiget explains the role of Christian missionaries, "One of the principal policies of the United States was to transform Native Americans into carbon copies of Anglo-Americans, and one of the principal ways that they hoped to accomplish this, ever since the Grant administration of the 1870s was through religion.... The objective was to get rid of the Indian while saving the man. Culture was imagined as a number of practices and behaviors and customs, which—if they could be changed—would eliminate all the historic obstacles to the Indians' participation in Anglo-American culture. Of course, if they were eliminated, so would the Indian nest be eliminated. Religion then is hardly a simple spiritual force, but an agent of the interests of the Euro-American majority" (854).

6. One is here reminded of Nanapush, Pauline/Leopolda's nemesis in *Tracks,* who takes Lulu Lamartine out of a school that would try to drive her culture out of her.

7. This observation about Sister Josepha recalls the earlier discussion of the source of Pauline's behavior. She, too, lacked a communal sense when living among the Chippewa people, in her case because of their treatment of people with mixed blood living among them.

WORKS CITED

Dunbar-Nelson, Alice. Vol. 1 of *The Works of Alice Dunbar-Nelson.* 3 vols. Ed. Gloria T. Hull. Schomburg Library of Nineteenth-Century Black Women Writers Series. New York: Oxford University Press, 1988.

Erdrich, Louise. *Love Medicine.* New York: Bantam, 1984.

Fontenot, Chester J. "Alice Walker 'The Diary of an African Nun' and Dubois' Double Consciousness." *Journal of Afro-American Issues* 5 (1977): 192-96.

O'Leary, Rev. Donald J. "On 'The Diary of an African Nun.'" *Freedomways* 9 (1969): 70–71.

Peterson, Nancy J. "History, Postmodernism, and Louise Erdrich's *Tracks.*" *Publications of the Modern Language Association* 109 (1994): 982-94.

Walker, Alice. "Alice Walker's Reply." *Freedomways* 9 (1969): 71–73.

_____. *In Love and Trouble.* San Diego: Harcourt Brace Jovanovich, 1973.

Wiget, Andrew O. "Louise Erdrich (Chippewa) (b. 1954)." In *Instructor's Guide for Heath Anthology of American Literature.* 2nd ed. Ed. John Alberti. Lexington, Ma.: D.C. Heath, 1994.

Creating Generations: The Relationship Between Celie and Shug in Alice Walker's *The Color Purple*

E. Ellen Barker

As Alice Walker asserts in response to those who harshly criticized *The Color Purple* for its scenes of agonizing physical and emotional abuse, art should "make us better; if [it] doesn't then what on earth is it for"? (qtd. in Davis 42). It was Walker's contention that by presenting unrelenting portraits of human weakness, despair, and abuse, she could repair the damage done to the black community in the past, and through *The Color Purple* "right [or rewrite] the wrongs" (Sadoff 4) of social and literary history. As she firmly stated in a 1972 address to Sarah Lawrence graduates, "[T]he world is not good enough; we must make it better" ("A Talk: Convocation 1972" 37).

Walker describes the pattern like the quilt motif that provides symbolic structure for The Color Purple that has already gradually been making the world better: the unifying bond between black women. It is through "their friendships, their love, their shared oppression" (Smith 182) that they collectively gain the strength to separate themselves from the bondage of their past and piece together a free and equal existence for themselves and for those they love. These interactive relationships, as Walker notes, are preceded by similar connection among black foremothers and grandmothers. It is not just the love that exists between these black women as friends—or occasionally as lovers—that engenders a sense of self, but it is also through their relationship with their mothers, "the root-worker[s]" (Sadoff 5) of families and whole generations. Through her characterization of Celie, the symbolic embodiment of the black woman who grows from self-negation to self-actualization, and her relationship with Shug Avery, Walker traces the path of wellness culminating in the "survival whole" (qtd. in Parker-Smith 479) of the black community.

Shug Avery is at first a friend to Celie, eventually a lover, but always a subtly guiding "mothering" influence (Perry and Brownley) who, like the mothers of Walker's "generations," enables Celie to evolve into an independent, self-actualized woman, no longer benignly accepting the emotionally crippling conditions that have enslaved her. While Shug does not give literal birth to Celie, she does give her spiritual rebirth, freeing her to finally enter "into the creation" (170).

Celie becomes, then, the "new Black woman" who "recreates herself out of the creative legacy of her maternal ancestors" (Christian 470), more enriched and more empowered than before.

Walker called upon the influence of her maternal ancestor, her mother, and her literary ancestor, Zora Neale Hurston, as the collective models for Shug Avery, the woman who would inspire possibility in Celie the same way both women from Walker's personal history inspired possibility in her. The ability to nurture another, to inspire, to create possibility has been termed "mothering the mind" by Ruth Perry and Martine Watson Brownley in their book by the same title. "Mothering the mind," a process that begins very early, has its beginnings with the self:

An infant first experiences itself in the presence of—and in relation to—the mother or primary caretaker who holds it, feeds it, cleans it, and so on. This regular intervention permits the infant the experience of going–on–being, of a "self with a past, present and future" (Introduction 5).

Celie has been denied "a self" and is treated merely as an object. She has been repeatedly raped by her step-father and viewed as a necessary replacement for her own mother who was too ill and too weary of sex to act on her own. Later, when given to Mr. as his wife-slave, she is described by her step-father in terms of her ability to work and to attend to Mr. _____'s sexual needs, being viewed as mere property for exchange. Robbed of her self-esteem and reminded repeatedly that she is "black pore ugly a woman nothing at all" (176), Celie gradually begins to view herself in the same way: "I make myself wood. I say to myself, Celie, you a tree. That's how come I know trees fear men" (22).

She begins her letters to God as a form of therapy to relieve her from her isolation and to validate that there must be some divine plan for her miserable existence. She begins her epistles by asking and informing God that "I am I have always been a good girl. Maybe you can give me a sign letting me know what is happening to me" (3). Now, because of her wretched existence and because she believes she must have done something to anger God to deserve this punishment, she denies herself the privilege of "being" by crossing out "I am" and by speaking of herself in the past: "I have always been a good girl." For Walker, Celie embodies all black women. Like them, she too bears her pain unaware and unmindful of personal beauty and inner worth.

In part, Celie is denied a sense of self because she lacks a sense of belonging. Her mother was too much a product of an oppressive environment to provide the kind of nurturing that could "mother the mind" of anyone. She was not a caretaker; she was a victim. She chose death over a life of continued misery and disappointment, fearing that admitting the truth would force her to fight back. She only established for Celie a "past" and a prickly "present and future."

To further delay Celie's selfhood, she is removed from the only other person she loves, Nettie. While, in part, Mr. _____ tells Nettie she must go out of meanness and retribution, he sees Nettie and Celie's continued contact as a threat. If Celie is allowed to see Nettie or to correspond with her, she will have what he doesn't have: love and a sense of belonging. By depriving Celie of Nettie's letters, he can make her as emotionally bereft as he, and she won't have the will to fight back. Just like her mother, Celie will "stumble blindly" through life and perform whatever task necessary to survive. As she says to Nettie: "I don't know how to fight. All I know how to do is stay alive" (17).

The only way to resuscitate life back into Celie is through love, primarily with a mothering influence who could inculcate in Celie what her own mother could not. The functions of "mothering the mind" include "intercepting the world, conferring unconditional approval, regulating the environment, supplying missing psychic elements, and mirroring certain aspects of the self" (Perry and Brownley, Introduction 5). Shug does all of this for Celie. As a surrogate mother, she subtly nurtures Celie into self-acceptance and guides her through all the stages of self-actualization that most children go through early in their lives.

Shug Avery, as gutsy blues singer, mistress to Mr. and mother of his illegitimate children, may not initially appear to be the "mothering" kind. Even the image projected by the photograph Celie sees attests to that:

Shug Avery was a woman. The most beautiful woman I ever saw. She more pretty then my mama. She bout ten thousand times more prettier then me. I see her there in furs. Her face rouge. Her hair like somethin tail. She grinning with her foot up on somebody motocar. Her eyes serious tho. Sad some. (8)

She is a woman of questionable morals who the local preacher describes as "a strumpet in short skirts" (40), but even in Celie's initial description of Shug's photograph, she makes an unconscious comparison to her "mama," a comparison she makes several times throughout the novel. Unlike Celie's natural mother, who is dominated by gender and tradition, Shug is dominated by no one. She is a woman whose experience has given her an identity; as Celie notes: "When you look in Shug's eyes you know she been where she been, seen what she seen, did what she did. And now she know" (228). For all that Shug has been through, she still has the capacity to love herself, and in turn, someone else. Shug and other black women—like Hurston, Walker's mother, and Walker herself—become the collective spirit of "womanist fiction." In spite of Shug's external behavior, she is warm and compassionate and loves herself and other women "regardless." In "Breaking Chains and Encouraging Life," a title that is appropriate to the theme of Shug's effect on Celie, Walker speaks of the sincere reciprocal love that exists among African American women. Echoing this statement comes Celie's remark, "Hard not to love Shug. She know how to love somebody back" (239). One of the essential stages of "mothering the mind" is supplying "missing psychic elements," and Shug does this by loving Celie. Through her love, all of the other necessary stages of the "mothering" process come into focus.

At first, Celie acts as Shug's primary caretaker when she comes to Mr. _____'s to recuperate. Although Celie is attracted to Shug and has been infatuated since first eyeing her photograph, her feelings have no actual form; she cares for Shug out of duty, performing the task of nurse/mother. Shug is vulnerable and has also felt like a "motherless child" (167). When she was a young girl, she was often denied displays of affection from her mother: "She never love to do nothing had anything to do with touching nobody. I try to kiss her, she turn her mouth away" (103). The attention that Celie lavishes on Shug while she attempts to nurse her back to health is not only appreciated, but reciprocated; thus the attachment begins.

In these early scenes, when Celie is attending to Shug, she unconsciously juxtaposes her role with that of her "mama," realizing not only her response as caretaker, but the inexplicable comparison to her own mother. At first she notes Shug's vitality as it differs from her own mother's depleted spirit: "But she more evil than my mama and that keep her alive" (43). Later, when Celie combs Shug's hair and "loves every strand of it" (48), she notices that she "work on her like she a doll or like she Olivia—or like she mama" (48). At this point, her relationship with Shug becomes inverted; she originally acts as a mother attending a child, but this is replaced as she begins to subconsciously realize Shug's gradual nurturing effect on her. As Shug settles back into her new role of surrogate mother, snuggling against Celie's knees, the legacy of the healing process in generations of women and Shug's place in that legacy is verbalized. She almost echoes from the past: "That feel like mama used to do. Or maybe not mama. Maybe grandma" (48). When Shug settles into Mr. _____'s home and Celie's life, she, for the first time, experiences a feeling of connectedness: "Then I see myself sitting there quilting tween Shug Avery and Mr. For the first time in my life, I feel just right" (52). Interestingly, it is the quilt motif that reemerges, foreshadowing that the severed ties of the black community will be patched up, mended. In "Lettered Bodies and Corporeal Texts in *The Color Purple*," Wendy Wall calls *The Color Purple* "a quilt that exposes its seams and yet still may function to accommodate the human body, simultaneously rewriting coldness into warmth, disparate interpretative axes into a mosaic and dialogic voice, oppression into self-authorization" (96).

Shug and Celie's bond becomes stronger and their love and respect as friends begins to deepen, gradually transforming Celie's "oppression into self-authorization." Validating Shug's "unconditional" approval of Celie as friend and confidant, Shug dedicates a song to her: "Miss Celie's Song." This is not only the first time "somebody make something and name it after me [Celie]" (65), but it's the first time anybody has done anything for Celie.

Shug also acts to "regulate" Celie's environment, "intercepting the world" to protect her, an instinctive duty for most mothers. When Celie confides that Mr. _____ beats her because, to him, she is inadequate (she is not Shug), Shug promises not to leave until he reforms. When Shug discovers the cache of letters Mr. _____ has hidden as a cruel method of subduing Celie, and when while reading these letters, it is discovered that "Pa" was not Celie's biological father, proving that her children were not the product of incest, Shug's immediate reaction is to take Celie away to a purifying environment where she will be safe.

While carefully ensconced in Memphis, Shug encourages Celie to pursue her creativity through the design of "fancy pants." Shug conceives of the idea and is major investor in the business, seeing to it that Celie becomes a success. Shug not only invests her time and her money in Celie's business, she invests her love: "I brought you here [Memphis] to love you and help you get on you feet" (179). According to the pattern of "mothering," Shug wants to nurture Celie, help her define herself through love and achievement, and then let her go, sending her off to garner her own outside experiences. As Celie sits on Shug's dining room floor, visualizing patterns and sewing together fabrics of her own choosing, Celie begins to trust in her own creativity and her own existence as a vital, contributing member of society. Like a mother surveying her own handiwork, the successful cultivation of a child, Shug squeals, "Girl, you on your way" (181).

Of course, part of the identification process to self-actualization begins in establishing roots, knowing family and place. When Celie's mother dies, her roots vanish; Shug helps her to recover them. When Celie discovers that she has inherited her parents' property, she has a desire to view her past as a means of securing her future and wants to confront her stepfather. As further affirmation of "self," Celie wants to return to the graves of her parents. Her stepfather, of course, placed the bodies in unmarked graves, burying Celie's past and identification with her biological parents. The only family Celie has left is Shug, and she gladly assumes that responsibility, comforting Celie with a kiss, acknowledging that "[u]s each other's people now" (156).

The final and most important stage of "mothering the mind" concerns "mirroring certain aspects of self." When an infant grows up, the most familiar person it sees is usually its mother. This is the person who, through her facial expressions, indicates approval, disapproval, pleasure in the infant's activities, and so on. As Perry and Brownley indicate in *Mothering the Mind*:

[T]he mother [as] primary caretaker also provides the child with its first external verification of inner feeling by reflecting back to the infant its own behaviors and sensations. When a baby cries, its mother often shows concern; when a baby coos and gurgles, its mother smiles and talks to it. These mirroring responses give the infant its first "objective" access to its inner world, help it to explore that new terrain. If there is no responsiveness to the infant's expressions of feeling, if the infant looks and does not see itself feeling what it feels, its creative capacity begins to atrophy. (6–7)

Certainly at the beginning of the novel, Celie's creative capacity and capacity to sustain life in any vital way had withered, but through her observance of Shug and their interaction, Celie gets the mirrored responses she needs to restructure her "self." According to Jacques Lacan, Shug would qualify as a "(m)Other" (qtd. in Ross 78). Under Lacan's formulation of the "self," a subject first becomes aware of itself by identification with a person, usually the mother, "although the figure can be any constant nurturer" (qtd. in Ross 77). This mirroring with Shug manifests itself with Celie's identification of another whom she wishes to be or be like. Second, united with identification of another, or "(m)Other," is the reclamation of the body. Celie has no concept of her own body, only that it—and she—are "ugly." Third, Celie forms personal beliefs and philosophies by mirroring and then evaluating Shug's beliefs. And, fourth, and most important, because Shug "knows how to love and give love back," Celie learns not simply to mirror the actions of love, but to genuinely feel love.

When she was a young girl, Celie was described as being hopelessly ugly, and after years of abuse, she nearly makes herself invisible. She has neither the time nor the desire to care for her appearance; she has been made to believe that such a concern would be self-defeating. When Celie sees Shug for the first time, she is enamored with the vision of a woman who is "bout ten thousand time more prettier than me" (8) and is so enamored that she stares at her photograph all night long. Later, when Celie goes to the local store to buy fabric, she pauses to "think what color Shug Avery would wear" (20), trying to mirror her appearance as a means of associating with a woman she admires.

Through Shug, too, Celie learns the universality of shared experiences. When Celie is being given away to Mr._____, she takes out the worn photograph of Shug for reassurance: "I look into her eyes. Her eyes say Yeah, it bees that way sometime" (10). She learns an early lesson verified through Shug's world-weary wisdom. During sex with Mr._____, Celie makes herself numb to mediate the pain of this violation. She thinks about Shug "whirling and laughing" (8), desiring to react like she would: "I know what he doing to me he done to Shug Avery and maybe she like it. I put my arm around him" (13). Wendy Wall explains that "the image of Shug is an antiself, someone active and able to express herself; it is by clinging to this image that she is able to translate her feelings of inanimacy into passion" (84)—or at least pseudo passion—because Celie's response, at this time, is merely imitative. Yet, she makes an attempt to respond passionately to another human being because this is what Shug Avery would have done. These initial imitative expressions of feeling lead the way for genuine responses to follow.

When Shug moves into Mr._____'s home, Celie's reaction to her builds from infatuation to physical response. When she sees Shug's body for the first time, she is attracted and feels her first erotic stirrings: "First time I got the full sight of Shug Avery long black body with it black plum nipples, look like her mouth, I thought I had turned into a man" (45). Shug interrupts Celie's prolonged stare and snaps, "What you staring at? You never seen a naked woman before?" (45). In truth, Celie has never actually *seen* a naked woman before. Her own sense of body is void. Curiosity about Shug's body helps her to see her own. The importance of reclaiming one's own body for the purpose of self-actualization is outlined by Daniel Ross as follows:

One of the primary projects of modern feminism has been to restore women's bodies. Because the female body is the most exploited target of male aggression, women have learned to fear or even hate their bodies. Consequently, women often think of their bodies as torn or fragmented, a pattern evident in Walker's Celie. To confront the body is to confront not only an individual's abuse but also the abuse of women's bodies throughout history; as the external symbol of women's enslavement, this abuse represents for women a reminder of her degradation and her consignment to an inferior status. (70)

Because Celie has been the subject of repeated rapes and beatings, she has no desire to get to know her body. To protect herself, she has had to annihilate her body as well as her soul. It is not until Shug's arrival that she develops an interest.

At this stage, Shug's initiation of Celie to the body is one of the primary functions of mothering in the "mirror-stage experience" (Ross 77). At some point, early in a young girl's growth, she should identify with her mother's body: "This identification foregrounds the child's acceptance or nonacceptance of its sexual organs" (77). Seeing Shug's body begins the primary step toward this identification, but through Shug's guidance and a handheld mirror, literally mirroring Celie's genitalia, she views that sexual part of herself for the first time. While not enthralled with what she sees, she's able to assertively announce "It mine" (70). By discovering and then accepting her own body, Celie is able to initiate a desire for selfhood. The mirror reflection of her own body opens the door for possibilities in herself, and with her newfound identity, Celie is able to break free from male domination and join a community of women for support, and she begins to establish an identification through a network of female relationships with Shug.

Even though Celie has come to terms with her body, she is still a "virgin" (69), Shug exclaims, because she has never had a satisfying love relationship. Self-awareness of her body and exposure to Shug's love have stimulated sexual desire in Celie, so it becomes only a natural response that their relationship climaxes in love making. When Shug returns to Mr._____'s house with her new husband Grady, Shug and Celie develop a more stabilizing, intimate bond. Because she's cold sleeping alone in the absent Grady's bed, Shug sleeps with Celie, and like two school girls, they talk about their sexual experiences. Shug is appalled by Celie's history of sexual abuse. Like a mother, Shug envelops Celie in her arms, trying to comfort her, to make up for her past. For the first time in the novel, Celie is uninhibited enough to respond naturally through tears. As she tells her awful tale, she confides that no one ever loved her, but Shug reassures Celie that "I [Shug] love your, Miss Celie. And then she haul off and kiss me on the mouth" (97). Their homosexual union is a first for both of them, but it is natural and freeing and a culmination of their love for each other. For Shug, it is an ultimate gift of love, and for Celie, love making and being loved complete her spiritual journey to selfhood. When she wakes up with Shug the next morning, she says, "it feel like heaven" (98). This is the first time Celie has ever awakened in the morning feeling secure and loved.

The lesbian relationship that develops between Celie and Shug again reinforces the richness of female bonding. For Celie, such a relationship is her only choice. Men are brutal oppressors; they are the enemy. With regard to Celie's past, it would be illogical for her to choose sex with a man, and lesbianism can be a learned preference rather than a biological or genetic orientation (Siegel). Celie has never been loved by any man, only tormented and abused. In his article, Ross notes that "Celie's orgasm suggests a rebirth or perhaps an initial birth into a world of love, a reenactment of the primal pleasure of the child at the mother's breast" (72). Essentially Celie's life begins anew here.

Utimately, Shug teaches Celie to believe in herself and to see herself as an object of creation, free and equal to anyone or anything. With Shug's instruction on religion, Celie takes her final, liberating step. Celie has always sought solace from God, the white man's institutionally defined God. She envisions him rather typically as "big and old and tall and graybearded and white. He wear robes and go barefooted" (165). Ironically, this *white man* represents exactly the two things that have enslaved her for years. Celie has allowed herself to be a slave to this God, expecting him to help her through life, always tackling difficulties, proclaiming that "with God help" (42), she can accomplish what she has been told to do, seldom what she wants to do. Rather than looking to God for help, Celie needed to look to herself.

Finally, Celie comes to realize that this God has gotten her nowhere when she discovers that Mr._____ has maliciously hidden Nettie's letters. At this point, she rejects this traditional version of God by asking: "What God do for me" (164)? Shug explains that

God is inside you and inside everybody else. You come into the world with God. But only them that search for it inside find it. And sometimes it just manifest itself even if you not looking, or don't know what you looking for I believe God is everything. Everything that is or ever was or ever will be. And when you can feel that, and be happy to feel that, you've found It. (166–67)

When Celie discovers that she is a part of "the creation," that she fits into the natural order of the world, actual redemption occurs. "To enter into the flow of God's creativity is to know love and through love to know the meaning of selfhood, family, and community—in short to know true wisdom" (Hiers 3); thus she finally has self-reckoning and importance. Since Celie can love herself, she can love others. With the love from Shug, Celie earns the right to wear the royal robe of purple.

Robed in purple [women] receive and accept the right to love themselves and each other. Love of self energizes them to the point that they break their chains of enslavement, change their own worlds, time and Black men. They are prepared to fight—eye for an eye, tooth for a tooth. And they remain women—cry when they need to, laugh when they want to, straighten their hair if they take a notion. They change their economic, political, and moral status, with love. (Parker-Smith 483)

Shug has successfully guided Celie through the mirror stage of her development as a fully actualized, autonomous individual by helping her to discover her own body, by giving her the ability to love and see the creation in herself, and finally by giving Celie the capacity for speech.

In Celie's jubilant celebration of self, she rises from a family dinner determined for once to stand on her own, "to fight—eye for an eye, tooth for a tooth" She leaves Mr._____ and her sentence of slavery behind. When she defiantly announces, "It's time to leave you and enter into the Creation" (170), Celie is affirming her selfhood and announcing her rebirth into this creation, to be free, to be equal to every man, to every being. When Mr. defies her, she maintains her affirmative stance: "I'm pore, I'm black, I may be ugly and can't cook, but I'm here" (176). Celie has arrived, and realizing the goal of the ideal Walker heroine in fiction—and better yet, in life—she has the power to be "her own black self"

(Davis 46).

With any parent/child relationship there comes a time when both must realize that it's time to let go. This time comes when Shug wants the freedom to pursue her last fling with a boy half her age. Shug can part from Celie, knowing that, like any good mother, she has done all that she could to provide an environment of love and security so Celie can stand on her own two feet. Celie has learned that with or without Shug, she is now enough of a woman that she can survive on her own. When Shug writes Celie that her last fling has fizzled and that she's going to come home, Celie, with her newfound insight, writes:

Now. Is this life or not?
I be so calm.
If she come, I be happy. If she don't, I be content. And then I figure this the lesson I was suppose to learn. (240)

The bond between Celie and Shug enables the cycle of generations to go forward, only this time with more freedom and more humanity. Once Celie learns to love herself, she loves others—even Mr._____, the man who was partially responsible for her deterioration. She inspires in him enough redemptive spirit that he can salvage what's left of his manhood, and like Celie, emanate love to others. While standing on the porch with Celie, he admits that "this the first time I ever lived on Earth as a natural man. It feel like a new experience" (221). Indeed, it is a new experience, not just for Mr._____ but for all the individuals in this novel, or anywhere, who have suffered a similar oppression. These people have survived and have made a new life for themselves and for generations to come; they symbolize a larger hope for their community and for their race. At the close of the novel, while Celie, Shug, and Mr._____ sit on the porch together, basking in the luxury of just "being," Nettie and Celie's children arrive, making the final connection to generations. Finally, this is a family united, and in the spirit of affirmation that this novel invokes, Harpo wisely asserts: "White folks busy celebrating they independence from England. Us can spend the day celebrating each other" (243).

In Celie's last letter, she addresses it, "Dear God. Dear stars, dear trees, dear sky, dear peoples. Dear Everything. Dear God" (242). Celie's salutation is a celebration of life and of all humankind beginning and ending with God, in praise of the self and of creation. Celie's life has come full circle, from spiritual annihilation to rebirth, and this has been accomplished through the mothering influence of Shug Avery, and has been and will continue to be accomplished by all mothers, all women, joined in the common cause of unifying families, communities, "peoples." When Celie concludes with an affirmative "Amen" (243), Celie is blessing the power of the human spirit to overcome the horrors of oppression and the past and is rejoicing in the utter possibility of life.

It is true that *The Color Purple* is burdened by page-after-page description of human suffering and despair, but as Walker knows, the world is still "not good enough." The novel concludes on an affirmative note, suggesting a larger hope for humankind. In "Finding Celie's Voice," Walker explains her responsibility as an artist and predicts her hopeful vision for the future, insisting that Celie's redemption is concomitant with her own sense of healing. In the spirit of generations of women before her, Walker has left her own legacy in the truth of her pages. *The Color Purple* can "make us better," or at least make us see how far we have to go.

WORKS CITED

Christian, Barbara. "Alice Walker: The Black Woman Artist as Wayward." In *Black Women Writers (1950 1980)*. Ed. Mari Evans. New York: Anchor Books, 1984.

Cooke, Michael G. *Afro-American Literature in the Twentieth-Century The Achievement of Intimacy*. New Haven: Yale University Press, 1984.

Davis, Thadious. "*Alice Walker's Celebration of Self in Southern Generations.*" In *Women Writers of the Contemporary South*." Ed. Peggy Whitman Prenshaw. Jackson: Univ. Press of Mississippi, 1984. 39–53.

Gates, Henry Louis, Jr. *The Signifying Monkey: A Theory of Afro-American Literary Criticism*. New York: Oxford University Press, 1988.

Gilbert, Sandra M., and Susan Gubar. *The Madwoman in the Attic: The Woman Writer and the Nineteenth-Century Literary Imagination*. New Haven: Yale University Press, 1979.

_____. *No Man's Land: The Place of the Woman Writer in the Twentieth Century*. New Haven: Yale University Press, 1988.

Harris, Trudier. "Three Black Women Writers and Humanism: A Folk Perspective." In *Black American Literature and Humanism*. Ed. R. Baxter Miller. Lexington: The University Press of Kentucky, 1981. 50–74.

Hiers, John T. "Creation Theology in Alice Walker's *The Color Purple*." *Notes on Contemporary Literature* (Sept. 1984): 2–3.

Lenhart, Georgann. "Inspired Purple." *Notes on Contemporary Literature* (May 1984): 2–3.

Parker-Smith, Bettye J. "Alice Walker's Women: In Search of Some Peace of Mind." In *Black Women Writers (1950–1980)*. Ed. Mari Evans. New York: Anchor Books, 1984. 478–493.

Perry, Ruth, and Martine Watson Brownley, Eds. *Mothering the Mind*. New York: Holmes and Meier, 1984.

Prescott, Peter S. "A Long Road to Liberation." *Newsweek*, 21 June 1982: 67–68.

Ross, Daniel W. "Celie in the Looking Glass: The Desire for Selfhood in *The Color Purple*." *Modern Fiction Studies* 34.1 (Spring 1988): 69–83.

Sadoff, Diane F. "Black Matrilineage: The Case of Alice Walker and Zora Neale Hurston." *Signs: Journal of Women in Culture and Society* 11.1 (1985): 253–70.

Siegel, Elaine V. *Female Homosexuality: Choice without Volition*. Hillsdale, N. J.: Analytic Press, 1988.

Smith, Dinita. "Celie, You a Tree." *Nation*, 4 Sept. 1982: 181–83.

Stade, George. "Womanist Fiction and Male Characters." *Partisan Review* 52.3 (1985): 264–70.

Tate, Claudia, ed. *Black Women Writers at Work*. New York: Continuum, 1983.

Walker, Alice. "A Talk: Convocation 1972." *In Search of Our Mothers' Gardens: Womanist Prose*. San Diego: Harcourt, Brace, Jovanovich, 1983. 33–41.

_____. "Breaking Chains and Encouraging Life." *In Search of Our Mothers' Gardens: Womanist Prose*. San   Diego: Harcourt Brace Jovanovich, 1983. 278–289.

_____. *The Color Purple*. New York: Harcourt, Brace, Jovanovich, 1983. 231–243

_____. "In the Closet of the Soul: A Letter to an African-American Friend." *Ms*. Nov. 1986: 32–33.

_____. *In Search of Our Mothers' Gardens: Womanist Prose*. San Diego: Harcourt Brace Jovanovich, 1983.

Wall, Wendy. "Lettered Bodies and Corporeal Texts in *The Color Purple*." *Studies in American Fiction*, 16.1 (Spring 1988): 83–97.

Washington, Mary Helen. "Black Women Myth and Image Makers." *Black World*, Aug. 1974: 10–18.

_____. "I Sign My Mother's Name: Alice Walker, Dorothy West, Paule Marshall." *Mothering the Mind*. Ed. Ruth Perry and Martine Watson Brownley. New York: Holmes and Meier, 1984.

Alice Walker and the "Man Question"

Pia Thielmann

During the Marxist-Socialist revolution in Europe, the "Woman Question" was relegated as secondary vis-à-vis the primary goal of a classless society liberating everyone from various injustices. Though solving the "Woman Question" was put on hold, an unequal status between women and men was recognized. When issues of gender inequality are not recognized—are glossed over or frivolously redefined—and if women's oppression merely subserves a revolutionary dynamic instead of inspiring it, women's unchallenged subordination is absorbed as necessary solidarity "in light of the more pressing unified front." Imamu Amiri Baraka's position on this issue is a case in point. This member of the Black Liberation Movement of the 1960s in the United States expressed his conviction that the African American woman's role is to instill a positive racial consciousness based on Africaness in children. To Baraka, African American men are the teachers of African American women; they determine what women are allowed to pass on to their children. In his view they cannot be equals but are complements. Thus, the African American woman is supposed to remain man's helpmate to build a black nation, wherein the African American woman is one-half and the African American man the other half. However, the man is the more important half of the two (Baraka 7–11).

The resulting dilemma for African American women—of being expected to choose one cause over another—was a part of the discussion in the broader Civil Rights Movement of the 1960s as well as part of the feminist movements since. In contrast to Baraka, the African American feminist, civil rights activist, and co-founder of NOW, Pauli Murray, has argued that African American women cannot afford to ignore any facet of their triple discrimination—racism, sexism and classism—and especially not sexual exploitation, from which they have suffered due to stereotypes about African American women's sexuality (87–102).

When African American women do not conform to ideas such as Baraka's, and share Murray's argument, they often get into trouble. One nonconformist who got into trouble is the African American novelist, Alice Walker. Walker addresses this issue of self-empowerment versus subjugation of women in Part Two of her essay collection *In Search of Our Mothers' Gardens* (117–228). It mirrors her experiences with and reflections on the Civil Rights Movement and its effects on

African Americans. In "Coretta King: Revisited," Walker expresses that for her, woman-oriented politics is an important means by which the African American woman finds a sense of self; it is a means by which she protects herself from the African American man who takes out his anger against white discrimination on her (146–57).

True to her conviction, Walker has dealt explicitly with African American sexism in her fiction. Her commitment has sparked a controversy about the "Man Question" in her literary work as well as in her own unique personality. She has become the target of literary critics—many, but not all, African American men, who questioned the validity of her representation of African American men. From some critics' perspective, Walker's treatment of African American male characters indicates her lack of unconditional solidarity with "her men" in reality. She was accused of having turned against them and having become a liability to the African American community.

The controversy about Walker's supposed lack of solidarity with African American men lingered after the publication of her first novel, *The Third Life of Grange Copeland,* in 1970; peaked after the publication of novel number three; *The Color Purple* in 1982, and flared up again in 1986 following the adaptation of the novel into a Hollywood film by director Steven Spielberg. In 1989, Walker published her fourth novel, *The Temple of My Familiar.* The controversy about the portrayal of African American men continued after *The Temple,* and at the December 1990 Modern Language Association convention in Chicago, an informal poll declared Walker "out" (Matthews 43ff.). And in the spring of 1992, when Walker's fifth novel, *Possessing the Secret of Joy,* appeared on the literary market, she had hoped that this one would "not be thrown back in my face like all of the other books" (qtd. in Whitaker 88). However, it was, in a way: it ignited a discussion about her representation of African women and society by highlighting the issues of "female circumcision" and its assumed psychological and political consequences. Within this framework, however, the focus regarding *Secret of Joy* shifts dramatically again to the "melodramatic" way in which Walker represents her male characters.[1]

Important contributions to the controversy directly relating to Walker's treatment of men have been made by the African American scholars, Trudier Harris and Philip M. Royster. Both take *The Color Purple* as the ground of their discussion. Harris's negative response to the novel is built on the fear that it might call into life what she calls "spectator readers," European American readers who buy into the description of Daniel Patrick Moynihan's 1965 report on the "pathology" of the African American family and whose racist stereotypes she sees reinforced by Walker's presentation of the African American community and African American men. For Harris, it is, then, no wonder that European Americans praise the novel more often than African Americans. She sees this praise as an expression of European-American racism. Taking a review by Gloria Steinem, the former editor of *Ms.* magazine, as an example, she accuses Steinem of being surprised at "Walker's achievement; She praises Walker for generally being alive, black, and able to write well" (Harris 156). Harris also shows the reaction of another European American woman who is presented as being more sensitive toward racism than Steinem. This woman is paraphrased as having said that "if she had not been told the novel had been written by a black woman, she would have thought it had been written by a Southern white male who wanted to reinforce the traditional sexual and violent stereotypes about black people." Thus, Harris believes that

the book simply added a freshness to many of the ideas circulating in the popular culture and captured in racist literature that suggested that black people have no morality when it comes to sexuality, that black family structure is weak if existent at all, that black men abuse black women, and that black women who may appear to be churchgoers are really lewd and lascivious. (157)

Hence, Walker, an African American author committed to antiracism and antisexism, is charged with having written a novel that confirms a racist and sexist society's most debilitating and degrading stereotypes about African Americans.

Harris also presents the view of an African American man whom she sees as representing other men's sentiments about the novel. This particular student of hers insisted that the male characters in *The Color Purple* are "young and potheads or middle-aged and henpecked" and "stripped of their identity" (157):

No man in the novel is respectable. this student maintained, not even Albert (because he can only change in terms of doing things that are traditionally considered sissified. such as sewing and gossiping). And what about the good preacher who goes off to Africa. I asked him. He's not an exception, either, the response came back, because he must get down on his knees and ask a woman for permission to get married. All the men, the student concluded, fit into that froglike perception Celie has of them. And the problem with these frogs? None of them can turn into princes. (159)

The problem that becomes evident in this student's and Harris's perception is that Walker does not glorify African-American men. This "failure" to glorify, however, turns to Walker's advantage, since her intent is to clarify the ways, however overt or subtle, in which men as well as women are wounded by racism and how they may ultimately be healed. Another problem the previous quotation makes clear is that critics of Walker's representation of African American men do not acknowledge that the author implies the possibility of positive change and growth. What Walker presents as desirable activities in men—activities that should be encouraged because they deal with nurturing one's own or another's body and/or soul, such as sewing (nurturing of the body) and gossiping (nurturing of the soul via communication), are seen as negative for men and thus dismissed as "sissifyed." This attitude is also expressed when Harris summarizes, "All the good guys win, and the bad guys are dead or converted to womanist philosophy." Unlike Hollywood's fantasy world with its guaranteed happy ending, to which Harris implicitly compares *The Color Purple,* the "bad guys" do not die because it is convenient for the story or because of some sense of moral judgment, but because their violence destroys them. Their deaths are tragic and not a relief. Walker, then, has created anything but a melodrama. In regard to the "good guys" and those "converted to womanist philosophy" (160), Harris does not acknowledge the possibilities of a constructive cohabitation and communication between men and women. Society's topsy-turvy value system seems to make Harris sneer at Walker's womanism and indirectly dismiss "good" as "sissified," just as her student does.[2]

Philip M. Royster's response to *The Color Purple* is similarly hostile. Backing himself up with negative responses by African American women, such as Sonia Sanchez and Trudier Harris, Royster adds other aspects to the criticism of Walker's portrait of men: Walker's only positive description of African American men is of older men as father figures or sexual partners for women with a desire for a "sugar daddy." Discussing *The Color Purple*, Royster says:

Appropriate to the attitudes of the novel, the malevolent Alfonso dies while screwing a child wife. Celie is up for only violent, abusive, and manipulative sexual relationships with father figures or parental figures to justify the anger and sublimate the desires of the alienated darling in search of a father. Celie's homosexuality is clearly portrayed not as congenital but as a predilection or pathology that results from being the victim of not merely male but also father figure abusiveness: She is too afraid of her father to look at boys; she expresses a desire for only one person; and she seems unaware of the sexuality of other women. (368)

Further, Royster sees Walker as alienated from other African American people. For both assumptions Royster gives reasons based on Walker's private life. Although Walker uses autobiographical elements in her fiction, she certainly does not project her own life experiences without any literary alterations. Royster's approach throws Walker completely back on her private experiences and limits her creative and imaginative capabilities as an author. Indeed, Royster sees Walker's childhood experiences as her private problem and nothing to bother readers with. The alienation from other African Americans he links with the fact that Walker was married to a European American man, which he mentions three times in his article. One cannot help but get the impression that he strongly disapproves of this interracial relationship and implicitly accuses her of betrayal with the white enemy. While he inflicts guilt on Walker, he accuses her of riding "one of her hobbyhorses" (357) when she says that Black women alienate themselves from women's liberation, which for Walker is an intolerable situation because of the multiple oppression African American women experience. Royster turns the table on Walker when he claims that the author inflicts guilt on African American women by emphasizing that if black women do not associate with the women's movement, "they abandon their responsibility throughout the world" (Walker, *In Search* 379). An interesting contribution to the debate about the portrait of African American men in the novel *The Color Purple*, as well as in the film with the same title, is offered by Richard Wesley. As an African American man who might also have been offended by Walker, he takes a positive position and defends the author against charges of betrayal by pointing to the social conditions that might occasion characters such as Mister, and for that matter, Celie, who for a long time has had to endure stoically unmitigated spousal abuse. Wesley points out that the criticism of the character as voiced by Royster is a relic of the Black Power Movement. Not directly referring to Royster, but speaking in general terms about the kind of criticism the novel itself has been subjected to, Wesley declares:

For these men, the Black Power ideology of that time has remained sacrosanct and is in no need of revision. Part of that ideology requires black men and women to pull together. However, the unity of black men and women can only exist if the man *leads.* Therefore the woman must "submit": remain silent on sensitive issues. You do not "disrespect" your man in public, that is, criticize him in public, or speak too loudly about things that matter to you, or interrupt him when he is conversing with friends or colleagues on "serious" issues. A woman must always defer to her man and subjugate her will to his. (90)

Wesley acknowledges that this standpoint is still part of African American male thinking, even if it is not spoken out loud—an attitude that he believes is responsible for the "image tribunal," as he calls it, to which African American women writers like Walker are and must be subjected. For Wesley, Walker "is reminding many of us men of our own failures. She is reminding women of *their* failures as well. She is saying that Black Is Beautiful, but not necessarily always *right.* A lot of people do not want to hear that" (90). A similarly positive view is taken by a white woman, Jane Miller, who describes Walker's novel as "a story of rebellion, a regenerative and affirming turning of the tables on men, whose brutality towards women may be understood but must also be resisted" (241). Miller's response to Walker's most controversial novel seems to affirm Harris's observation that white women are quick to praise *The Color Purple.* Yet Miller has simply found it necessary to analyze negative behavior, recognizing that to change it is to the benefit of everybody. As Walker herself has said, she is "preoccupied with the spiritual survival, the survival *whole* of my people" (qtd. in O'Brien 192), and she believes in change,

change personal, and change in society. I have experienced a revolution (unfinished, without question, but one whose new order is everywhere on view) in the South. And I grew up—until I refused to go—in the Methodist Church, which taught me that Paul *will* sometimes change on the way to Damascus, and that Moses—that beloved old man—went through so many changes he made God mad. (qtd. in O'Brien 194)

Walker's belief in change, and commitment for a better world that enables better men (and women) of all colors to emerge is apparent in her dedications. The book *To Hell with Dying*,[3] beautifully illustrated by Catherine Deeter, is dedicated "To the old ones/of my childhood/who taught me/the most important/lesson of all:/That I did not need/to be perfect to/be loved./That no one/does." The "old ones" of Walker's childhood here can safely be assumed to include men, especially since the story "To Hell with Dying" is about an old man. The first novel, *The Third Life of Grange Copeland*, is written "For my mother,/who made a way out of no way/And for Mel, my husband." *Meridian* has a dedication for the civil rights workers "Staughton Lynd and Maryam L./and for John Lewis the unsung." And Walker's *The Temple of My Familiar* is dedicated to her friend "Robert,/in whom the Goddess shines." If Walker were not concerned about the well-being of all human beings, female and male, but were interested in putting (African American) men down, she most likely would not have dedicated some of her works to men; or, put differently, Walker dedicates her works to men and women, young and old, Africans and European Americans alike, as an expression of her loving inclusion of all human beings in her concern for wholeness/survival whole. This concern for human well-being is also expressed—successfully or not—in her latest novel *Possessing the Secret of Joy*, whose dedicatory note reads: "With Tenderness and Respect/To the Blameless/Vulva."

The male characters in Walker's fiction that have caused the most heated controversy because of their combined age and positive attributes include Mr. Sweet in her first published short story, "To Hell with Dying," the father and grandfather of Sarah in "A Sudden Trip Home in the Spring," and Grange Copeland in *The Third Life of Grange Copeland*. As mentioned above, Royster sees the positive portrait of these old men as the "castration" of young men. He implies that only when physically nonthreatening or weakened are men portrayed by Walker in any way other than as brutes and rapists. However, Mr. Sweet is not shown as having been a brutal young man, but as one who has experienced racism. He "had been ambitious as a boy, wanted to be a doctor or lawyer or sailor, only to find that black men fare better if they are not" (*In Love and Trouble* 130). And despite the fact that he is not a faithful husband, he is not shown as a physical wife abuser but rather as a person who falls victim to drinking out of frustration caused by the limitations put on him because of his color. Further, the tenderness between the old man and the children does not necessarily have to be interpreted as Walker's "hang-up" on older men but can, especially if one considers Walker's commitment to wholeness, be interpreted as a symbol of the human life cycle. While the old man is about to "give back"—or to die—he gives tenderness to the children, and the children give tenderness to him. There is no strict hierarchy between the young and old; they have related souls and prepare each other for their respective futures with the mutual sense of responsibility: individuals have to take care of each other, especially in difficult times, such as growing up or dying. Further, they can learn from each other, learn openness and trust from children and life experiences from the old.

In "A Sudden Trip Home in the Spring," the young college student, Sarah, travels South to the funeral of her father. This funeral gives her the opportunity of coming to terms with him. By asking her brother the question Richard Wright had asked himself in regard to his father about "the duty of the son of a destroyed man" (Washington, *Black-Eyed Susans* 145), she is trying to understand the life circumstances of her father that made him the man he was: the "man whose vision had stopped at the edge of fields that weren't even his" (Washington, *Black-Eyed Susans* 145). Thus she includes her father's history as well as the history of all African American men into her understanding of her relationship toward him. He is not the villain who cannot and will not relate to his daughter. Rather, he is one of those African American men whose face the young artist cannot paint—one of the victims of racism: a person who is sensitive enough to acknowledge that poverty based on racism destroyed his wife, a person who could not bear the excruciating burden of endless overwork and constant uprooting in the hunt for scarce job opportunities. The tender description of Sarah's proud, patriarchal grandfather stresses that he is very family oriented. He has not deserted his wife or children; he and his wife have earned a living for their family; he is not defeated. This undefeated attitude is also expressed by the grandmother, who would like to have a great-grandchild. This longing for a new life expresses hope in the future and a positive attitude toward life despite life's hard circumstances.

In *The Third Life of Grange Copeland*, Grange is another positive portrayal of Walker's men who is old. Different in some respects from Sarah's grandfather in "A Sudden Trip Home," Grange is described as a brutal young man who unwittingly leads his neglected wife to commit suicide, who raises a son, Brownfield, who in turn brutalizes others over the course of the novel, and who ultimately sacrifices himself at the end. Yet the relationship between Grange and his granddaughter, Ruth, is whole. It is a tender, respectful relationship, one of give and take, as between Mr. Sweet and the children who are frequently called to his deathbed in "To Hell With Dying." While Ruth learns from Grange the spiritual and practical tools necessary for survival, he learns from her to love, that indiscriminately hating European Americans does not solve racism, and that not all European Americans are villains. Grange has to go through changes in order to be able to allow himself to grow and reach his third, positive, but short stage of life. And these changes literally take a lifetime. Again, it seems that Walker implies that old people are close to the spirits, the truth of life, and can see the mistakes of European Americans as well as their own.

In *Meridian*, Walker takes up the topic of sexual pressure imposed on younger African American men and the consequences, both for African American men, and all women. Sexual pressure, based on white stereotypes about black male sexuality, can lead to rape, as Walker indicates in creating the volatile situation between Tommy Odds and Lynne Rabinowitz. Lynne, the European American exchange student, friend of Meridian and wife of Truman Held, first sees African Americans as art rather than as full human beings and feels pity for Tommy Odds as a member of an oppressed/"handicapped" group, and because he has literally lost an arm. In turn, Tommy Odds does not see his rape as a rape because Lynne has not screamed at all. Walker also suggests that Truman Held "feeds" on white virgins, as Lynne puts it in her moment of frustration. There is no excuse for rape, and Walker makes no attempt to offer one. What she appears to do is not to show a black brute, but to make visible the interlocked patterns of misconceptions about black and white sexuality, misconceptions that have existed for hundreds of years and have been perpetuated by society. The anger of Tommy Odds against European Americans and his lack of knowledge about them as human beings lead to the vicious circle of self-fulfilling prophesy that turns him into the rapist of a European American woman and allows him to justify his actions.

Truman Held, however, is one of Walker's male characters who learns and changes. He does, however, come under severe scrutiny by Walker. For example, his unbecoming treatment of his wife, Lynne, and his friend and lover Meridian; and his demeaning of African American women, whom he sees largely as specimens for his eccentric art, are some of the less charitable aspects of his personality. Toward the end of the novel, Meridian tells him: "You are free to be whichever way you like, to be with whoever of whatever color or sex you like—and what you risk in being truly yourself, the way you want to be, is not the loss of me. You are *not* free, however, to think I am a fool" (*Meridian* 216). Truman thus comes to understand that Meridian is not there at his beck and call; nor is any other woman, black or white. He simply has to learn to see the human being in the woman instead of merely the sexual artifice of his deadened fancy.

Mr._____ in *The Color Purple*, probably the most controversial male character in all of Walker's works, comes a long way from cheating on his wife Celie, abusing her, keeping her sister's letters from her, and telling her "You black, you pore, you ugly, you a woman. Goddam you nothing at all" (213), to being able to communicate with her, tell her his thoughts, and ultimately learn to love:

I start to wonder why us need love. Why us suffer. Why us black. Why us men and women. Where do children really come from. It didn't take long to realize I didn't hardly know nothing. And that if you ast yourself why you black or a man or a woman or a bush it don't mean nothing if you don't ast why you here, period.

So what you think? I ast.

I think us here to wonder, myself. To wonder. To ast. And that in wondering bout the big things and asting bout the big things, you learn about the little ones, almost by accident. But you never know nothing more about the big things than you start out with.

The more I wonder, he say, the more I love.

And people start to love you back, I bet, I say.

They do, he say, surprised. (289–90)

When Mr._____ learns to wonder and begins to change, he learns the art of tolerance, and at that point, actually becomes an authentic friend with a name—Albert. Learning this art has become a sine qua non for the cultivation of positive characters; they learn to respect and care for each other. Such care can be expressed when men take on nurturing work, the kind of work that Harris's African American student had called "sissified." What is traditionally women's work, seen as degrading for men, is here propagated as work done by people who like to do it rather than as being gender specific. It is also work that expresses the possibility of communication, and work that can lead to a common goal. For example, as long as Harpo, Albert's son, does the work he loves— house work—despite the fact that it is not defined as man's work, and as long as he lets his wife, Sophia, be the strong and independent person she is and always wants to be, the two of them are happy. Only when he tries to control her and starts to beat her as a means of submitting her to his will does their marriage begin to falter. As soon as Albert starts to see Celie as a human being rather than his personal property (which he received, along with a cow, from her stepfather to substitute for his dead wife) is he able to stop hating her and even take humorously her view of his genitals as being froglike. By carving her a wooden purple frog, which Celie keeps on her mantlepiece, Albert takes the sting out of her view. As the white feminist science fiction writer, Ursula K. Le Guin, says in her review of Walker's fourth novel, *The Temple of My Familiar*, the novel's richness is "amazing, overwhelming. A hundred themes and subjects spin through it, dozens of characters, a whirl of times and places. None is touched superficially: all the people are passionate actors and sufferers, and everything they talk about is urgent, a matter truly of life and death" (12). Similarly positive views of this book are voiced by the African American critic, Doris Davenport and by the Native American poet, Luci Tapahonso. Davenport calls *The Temple of My Familiar* "one of the most important books of the late eighties because of Walker's "messages," her possibility of "saving" a large number of us—or of enabling us to see and save ourselves, through an Afracentric vision" (14). Tapahonso calls this novel "a celebration of ordinary life and of everyday emotions" (13) and

a novel about love—in all its forms: love for spirits and spirituality, love for the land and plants, love for all people—regardless of color, sexual preference or age—and love for all loving things. It is about compassion for the oppressed, the grief of the oppressors, acceptance of the unchangeable and hope for everyone and everything. (13)

In this novel, Walker pulls together the strings from her previous work, by having a central character, Miss Lissie, who remembers her former lives as women, men, black, white, and animal (lion). This technique allows Walker to revive characters from *The Color Purple*. In addition, it allows her to place the novel in several locations and at several different times. Further, Walker can put important and extensive parts of the novel from male points of view, namely, those of the characters Suwelo and Arveyda. Thus the reader is presented with a holistic approach to life, with an attempt to eliminate boundaries and hierarchies among different species, different historical times, and different geographical places. She can fictionalize people's roots in Africa, trace myths, and give "the familiar," the friend—everybody, that is—a temple, a home. So the book itself is a temple, a place in which to learn to value and respect life—and death—as part of the life cycle. The dedication in *The Color Purple* reads: "To the Spirit:/without whose assistance/Neither this book/Nor I/Would have been/Written" and the post script reads: "I thank everybody in this book for coming. A. W., author and *medium*" (emphasis mine). In *The Temple*, Walker gathers the spirits again who are meant to guide her readers in understanding our stories and each other.

 The Temple is an optimistic book with positive portraits of men—but the controversy around Walker's portrayal of men continues as her critics now focus on characters "too good" for reality. In an ironic tone, critics Merle Rubin, J. M. Coetzee, and James Wolcott, to mention only a few, discredit Walker. Rubin talks about the character Suwelo as "a model 'womanist,' who feels bad about the way he used to treat women and hopes to make things up with Fanny," his ex-wife; she summarizes Walker's development and study of myths as "[b]adly put: Women had things right; men took over and, to justify themselves, invented stories presenting women (and, Walker adds, animals and blackness) as evil: Eve and the serpent; witches and their animal 'familiars'" (13). Via the permanent use of quotation marks throughout her review and the very casual tone, Rubin distances herself from the author and the book and leaves an impression of ridicule. Ridicule of Walker and her work also seems to be the main objective of the South African white novelist Coetzee's review, "The Beginnings of (Wo)man in Africa." By using the word "woman" in deconstructive terms, he not only ridicules but also seeks to marginalize women—in stark contrast to the egalitarian approach of the novel itself. If he had not wanted to distort Walker's vision, he could simply have used the terms "people" or "humankind." He brushes the book aside when he says, "But whatever new worlds and new histories we invent must carry conviction: they must be possible worlds, possible histories, not untethered fantasies; and they must be born of creative energy, not of dreamy fads" (7). By calling her book a "workshop" of all kinds, James Wolcott, the most biting reviewer thus far, not only attacks Walker as a skillful author but also implies that the novel has no literary value. He is also hard on Walker's male characters, who are portrayed, after all, as either positive or as capable and willing to challenge their old views and kinds of behavior. He ridicules the singer Arveyda, who is presented as a sensitive person with a healthy center who thus can move his audience with his music; he is not, as Wolcott sees him, a Jimmy Hendrix imitation who "makes women weep and moan with his guitar and flute" (28); nor is he "secure with himself; man enough to be a woman" (29). As Wolcott sees it, "he's rewarded with the novel's showcase prize of penetration" (29). While the reviewer's perspective on intercourse remains that of the male, Walker describes the scene to which he is referring from both Arveyda's and Fanny's perspective, as a mutual, enjoyable, shared experience, only possible after difficult self-recognition and respect for one's self, one's past and each other:

Fanny feels as if the glow of a candle that warms but could never burn has melted her, and she drips onto Arveyda. Arveyda feels as if he has rushed to meet all the ancestors and they have welcomed him with joy. It is amazing to them how quickly—like a long kiss—they both come. (408)

However, Wolcott's primary focus is on Suwelo, who he claims "grows as a person, but his growth is entirely on Walker's terms—he comes around to her way of thinking" (29). He contends that the novel "tutors him and in tutoring him becomes tedious" (29). Suwelo, the history teacher, does in fact grow as a person. He grows as he relearns history, his own and his people's. He has to learn that there is more to history than the perspective of the dominant group—that it is essential, both literally and figuratively, "to consider African women writers and Kalahari Bushmen," which initially he sees as "a bit much" (178).[4] He has to learn to make the connection between colonialism and his relationship to his wife's physical sensations. Only when he can analyze his fascination with pornography and his demand that Fanny direct her attention to his sexuality rather than to her own or shared needs can he develop respect and come to the conclusion that "[e]ach person must remain free. That is the main thing" (396). Equally ironic is Wolcott's review of Miss Lissie, the painter-storyteller who, via her incarnation as multiple beings–including a white man and a lion—is the link to the past and to the understanding of victims and victimizers. Yet Wolcott, who calls her "Mother

Africa's kharmic ambassadress, a woman [who] has never changed sex or hue" (30), cannot recognize Miss Lissie's function in the book and thus Walker's unique holistic vision of the world. Since he sees Walker as a "hippie artifact," he dismisses her literary product as "counterculturalism [:] too dreamy-floaty to connect with the crackhead immediacies of the times" (30). One imagines him to agree with another disgruntled critic who dismisses *The Temple* as nothing but a "sorry sack of silliness" (Iannone 59).

Tina McElroy Ansa invents a new form of attacking or dismissing Alice Walker: the breaking of another taboo, this time by writing about something as seemingly private and embarrassing as female "private parts." She introduces her review of Walker's fifth novel, *Possessing the Secret of Joy*, with the following anecdote:

A month ago, I heard an African-American male scholar/writer say in the manner of a comic throwing away a line, "Hey, did you hear that Alice Walker dedicated her latest novel to 'the innocent vulva?'"

He sort of pursed his lips and looked slowly around the room. Then, he raised one eyebrow, sort of chuckled and went on to another subject. As if to say, "Nough said."

His gesture was part amusement, part embarrassment, part incredulity, part derision. (4)

This reaction might give an indication as to why most reviews of Walker's most recent novel are written by women, one of whom calls it "idiotic" (Shapiro 56). Women do not remain silent on the issue of "female circumcision," since the philosophy and justification as well as the condemnation of this practice impact all women, directly or indirectly. Further, one could speculate that the representation of this small (t)issue does not directly threaten the reputation of men in general, since, as one common argument goes, it is women who are the guardians of this cultural practice. Neither does it threaten the reputation of African American men, since none of its three forms—excision, clitoridectomy, and infibulation—are a common practice in the United States. If such were the case, one wonders whether there would not be more (defensive) reactions by men to Walker's last novel.[5]

The question the reader is led to ask, and one that might be another reason why the book does not seem to be of urgent interest for male critics, is, How can women do something like this to each other? The answer Walker suggests in her novel lies in patriarchy, "African corruption," and "primitivism." This triune implication leaves room for a critical debate about Walker's representation of black male characters—including African men, such as the president of the fictive state of Olinka. Yet a controversial representation of African men apparently poses no threat to African Americans, since they are not part of the group that demands solidarity and loyalty from African American women. And with the "insignificant morsel" (72), the clitoris, at the center of attention, even the debate about her representation of African American male characters appears to have waned.

As far as the representation of African American men goes, one should be concerned about Walker's positive representation of Adam, the husband of the African woman, Tashi. With Adam, Walker picks up a character whom the reader of *The Color Purple* knows as a loving, lovable man. In *Possessing the Secret of Joy*, Adam is portrayed as supportive of Tashi. He goes with her to Zurich to see "The Old Man," the depth psychologist himself——Carl Jung. And he stands by her in her trial for the acclaimed murder of the circumciser, M'Lissa. Through all these sensational events, Walker shows another side of Adam, yet glosses over this persona in such a way that being an adulterer who frequently leaves his wife and has a son with his white French lover does not call for protest. In the sections that are devoted to Adam's perspective, we learn that the young French woman, Lisette, who becomes his lover of many years, is an early attraction for Adam, even before his marriage to Tashi.[6] Although he acknowledges how painful this relationship is to Tashi, he does not end it. Tashi's reactions to Lisette and later, to Adam's love son, Pierre, are simply fits of jealousy to Adam. Each of Adam's visits to Paris is another turn of the knife in Tashi's wound. Yet he does not discontinue them because he needs a friend with whom he can release his pain about Tashi (renamed Evelyn in the United States) and their burdened marriage.

When Adam is relieved that Tashi and "The Old Man" get along, his perception reveals the limitations of his male perspective. Writing to Lisette, who had recommended her uncle, "The Old Man," as a therapist, Adam says, "At least the two of them get along. As you know, I had feared they would not; Evelyn does not take easily to doctors of any sort, and has, over the years, tended to leave her therapists prostrate in her wake" (74). This seemingly positive creation of Walker's is in fact a condescending, prejudiced, disloyal man. He expresses more understanding for the doctors' "hopeless case," Tashi, whom he treats like a child. He reports to Lisette that "[s]he is sometimes merry just at the sight of him, and thinks of him, I believe, as a kind of Santa Claus. As such, he is another representative of the exotic Western and European culture she so adores" (74). He feels free to talk about his wife to his lover. Adam is not critically approached within the novel: Walker shows empathy with this poor man who got such a bad deal of a wife. Through the representation of Adam, the prototypical male, Walker appears to give men license to cheat, because, after all, men need good sex (and Lisette even has an orgasm giving birth to their son). Since Walker chooses to make Tashi a mad child, she gives Adam license to fulfill his needs for good conversation with a would-be wife. And since Tashi's "condition" provides most of their topics, Tashi is, once again, exploited——by Adam and by Walker.

With the representation of African American men in *Secret of Joy*, Walker continues the trend begun with *Temple*. While the positive portrayal of black men in this novel is part of her literary vision in which a loving life becomes possible for everybody, Adam's positive image portrayal reeks of giving in to the desire to be "in" again, to have her book accepted rather than thrown back in her face. *Possessing the Secret of Joy* is clearly a less successful segment of Walker's otherwise holistic literary approach to diverse experiences of human life. As Walker will continue to write, the controversy is likely to continue also, if not escalate: be it about her portrayal of African American men or about new issues relating to the politics of gender. One of Walker's supportive critics, Richard Wesley, says, "Writers are the antennae of any society" (91). If that is so, Walker did pick up on a marketable issue, "female circumcision." She also picked up on—or rather, caught up with—conservatism that is lenient on women-degrading attitudes and actions. Wesley further states that "they [the writers] have to speak when others dare not" (91). Regarding her transformed representation of African American men, Walker apparently has stopped being daring: with her new handling of the "Man Question," by presenting acceptable African American male characters unlikely to rekindle old controversy, she appears to relegate the "Woman Question" to its historical subordinate position.

NOTES

1. I assess Walker's latest novel, *Possessing the Secret of Joy*, as a problematic representation of infibulation, one of three different forms of the so-called female circumcision. Briefly, some of my questions and concerns include: (1) The life and mental health of the African protagonist, Tashi, are entirely determined by the absence of her clitoris. Does that mean that "circumcised"women/African women are mental wrecks? Tashi is, in fact, reduced to her clitoris, that is, in my view, to nothing. (2) The African woman has no (positive) identity—she is stripped of her name and renamed in the United States. (3) Though appropriated, she seems to be a burden to everybody, including herself. (4) Walker does not cast the subject in a thoroughly credible, investigative social and cultural context; her main source is a dead, white European anthropologist, rather than African women and men. (5) Tashi's "case" demonstrates the benefits, perhaps primacy, of "civilized" society (the Western world) over a backward, even barbaric setting (dark Africa). For an excellent discussion of Walker's vision of Africa and African women, see Omofolabo Ajayi's article, "Transcending the Boundaries of Power and Imperialism: Writing Gender, Constructing Knowledge" in Obi Nnaemeka and Ronke Oyewumi, eds., *African Women and Imperialism* (Trenton, N.J.: Africa World Press, forthcoming).

2. For Walker's definition of womanism, see *In Search of Our Mothers' Gardens*, xi—xii.

3. This book is the short story with the same title included in Walker's collection *In Love and Trouble: Stories of Black Women*.

4. The people Suwelo calls Kalahari Bushmen call themselves Basarwa.

5. Some reviews by women not previously mentioned include: Carol Anshaw, "The Practice of Cruelty," rev. of *Possessing the Secret of Joy*, by Alice Walker (*Chicago Tribune*, 21 June 1992: sec. 14.3); Karen Grigsby Bates, "Possessing the Secrets of $uccess: Toni Morrison is the Senior Member of a Triumphant Trio of Best-selling Writers" *(Emerge: Black America's Newsmagazine* 4.1 October 1992): 47–9. Pearl Cleage, "A Stunning Journey for 'Joy,'" rev. of *Possessing the Secret of Joy*, by Alice Walker *Atlanta Journal* June 14, 1992: N8); Diedre Donahue, "Walker's Disturbing 'Secret': Novelist explores trauma of the mutilation of women," rev. of *Possessing the Secret of Joy*, by Alice Walker, *(USA Today* 18 June 1992): D1; Janette Turner Hospital, "What They Did to Tashi," rev. of *Possessing the Secret of Joy*, by Alice Walker *(New York Times Book Review* 28 June 1992 : 11–12); Susan McHenry, "A Dialogue with Alice Walker," *Emerge: Black America's Newsmagazine* 3.10, September 1992: 9–10); Patricia A. Smith, "'Secret of Joy': Walker's Tender, Terrifying Tour de Force," rev. of *Possessing the Secret of Joy*, by Alice Walker, *Boston Globe* (6 July 1992): 38. Some reviews by men not previously mentioned include: Charles R. Larson, "Against the Tyranny of Tradition," rev. *Possessing the Secret of Joy*, by Alice Walker *(Washington Post* 5 July 1992: WBK1, 14); Mel Watkins, "A Woman in Search of Her Past and Herself," rev. of *Possessing the Secret of Joy*, by Alice Walker *(New York Times* 24 July

1992: C20). Charles Whitaker's previously quoted article in *Ebony*, based on a talk with Walker, takes an overall positive attitude toward Walker and her work and focuses a good deal on Walker's apparently unexpected nonthreatening appearance and friendliness.

      6. As an aside, it might be interesting to note that Walker has three females with similar names: Miss Lissie in *Temple*, and M'Lissa and Lisette, both in *Secret of Joy*. While Miss Lissie is the incarnation of positive change, the circumciser M'Lissa is a villain, and Lisette is positioned between these extremes, as a real human being. The ending—*ette*—in her name means "little." Thus the potential for growth is allocated to this person, a white European. Miss Lissie is perfect and does not need to grow. M'Lissa dies and so cannot grow anymore.

WORKS CITED

Ajayi, Omofolabo. "Transcending the Boundaries of Power and Imperialism: Writing Gender, Constructing Knowledge." In *African Women and Imperialism*. Ed. Obi Nnaemeka and Ronke Oyewumi. Trenton, N.J.: Africa World Press, forthcoming.

Ansa, Tina McElroy. "Taboo Territory." Rev. of *Possessing the Secret of Joy*, by Alice Walker. *Los Angeles Times*, 9 July 1992: BR 4,8.

Anshaw, Carol. "The Practice of Cruelty." Rev. of *Possessing the Secret of Joy*, by Alice Walker. *Chicago Tribune*, 21 June 1992: sec. 14.3.

Baraka, Imamu Amiri. "Other Aspects, Single Entity: Black Woman." *Black World* 19.9, July 1970: 7–11.

Bates, Karen Grigsby. "Possessing the Secrets of $uccess: Toni Morrison Is the Senior Member of a Triumphant Trio of Best-selling Writers." *Emerge: Black America's Newsmagazine* 4.1 October 1992: 47–49.

Berry, Faith. "A Question of Publishers and A Question of Audience." *The Black Scholar* 17.2 March-April 1986: 41–49.

Bloom, Harold, ed. *Alice Walker*. New York: Chelsea House, 1989.

Bobo, Jacqueline. "Sifting through the Controversy: Reading *The Color Purple*." *Callaloo: A Journal of Afro-American and African Arts and Letters* 12.2 (Spring 1989): 332–42.

Byerman, Keith. "Desire and Alice Walker: The Quest for a Womanist Narrative." *Callaloo: A Journal of Afro-American and African Arts and Letters* 12.2 (Spring 1989): 321–31.

Christian, Barbara. "Novels for Everyday Use: The Novels of Alice Walker." *Black Women Novelists: The Development of a Tradition, 1892 1976*. Westport, Conn: Greenwood Press, 1980.

Cleage, Pearl. "A Stunning Journey for 'Joy.'" Rev. of *Possessing the Secret of Joy*, by Alice Walker. *Atlanta Journal*, June 14, 1992: N8

Coetzee, J. M. "The Beginnings of (Wo)man in Africa." Rev. of *The Temple of My Familiar*, by Alice Walker. *New York Times Book Review*, 30 April 1990: 7.

Davenport, Doris. "Afracentric Visions." Rev. of *The Temple of My Familiar*, by Alice Walker. *The Women's Review of Books* 6.12 (September 1989): 13–14.

Donahue, Deidre. "Walker's Disturbing 'Secret': Novelist Explores Trauma of the Mutilation of Women." Rev. of *Possessing the Secret of Joy*, by Alice Walker. *USA Today*, 18 June 1992: D1.

Ebony Book Shelf. *The Color Purple*. Rev. of *The Color Purple*, by Alice Walker. *Ebony* 37.12, Oct.1982: 26.

Evans, Mari, ed. *Black Women Writers (1950 1980): A Critical Evaluation*. Garden City, NY: Anchor-Doubleday, 1984. Section on Walker: 453–95.

Giddings, Paula. "Alice Walker's Appeal." Interview with Alice Walker. *Essence* July 1992: 58ff.

Graham, Maryemma. "Skillful but Disturbing Novel." Rev. of *The Color Purple*, by Alice Walker. *Freedom-ways: A Quarterly Review of the Freedom Movement* 23.4 (1983): 278–80.

Harris, Trudier. "On *The Color Purple*, Stereotypes, and Silence." *Black American Literature Forum* 18.4 (1984): 155–61.

hooks, bell. "Writing the Subject: Reading *The Color Purple*." In *Reading Black, Reading Feminist: A Critical Anthology*. Ed. Henry Louis Gates, Jr. New York: Meridian, 1990. 454–70.

Hospital, Janette Turner. "What They Did to Tashi." Rev. of *Possessing the Secret of Joy* by Alice Walker. *New York Times Book Review,* 28 June 1992: 11–12.

Iannone, Carol. "A Turning of the Critical Tide?" Commentary, November 1989: 57–59.

Jackson, James E. "The Destructive Design of *The Color Purple*." *Political Affairs*, March 1986: 26–30.

Kelly, Ernece B. "Walker Spins Moral Themes in Rich Tale." Rev. of *The Temple of My Familiar*, by Alice Walker. *New Directions for Women* 18.3 (May-June 1989): 17.

Landner, Joyce A. *Tomorrow's Tomorrow: The Black Woman*. Garden City, N.Y.: Doubleday, 1971.

Larson, Charles R. "Against the Tyranny of Tradition." Rev. of *Possessing the Secret of Joy*, by Alice Walker. *Washington Post*, 5 July 1992: WBK1,14.

LeGuin, Ursula K. "All Those at the Banquet." Rev. of *The Temple of My Familiar*, by Alice Walker. *San Francisco Review of Books* 14 (Summer 1989): 12–13.

Mason, Theodore O., Jr. "Alice Walker's *The Third Life of Grange Copeland*: The Dynamics of Enclosure." Callaloo: A Journal of Afro-American and African Arts and Letters 12.2 (Spring 1989): 297–309.

Matthews, Anne. "Deciphering Victorian Underwear and Other Seminars; or How to be Profane, Profound and Scholarly—All the While Looking for a Job at the Modern Language Association's Annual Convention." *The New York Times Magazine*, 10 February, 1991: 43 ff.

McHenry, Susan. "A Dialogue with Alice Walker."*Emerge: Black America's Newsmagazine* 3,10, September 1992: 9–10.

Miller, Jane. *Women Writing about Men*. London: Virago, 1986.

Murray, Pauli. "The Liberation of Black Women." In *Voices of the New Feminism*. Ed. Mary Lou Thompson. Boston: Beacon Press 1970. 87–102.

Nyabongo, V. S. "Rev. of *In Love and Trouble: Stories of Black Women*, by Alice Walker. *Books Abroad* 48.4 (Autumn 1974): 787.

O'Brien, John, ed. *Interviews with Black Writers*. New York: Liveright, 1973. Section on Walker: 186–211.

Ogunyemi, Chikwenye Okonjo. "Womanism: The Dynamics of the Contemporary Black Female Novel in English." *Signs: Journal of Women in Culture and Society* 11.1 (1985): 63–80.

Pinckney, Darryl. "Black Victims, Black Villains." Rev. of *The Color Purple*, by Alice Walker and "The Color Purple," by Steven Spielberg. *New York Review of Books,* 29 Jan. 1987: 17–22.

Rev. of *In Love and Trouble*, by Alice Walker. *Library Journal* 98.20 (15 November 1973): 3476.

Royster, Philip M. "In Search of Our Fathers' Arms: Alice Walker's Persona of the Alienated Darling." *Black American Literature Forum* 20.4 (1986): 347–70.

Rubin, Merle. "Alice Walker Reimagines the World." Rev. of *The Temple of My Familiar*, by Alice Walker. *Christian Science Monitor,* 4 May 1989: 13.

Sadoff, Dianna F. "Black Matrilineage: The Case of Alice Walker and Zora Neale Hurston."
    Signs: Journal of Women in Culture and Society 11.1 (1985): 4–26.
Shapiro, Laura. Rev. of *Possessing the Secret of Joy,* by Alice Walker. *Newsweek* 8 June
    1992: 56–57.
Smith, Barbara. "The Souls of Black Women." Rev. of *In Love and Trouble: Stories of Black
    Women,* by Alice Walker. *Ms.,* February 1974: 42–44, 78.
Smith, Patricia A. "'Secret of Joy': Walker's Tender, Terrifying Tour de Force." Rev. of
    Possessing the Secret of Joy, by Alice Walker. *Boston Globe,* 6 July 1992: 38.
Stade, George. "Womanist Fiction and Male Characters." *Partisan Review* 52.3 (1985):
    264–70.
Tapahonso, Luci. "Learning to Love through Storytelling." Rev. of *The Temple of My
    Familiar,* by Alice Walker. *Los Angeles Times Book Review,* 21 May 1989: 1, 13.
Tate, Claudia. "Alice Walker." In *Black Women Writers at Work.* Ed. Claudia Tate. New
    York: Continuum, 1983. 175–87; 193.
Towers, Robert. "Good Men Are Hard to Find." Rev. of *The Terrible Two,* by Ishmael Reed,
    and *The Color Purple,* by Alice Walker. *New York Review of Books,* 12 August
    1982: 35–36.
Walker, Alice. *The Color Purple.* New York: Pocket Books, 1982.
_____. Meridian. New York: Washington Square Press, 1976.
_____. *In Love and Trouble: Stories of Black Women.* New York: Harcourt Brace
    Jovanovich, 1973.
_____. *In Search of Our Mothers' Gardens.* San Diego: Harcourt Brace Jovanovich,
    1983.
_____. *Living by the Word: Selected Writings 1973 1987.* San Diego: Harcourt Brace
    Jovanovich 1988.
_____ *Possessing the Secret of Joy.* New York: Harcourt Brace Jovanovich, 1992.
_____. *The Temple of My Familiar.* New York: Pocket Books, 1989.
_____. *The Third Life of Grange Copeland.* New York: Pocket Books, 1970.
_____. *To Hell with Dying.* San Diego: Harcourt Brace Jovanovich, 1988.
Walker, Melissa. *Down from the Mountaintop: Black Women's Novels in the Wake of the
    Civil Rights* Movement, 1966– 1989. New Haven: Yale University Press, 1991.
Washington, Mary Helen, ed. *Black-Eyed Susans: Classic Stories by and about Black
    Women.* Garden City, N.Y.: Anchor-Doubleday, 1975.
_____. "An Essay on Alice Walker." In *Sturdy Black Bridges: Visions of Black Women
    in Literature.* Eds. Rosean P. Bell, Bettye J. Parker, and Beverly Guy-Sheftall.
    Garden City, N.Y.: Anchor-Doubleday, 1979. 133–49.
Watkins, Mel. "A Woman in Search of Her Past and Herself." Rev. of *Possessing the Secret
    of Joy,* by Alice Walker. *New York Times,* 24 July 1992: C20.
Wesley, Richard. "Can Men Have It All? *The Color Purple* Debate: Reading Between the
    Lines." *Ms.,* September 1986: 62, 90–92.
Whitaker, Charles. "Alice Walker: *The Color Purple* Author Confronts Her Critics and Talks
    about Her Provocative New Book." *Ebony* May 1992: 86–90.
Wolcott, James. "Party of Animals." Rev. of *The Temple of My Familiar,* by Alice Walker.
    New Republic, 29 May 1989: 28–30.

Revolutionary Stanzas: The Civil and Human Rights Poetry of Alice Walker

Jeffrey L. Coleman

The tongue mounts the hand and produces writing. When tongue and hand work together, they unite art and politics and attack the dominant ideology. For many of us the acts of writing, painting, performing and filming are acts of deliberate and desperate determination to subvert the status quo. Creative acts are forms of political activism employing definite aesthetic strategies resisting dominant cultural norms and are not merely aesthetic exercises.
— *Making Face, Making Soul*, Gloria Anzaldua

I think it is more than safe to assume that when one hears/reads the name Alice Walker, it is the genre of fiction that immediately comes to mind; most likely it is *The Color Purple* one initially thinks of. Justifiable or not, this privileging of Walker's fiction will perhaps forever be with us. After all, it is this genre, the novel, that garnered Walker the American Book Award and the Pulitzer Prize. However, such achievements should not necessarily preclude or exclude serious attention toward Walker's other creative and cultural productions. I am thinking mainly, but not exclusively, of Walker's poetry especially those poems that directly address the themes of civil and human rights, which can be found in abundance throughout *Her Blue Body Everything We Know: Earthling Poems, 1965–1990.*

Her Blue Body includes poems from Walker's four collections of poetry—*Once*; *Revolutionary Petunias and Other Poems*; *Good Night, Willie Lee, I'll See You in the Morning*; and *Horses Make a Landscape Look More Beautiful*—in addition to a final section titled "We Have a Beautiful Mother: Previously Uncollected Poems." Walker's poetry, however, is not as widely acknowledged or recognized as her fiction and essays, which constitutes a substantive disservice to the author. Nor does her poetry deserve the disturbing and overwhelming amount of silence and critical neglect it has received. For example, when Henry Louis Gates, Jr., and Kwame Anthony Appiah published *Alice Walker: Critical Perspectives Past and Present* in 1993, they found only two essays either available or worthy of inclusion that directly concerned Walker's poetry. Aside from Hanna Nowak's "Poetry Celebrating Life" and Thadious Davis's "Poetry as Preface to Fiction," none of the twenty-three reviews, essays, and interviews included in that collection positions Walker's poetry as centrally or significantly relevant to her development as a writer. And as indicated by Davis's title—"Poetry as Preface to Fiction"—she views the author's poetic output as a mere stepping-stone to the more "important" or "serious" creation of fiction.

Consider this essay as a "chalk mark in a rainstorm" of sorts, for not only has Walker's poetry been tentatively placed in a position of erasure in relation to the downpour or onslaught of her fiction and essays, but the critical attention given to her poetry (or the lack thereof) has also suffered the same tenuous fate. I can only hope that this trend does not continue and that this essay helps to (re)establish an elevated degree of interest in Walker's often revolutionary stanzas.

My primary intention is to examine, explicate, and historicize the corpus of poetry written by Alice Walker that offers itself to an interpretation within a framework of rights: the Civil Rights Movement in specific, and human rights in general. This is a structure directly constructed by way of the poems themselves; poems that indeed speak for themselves, and are intended to speak to others—poems that make vital connections between past and present struggles for the rights of people everywhere. This is not to say that all of her poems fall into the category of political agency. However, there exists in her work a substantial amount of themes and ideas that directly address both the history and concerns of humanity and (in)justice in the United States and the world at large during the Civil Rights Movement of the 1950s and 1960s, as well as in the contemporary scene. I will, for the most part, avoid relying upon abstract, alienating theory, for as Nancy K. Miller reminds us, "theory" of this variety "exacts as its price the repression of feelings: and the price is too high" (Miller 5). Instead, I will utilize Hazel Carby's approach to the works of "black women intellectuals." Carby writes, in *Reconstructing Womanhood,* that her concern is to examine such works "within the theoretical premises of societies 'structured in dominance' by class, by race, and by gender," which, for the purposes of this essay, will result in "a materialist account of the cultural productions" of Walker "within the social relations that inscribed them" (17). This approach, I feel, closely mirrors the overall intent of the poems themselves, and places them in relevant social and historical contexts which do not, in keeping with Miller's concerns, repress feelings.

Walker published *Once,* her first book of poetry, in 1968. This, of course, was the year Martin Luther King, Jr., was murdered, and the year the Civil Rights Movement supposedly suffered a similar "death." And while *Once* does include poems relevant to the movement, it is interesting to observe that Walker does not structure the book in a fashion that places those poems in a privileged position. By this I mean that the opening pieces do not directly concern themselves with the movement or even with the United States. Instead, Walker initializes the text with poems distinctly set in Africa. This is more than appropriate since at least some of the poems in *Once* were written while the author was visiting the continent. In the brief preface to the collection, Walker reveals that every single one of the poems in *Once* was written either in Africa or at Sarah Lawrence College in New York.

Walker aptly and humorously titles the opening poem "African Images: *Glimpses from a Tiger's Back.*" The humor here rests in the fact that, as the author notes in the introduction to *Her Blue Body,* a friend later informed her that she could not give the poem this title, since there were no tigers in Africa. Walker responds by insisting that notwithstanding the animal remains majestically beautiful. After this touch of playfulness the writer begins the book by giving the reader a succession of terse "glimpses" and images from her stay in Africa. Among them is a section that alludes to early African and European contact. For starters, these two stanzas definitely add a fresh if not disturbingly comical twist to bell hook's metaphorical notion of "Eating the Other." But what is not quite as humorous is the fact that once upon a time both Africans and Europeans conceived of and referred to each other as cannibals. These impressions mainly came about as a result of misperceptions and lack of familiarity with each other or out of a need to identify one in opposition to the other.

The late Afro-Caribbean historian Walter Rodney notes at various points in *A History of the Upper Guinea Coast: 1545—1800,* that both the Sumba and Bijago ethnic groups of West Africa were often thought to be cannibals by Portuguese navigators, but that those claims were greatly unwarranted. For example, Rodney writes:

Both among the Sapes and the Europeans, the notoriety of the Sumbas probably far out stripped their performance. It was said that they would sometimes appear brandishing a human joint for effect and that they ate the flesh of their enemies "for courage and ferocity," and for the psychological effect it would have on their future opponents. (56)

As for the Bijogos, Rodney claims, "The cannibalism ascribed to the Bijogos is a red herring," and that no proof of the ethnic group consuming human flesh exists (116). Nonetheless, this notion of literally eating the other was quite a prominent and widespread rumor in relation to both Africans and Europeans. For those unaware of this historical misperception, Walker's lines concerning Negroes as food and of the young girl fearing the speaker's white friend may come across as rather strange or paranoiac. But contemporary scholars such as Jan Nederveen Pieterse and Patricia A. Turner still view the phenomenon as crucial to understanding the exchange of views and perceptions that resulted from initial contact between Africans and Europeans.

Pieterse's view is that "[t]he most common explanation for the accusation of cannibalism is that it served, above all, as a justification for conquest—as it did in the conquest of the Americas. It forms part of an enemy image which colonialism fashions of the colonized." Pieterse goes on to say

At a time when the cosmography of Christendom had been visibly shaken by the encounter with the "New World," the new continent evoked profound ambivalence, ranging from Utopianism (Montaigne, Thomas More) to aversion (Shakespeare, Hobbes, Defoe). At this juncture the "new cannibalism" inserted itself as a strategic topos. (Pieterse 115)

Judging from Pieterse's account of the assertion of cannibalism on behalf of Europeans in relation to Africans, the primary objective was to posit Africans as savages in order to justify capturing, enslaving, and colonizing them. This denial, deflection, transference of sorts, is also mentioned in Turner's 1993 publication of *I Heard It through the Grapevine: Rumor in African-American Culture.* She states that:

> rumors on both sides sprang from circumstantial and psychological "evidence" about the other. Since [Africans] were base enough to indulge in cannibalism, the reasoning went, they deserved to be forced to serve the Europeans. For the blacks: slave traders kept coming back for more live bodies to satisfy their hunger for human flesh. (30-31)

These exchanges and misperceptions, I feel, are crucial to understanding how language and discourse, in addition to tactile and physical abuses, also had (and still have) a tremendous impact in regard to human and cultural (mis)-appropriations; that is, hegemonic exploitations of one racial or ethnic group of another are not always solely perpetuated by way of the physical. As Carby sees it, "Language is accented differently by competing groups, and therefore the terrain of language is a terrain of power relations. This struggle within and over language reveals the nature of the structure of social relations and the hierarchy of power, not the nature of one particular group" (17). Or, in short, words as well as tangible acts can serve the purpose of maiming or "consuming." Words, as Walker well knows, can injure, either literally or metaphorically, especially when they are utilized to justify or distort the course of history. Distortion of this sort falls into the realm of what Judith Butler terms "presentist" discourse. As Butler puts it, "My under-standing of the charge of presentism is that an inquiry is presentist to the extent that it (a) universalizes a set of claims regardless of historical and cultural challenges to that universalization or (b) takes a historically specific set of terms and universalizes them falsely. It may be that both gestures in a given instance are the same" (282). It is difficult to adequately place the charges of mutual cannibalism in either the "a" or "b" rubric Butler puts forth, for perhaps the claims occurred simultaneously on two very different continents, making accurate historicization of the assumptions virtually impossible. It may be, as Butler suggests, "that both gestures in [this] given instance are the same." Regardless, the naming of the other as cannibal helped to set in place a false and damaging perception of both Africans and Europeans. So it is not altogether surprising that the "little African girl" in Walker's poem assumes she will serve as dinner for the white man, and then runs away in a frightened state.

After giving the reader several more glimpses of Africa, Walker and her poems find their way to America (does this make Walker an Afro-centrist: one who first acknowledges or comes to terms with one's African heritage in order to ground and center one's self in the new world?), where the title poem of the book *Once* opens with a stereotypical depiction of the mythical American Dream: "Green lawn/a picket fence/ flowers—/My friend smiles" (1–4: 72).

The fact that Walker opens her poem with this image is significant, for it calls into question the entire concept of what makes one American or an American dreamer who has transferred such a desire into physical reality. But who, historically, has had access to the means of economic potency required to inhabit or actualize such a dream motif or space? And does an acquisition of this nature make one more American, or desirable? These are pertinent questions in relation to Walker's opening lines to the poem "Once," for the idea of the American Dream is and perhaps forever will be a site of heated contestation.

In terms of the distribution of wealth around the time Walker published *Once,* Rashi Fein claims that

[i]n 1964 7.7 percent of Negro families had incomes below $1,000 but this was true of only 2.7 per cent of whites. [A Negro] child had a twenty-two in one hundred chance of being born to a family with an income below $2,000. A white child would have an eight in one hundred chance. [A Negro] child has only a two in one hundred chance of being born in a family with income over $15,000. For a white child the chances are seven in one hundred.

Not surprisingly, Fein's findings indicate that the chance of owning a home with a proverbial white picket fence was highly unlikely for "Negro" families in the 1960s, as I'm sure Walker was well aware of.

Evidence of the ambivalent position regarding this American Dream world can be found in contemporary African American popular culture. I am thinking mainly of the so-called gangsta rapper, Snoop Doggy Dogg, and his lyrics to "Bathtub," which serve as a brief, introductory text to his often misogynistic and arguably racist (yet intensely popular) 1993 album titled *Doggystyle.* Aside from the polemical, problematic nature of his album, Snoop shares the irony of Walker's description of the American Dream. In the song, an uninvited male guest drops by Snoop's home, and in a soft-spoken voice, wonders why Snoop would even contemplate giving it up. To this inquiry, Snoop assumes a state of speechlessness. And in this space of silence in relation to the American Dream, lingering questions exist and persist: What exactly is the American Dream with respect to late-twentieth-century American capitalism? Whose job is it to tell us if we have attained it or not? On whose standards is it based? Snoop's narrated friend seems to think that if you can afford to get high everyday, own an expensive wide-screen television, and make "dope" music, then you've achieved the Dream. For others, of course, those items would be unrealistic, while for still others, only the beginning. But regardless of how one looks at the American Dream, its myth is very pervasive and it is founded on the capitalistic principles of earning potential and accumulated wealth, at times by any means necessary.

This statement by Snoop Doggy Dogg, in relation to cornering or monopolizing personal or community capital for the sake of confronting and overcoming historically white hegemonic economic power, comes exceedingly close to what Huey P. Newton of the Black Panther Party once called for in his essay "Black Capitalism Re-Analyzed I: June 5, 1971." Newton asserts, "We have been subjected to the dehumanizing power of exploitation and racism for hundreds of years; and the Black community has its own will to power also. What we seek, however, is not power over people, but the power to control our own destiny" (Morrison 101). Snoop in his song is (in)directly acknowledging the historical position of the African American community as it concerns the larger, external, and exploitative capitalistic white power structure Newton speaks of. He is acknowledging the concept of the American Dream, the ways in which Americans are conditioned to attack and consume fiscal authority at the expense of others. This, perhaps, is why he titles one of his songs "Doggy Dogg World"—which carries a great amount of resonance when one considers the age-old catchphrase that depicts America as a "dog-eat-dog world."

Likewise, while depicting the amount of control whites have historically held over African American personal, legal and economic aspirations, Walker not only ironically conflates the historical and often racially repressive nature of the American legal, and judicial system, but also points up the way in which the system has contributed to the physical, fiscal and personal "protection" of whites from blacks or African-Americans. The strong arm of the law, be it illegal (e.g., the KKK) or legal (e.g., the Constitution of the United States of America), has traditionally, historically worked in opposition to the civil and human rights of African Americans and other Others for the sake of instilling within white Americans a presumed and assumed sense of privilege and "rights" to all the fruits and benefits America has to offer—such as the hypothetical, mythical American Dream.

Walker also assumes of and for the reader the knowledge that the legal system works for *some* Americans (but which Americans?). However, once she includes the parenthetical line "(from me)" it becomes all but lucid that the speaker of the poem is speaking from a marginalized, unprotected perspective, from a perspective in which the American judicial system views the speaker as always already guilty or unworthy of due process of law.

Later, Walker returns to this quest for democracy when she writes of the painful irony of a black girl waving the American flag. This section of the poem, especially the conclusion, receives sharp criticism from Hanna Nowak in her essay "Poetry Celebrating Life." Nowak asks: "Why does the poem end with the detailed description of a small black girl waving the American flag? The penultimate stanza would have been more forceful and evocative: in a few words it recounts the death of a little black girl, an episode that subtly depicts the cruelties of the time without any bland flag-waving" (Gates and Appiah 191). The "penultimate stanza" Nowak refers to here occurs in the previous section of the poem, wherein a young black girl is run over and killed by a racist truck driver who justifies his actions by claiming to sympathetic cops "that nigger was/in the way!" (xiii, 8–9: 93). What Nowak fails to derive from the poem in which the girl "gingerly" waves the American flag with is that this depiction is probably given in order to underscore the tentative relationship the young girl shares with America, American "democracy," and the American Dream. Thus the lines Nowak dismisses strike me as extremely relevant and centered in American and African American history, and relate to the problematic notion of inclusion, especially in relation to the symbolism of the American flag. African Americans' apprehension in regard to such idealized American ideology (i.e., freedom, inclusion, and fairness) is deeply rooted in our sense of peace (or the lack of it) in the history of this country. Many African Americans have never felt fully *included* in this country. One troubling yet pertinent and relevant justification for this sense of exclusion can be found in the Constitution of this country. As Lawrence H. Fuchs points out in *The American Kaleidoscope:*

Race, Ethnicity, and the Civic Culture, "[T]he authors of the Constitution themselves recoiled from the word 'slave.' They wrote of 'three-fifths of all other persons'" (31). Also, as Gates writes in *"Race," Writing, and Difference:*

When Abraham Lincoln invited a small group of black leaders to the White House in 1862 to present his ideas about returning all blacks in America to Africa, his argument turned upon "natural" differences. "You and we are different races," he said. "We have between us a broader difference than exists between any other two races." Since this sense of difference was never to be bridged, Lincoln concluded, the slaves and the ex-slaves should be returned to Africa. (3)

With this in mind, is it difficult to understand why the young black girl in Walker's poem holds the American flag rather lightly at fingers' ends as if to signify the very uneasy, uncomfortable relationship blacks or African Americans—especially females—have shared with the idealism of American culture? According to Carby, African American women have never fallen into the purported realm of "true womanhood," which she terms as a "dominating image, describing the parameters within which women were measured and declared to be, or not to be, women" (23).

Yusef Komunyakaa, who in 1994 became the first African American male to win the Pulitzer Prize for poetry, discusses his personal relationship with the American Dream by saying:

I grew up in a poor and impoverished neighborhood in the deep South [Bogalusa, Louisiana], dominated by the typical American, Calvinistic work ethic for the most part. People around me believed that if they worked hard enough they could get ahead in the "American Dream," which of course was a complete myth. When I was growing up, I did not see it as a myth, but having been away from that part of my life for so long now, and in trying to establish some kind of intellectual equation, the "American Dream" seems to have been very much a myth. (Carroll 130–31)

The truth of the matter is that—especially for many women, people of color, and others who have traditionally found themselves near or at the bottom of the socio-economic ladder—the hypocritical, hypothetical Dream will unfortunately never be realized due to America's long-standing sexist, racist, and classist hierarchical structures of dominance, accessibility and marginalization. Or, as Walker writes in regard to these structures and the practice of Othering, in "First, They Said": "First, They said we were savages/But we knew how well we had treated them/And knew we were not savages." These lines from the first stanza in Walker's *Horses Make a Landscape Look More Beautiful*, plus the other six stanzas—especially the final sentence of stanza seven—not only subsume or reinforce many, if not all, of the arguments previously presented, but also serve as a manifesto of sorts in regard to Walker's civil and human rights ideology. Implicit in the lines from "Once" (ii, 1–9) in which Walker talks of a black person fraternizing with white folks is the act of naming and the resistance to naming. More specifically, the name "nigger" is given to the "dark" male friend of the speaker of the poem (and to the speaker as well?). The friend humorously yet defiantly asks,

"Where?", which implies a resistance to such naming. This naming, as Butler asserts, "is at once the setting of a boundary, and also the repeated inculcation of a norm" (Butler 8). The subject in Walker's poem questions and shatters these "boundaries" and norms by way of a humorous trope of sorts. Walker often invokes a sense of humor in her poetry, especially during events or acts that seem dire in relation to race or racial affronts. She uses humor in order to "talk back" as a writer, or invests the subjects in her poems with this same defiant resistance. The notion of "talking back" or confronting and combating nominal abuse is performed by the subject in Walker's poem just cited above who is called a "nigger." As mentioned earlier, this performativity takes place by way of the subject's vocal interjection of "Where?" which also carries with it more than a hint of humor. This questioning of historical subordination is in concert with the King-centered notion of nonviolent resistance and civil disobedience. Likewise, the humor embedded in the questioning of the supposed authority of the one who names is in concert with what John Lowe, in his 1994 publication of *Jump at the Sun: Zora Neale Hurston's Cosmic Comedy,* terms "liberating." Lowe advances this argument by quoting Freud's "Humour" essay:

Humour has in it a *liberating* element. But it has also something fine and elevating, which is lacking in the other two ways of deriving pleasure from intellectual activity. It refuses to be hurt by the allows of reality or to be compelled to suffer. It insists that it is impervious to wounds dealt by the outside world, in fact, that these are merely occasions for affording it pleasure. Humour is not resigned; it is rebellious. It signifies the triumph not only of the ego, but also of the pleasure-principle, which is strong enough to assert itself here in the face of the adverse real circumstances. (25)

The subject in Walker's poem indeed uses "Where?" as humor for the sake of liberation, and in this sense the word is rebellious "in the face of the adverse real" circumstance in which he finds himself labeled a nigger for associating with white folks. Another example of Walker's use of humor in order to defy or subvert racist, hegemonic notions concerning African Americans can be found in section "xi" of the poem "Once." In this section Walker posits a fascinating imbecile, an African American character in a court of law. Standing before the judge, in defense of charges of indecent exposure, the blockhead protests skin color discrimination.
    Aside from the obvious—that is, these lines coincide with and reinforce the "Black Is Beautiful" mantra of the Black Power Movement—the lines also quite blatantly put the black or African American body, in its entirety, in a position of social display and confrontation, a body which has traditionally been "abjected" by "regulatory norms failing to qualify as fully human" (Butler 16). And once the imbecile refers to the judge as a bastard, the entire situation takes on a sense of the absurd. By this I mean that a half-wit African American (one not completely responsible for one's actions) naming the law of the land (one who has been chosen to deem who is responsible or what is responsible behavior) as a "bastard"—while in a court of law—strikes me as absurd, in the traditional and comedic sense of the term. Lawrence W. Levine refers to this particular strand of humor when he writes:

The humor of absurdity worked through a straight-faced assumption of the rationality of the system and the belief structure upon which it rested. Events could then be unfolded which exposed the system and its underlying beliefs by accepting them with complete and faithful literalness. No institution or custom, South or North, lent itself better to this humor than segregation (310)

Walker definitely places the subject of her poem, the half-wit, in a position to question the "straight-faced assumption of the rationality of the system and the belief structure" that blackness was something to hide or be ashamed of, by having the half-wit literally confront and denounce the judge in relation to the judge's assumed notion concerning the beauty or validity of the African American's natural, naked human body. Walker then goes on to conclude the poem, with what I consider to be more of a playful coda than a connective finale, when she reflects on the problem of human prejudice.

Walker's insertion of the word "prejudice" in the context of this poem as well as the themes of previous sections ties into Levine's notion that the humor of the absurd could usually be found in its most potent form within the institution of segregation. Furthermore, the poet's concluding lines call to mind not only the absurdity of segregation and interrogation inherent in previous lines, but also to the innocent nature or imagery of a half-wit mistakenly taking a stroll in her/his most natural and, presumably, most comfortable form.

A decidedly less humorous but equally troubling or problematic section can be found immediately following (lines 91–92). The overall message embedded in these lines is troubling, yet historically intriguing. By this I mean that if the reader is to take the lines on face value, void of such common poetic practices as inversion, metaphor, irony, and so forth, the reader has to confront and come to terms with the fact that the white female speaker expresses grave and fatal concerns in relation to dating or copulating with a nonwhite male. (Of course, the act of ironic inversion Walker has performed in previous sections could also apply here; however, another reading/interpretation, such as the *literal* for instance, proves to be as equally useful and valid, if not more problematic). Perhaps the fear on behalf of the female speaker stems from "the doctrine of true womanhood," wherein "death itself was preferable to a loss of [white] innocence" (Carby 59). In any regard, the obvious problem the reader/interpreter is presented with, in terms of the literal, is that traditionally it has been non-white males who have been in the most danger for considering or indeed dating and copulating with white females. Additionally, it has historically been the nonwhite male, especially the African American, who has had to fear the *assumption* of "getting too close" to white females or even *looking* at a female of the white race "in the wrong way." These "acts" have traditionally been greeted with intimidation and lynchings or, as Carby states in relation to accusations of rape leveled against African American males, "the charge" often "became the excuse" for lynching (Carby 111). Nonetheless, Walker posits the female in an endangered light.

One reason for this on Walker's behalf may have to do with events that took place on March 25, 1965. On this day, Viola Gregg Liuzzo, "a [white] 39-

year-old mother from Michigan" and a Civil Rights Movement activist, was in the process of driving to Montgomery, Alabama, for the sake of gathering and returning other Civil Rights Movement workers and activists back to Selma, Alabama. The workers/activists had spent three days marching to and in Montgomery. Liuzzo, on this day, was accompanied by an African American male. During their travel, according to Sara Bullard's *Free at Last: A History of the Civil Rights Movement and Those Who Died in the Struggle,* a "carload of Klansmen pulled up alongside Liuzzo's Oldsmobile." Bullard then states that "Liuzzo turned and looked straight at one of the Klansmen, who sat in the back seat with his arm out the window and a pistol in his hand. He fired twice, sending two .38-caliber bullets crashing through the Oldsmobile window and shattering Viola Liuzzo's skull" (80). While this blatant and racially motivated murder does not fall into the traditional category of lynching—in terms of hanging—it does shed light on the fact that white females have suffered for their associations with African American males, for their fall from the graces of "true womanhood."

And while accounts of female hangings may be difficult if not impossible to obtain in formal writings, at least one example can be found in popular culture. I am thinking here of the classic Cole Porter tune, "Miss Otis Regrets," as recorded by Ella Fitzgerald in 1956. The song is a tale of infidelity rendered in oral epistolary fashion to an anonymous "Madame." She is informed, by way of a refrain that establishes the smooth, understated nature of the narrative, that Miss Otis regrets she would not be attending lunch today. Listeners, as well as the "Madame," discover that her absence is due to the fact she has been lynched for shooting an unfaithful lover. While this song is lyrically and thematically painful, Fitzgerald's rendition of it is nothing short of sonically beautiful. And as Geoffrey Mark Fidelman points out in his 1994 biography, *First Lady of Song: Ella Fitzgerald for the Record,* the song was immensely popular with Fitzgerald's audience. Fidelman writes, "Over thirty-five years later, audiences still screamed for Ella to sing the [tune] in her concerts" (91). Fidelman goes on to say that "Miss Otis Regrets" is one of "the ten best songs [Fitzgerald] ever recorded in the studio" (300). How should we read the popularity of this song, a song in which a woman is brutally murdered at the hands of a mob (all-male?) without ever having an opportunity to plead her case?

Although the race of Miss Otis is not explicitly stated, such signs as class and material goods and the fact that an enraged mob whisked her from jail, suggest that perhaps Miss Otis, as well as her estranged lover, was white. I address these identificatory markers, especially the material, because, as Carby insists, "Any feminist history that seeks to establish the sisterhood of white and black women as allies in the struggle against oppression of all women must also reveal the complexity of the social and economic differences between women" (Carby 53). After all, how many angry mobs have ever persecuted an African American woman for murdering an African American male (unless we count the so-called high-tech lynching accusation leveled against Anita Hill and members of Congress by Supreme Court Justice nominee Clarence Thomas for supposedly metaphorically attempting to murder his law career)? Perhaps also plausible in the song's scenario is the proposition that Miss Otis was African American and her lover, white. Would she have suffered this fate if the latter were true? These speculations, of course, serve only as an attempt to derive some sort of precedence for Walker's white female subject fearing a lynching for dating or copulating outside of her race. The poem and the song share gender violence, but not necessarily interracial violence.

As stated earlier, it is usually the African American male who has most to fear as a result of interracial encounters. But the fact that Walker's white female subject specifically mentions something resembling a body swinging loosely from a tree sounds indeed interesting, and conjures up memories of Billie Holiday's 1939 classic, "Strange Fruit." In this particular tune, as Patricia Hill Collins points out in *Black Feminist Thought: Knowledge, Consciousness, and the Politics of Empowerment,* we discover that "Sometimes the texts of Black women blues singers take overtly political forms." The author cites Holiday's "Strange Fruit" as an example. Here, as in Walker's poem, the tree of choice for lynching is the poplar, whereas in the Porter/Fitzgerald piece it is a weeping willow (both trees happen to belong to the cottonwood family). I do not feel this is a result of pure coincidence, per se, for Walker has later (i.e., since the publication of *Once)* made clear her love for Holiday. While speaking of Holiday, Hurston, and Bessie Smith, Walker stated that it would have been preferable, even psychologically uplifting, if the three women had had one another to turn to in time of adversity and great personal need (*Gardens* 91–92).

This sense of sisterly, feminist, or womanist affection, protection or camaraderie could possibly help explain the fear Walker invests in the white female of the poem under discussion. Perhaps Walker felt a need to perform a trope or turning of tables in order to suggest or express the historical abuse of women and the fear such abuse undoubtedly instills in most, if not all, women to this very day. (This analysis, of course, is prefaced by the lack of historical accounts of white women lynched as a result of interracial encounters—or, I should say, by my inability to find such accounts, if indeed, they exist.) After all, Miss Otis, who pulled from underneath her "velvet gown" a gun and "shot her lover down," was eventually lynched. In contrast to her fate, in popular culture, Jimi Hendrix's song "Hey Joe" was released in 1967, the year prior to the publication of Walker's *Once.*

An analysis of "Miss Otis Regrets," "Hey Joe," and Walker's *Once/* "Once" makes for an intriguing historical capsulation of the different treatments or forms of justice visited upon women and men. In the Hendrix tune, the narrator initializes the sonic text by twice asking Joe where he might be headed with a gun. Joe responds that he plans to shoot his cheating lover. He succeeds and then reveals plans to cross the Mexican border to prevent being lynched for his crime.

Unlike Miss Otis, who is lynched for shooting her lover down, or the white female in Walker's poem who has anxieties of being lynched, Joe seems to find his way down to Mexico where he presumably can be "free" of and from the bothersome nature of American jurisprudence. The strategic placement of the fade-out in Hendrix's tune seems to acknowledge and support the claim that male-on-female violence is escapable or not as serious or punishable as female-on-male violence (e.g., the fate of Miss Otis). Likewise, whereas Joe does express anxiety in regard to being lynched, he does so after the fact of homicide, while the female in Walker's poem is somewhat paralyzed by such fear, preventing her from acting on her innocent, mutual desire for a nonwhite male.

An interesting footnote to this discussion of assumed and practiced "justice" in relation to male and female violence can be found in the October 17, 1994, ruling of Judge Robert E. Cahill, Sr. The judge presided over a case involving Ken Peacock of Maryland, who was found guilty of murdering his wife, Sandy, after he found her in bed with another man. Peacock, however, did not immediately perform this act. He first went out, began drinking heavily for approximately three hours, then returned home to drink another gallon of wine and a couple of beers over the next several hours. All the while, Peacock was brandishing his .30–.30 Marlin hunting gun. It was reported that [a]t one point, Ken fired the rifle once into a wall behind Sandy. Then, about 4:20 a.m. [February 9, 1994], as Sandy lay on the living-room sofa, Ken was 'toying' with the gun, he told police, when it discharged accidentally, killing his wife. Shortly afterward he called 911 to report the shooting.

For this premeditated, aggravated murder, Peacock was sentenced to three years in prison, which was then suspended by Judge Cahill to half the sentence, which makes it possible for Peacock, the murderer, to serve his time in a detention center as opposed to the state penitentiary. Additionally, Judge Cahill recommended that Peacock be made eligible for a work release program as soon as possible. The judge made this recommendation because, as he reportedly stated later, "[He] seriously wonder[s] how many married men would have the strength to walk away without inflicting some corporal punishment." Later Judge Cahill said, "I shudder to think what I would do. I'm not known for having the quietest disposition."

Aside from the blatant subjectivity of the judge, who obviously saw the case through and from his own privileged white male gaze, this occurrence makes clear how "the system" works against so-called Others, in this case a white female. But regardless of the race of the murderer (who was also white) or the victim, this points to the fact that when we Others complain of mistreatment or discrimination of any kind, we are doing so out of a result of historical or present-day atrocities. Whether these atrocities occur in the "make-believe" world of popular culture, formal or informal art genres, or in the "real" world, the unfortunate and intolerable truth of "the white (man's) law" seemingly remains intact. Perhaps this helps explains why the female in this section of Walker's poem, regardless of the privilege of her white skin, fears being lynched. Indeed, perhaps this also explains why Miss Otis, regardless of her race, was lynched, and why the character Joe in Hendrix's narration never faces the American judicial system.

Along these same lines (i.e., murder, lynching, and justice), Walker later includes the poem "South: The Name of Home." In the second and third stanzas of this poem, we find the poet lamenting the tragic sense of loss occasioned by lynching and other murderous acts. The third stanza clearly makes a reference to bloodshed and lynchings, but the last four lines also allude to the silence or lack of justice that often followed such acts. Likewise, the last four lines of the second stanza connote the fact that dead African American bodies were often found in swamps, rivers, or earthen dams in the South, especially Mississippi. Among the documented and interned bodies found in this condition and linked to Mississippi and the Civil Rights Movement were those of Emmett Till in 1955; Mark Charles Parker in 1959; Charles Eddie Moore and Henry Hezekiah Dee in 1964; CORE (Congress of Racial Equality) workers James Chaney, Andy Goodman, and Michael Schwerner during the same year; and Ben Chester White in 1966. By Sara Bullard's accounts alone, in *Free at Last* Till was "shot in the head" by white supremacists who "wired a 75-pound cotton gin fan to his neck and dumped his body in the Tallahatchie River" (44); Parker was accosted by "eight masked white men [who] dragged him from his cell [due to allegations of raping a white female], beat him, shot him in the heart and threw his body in the Pearl River, where it was found 10 days later" (50); Moore's and Dee's "mutilated bodies were discovered in the Mississippi River," after the "White Knights [of the Ku Klux Klan] had "abducted [the men] from a roadside and taken them deep into the Homocitto National Forest, where they tied them to trees and beat them unconscious." Bullard says that Moore's and Dee's bodies were detected as a result of rescue workers searching for the bodies of Chaney, Goodman, and Schwerner (68), who were later found in an earthen dam after "an anonymous informer revealed the location of the bodies in exchange for $30,000 in federal reward money." Bullard later states that "a team of FBI agents and a hired bulldozer dug up 10 tons of soil to uncover the decomposed bodies" (72); and White, who was approached at his home by three Klansmen [James Jones, Claude Fuller, and Ernest Avants], was shot at close range by Fuller, who then "ordered [Avants] to shoot into White's bullet-riddled body. Avants fired a shotgun blast that tore apart White's head. The men then dumped the remains in a creek" (92).

Thus, Walker's poem "South: The Name of Home," ends with echoes of rivers (especially the Mississippi), earthen dams, and creeks that have served as burial grounds for many African Americans, especially those directly associated with the Civil Rights Movement or those who just happened to be African Americans during that period of American history.

In *Revolutionary Petunias and Other Poems,* which the author, in part, dedicates to her heroes, heroines, and friends of the early SNCC (Student Nonviolent Coordinating Committee), Walker makes an indirect reference to yet another memorable and despicable event that occurred during the Civil Rights Movement in her poem "Winking at a Funeral." The poem, innocently enough, begins by asserting that the ceremonies of burying the dead contrast sharply with the sense of warm attachment and general feeling of love and affection that seem to exude from both the congregation gathered at a church for the funerals and the hymnal melodies that rise from their lips. The poem then continues and concludes by way of recounting the tragic event of September 15, 1963. It was the bombing of the Sixteenth Street Baptist Church of Birmingham, Alabama, on September 15, 1963, in which four young African American females lost their lives at the hands, and bomb, of Robert Edward Chambliss. Henry Hampton and Steve Fayer's account of the event found in *Voices of Freedom: An Oral History of the Civil Rights Movement from the 1950s through the 1980s* is worthy of quoting at length:

Eighteen days after the euphoria of the March on Washington, four hundred worshippers crowded into the Sixteenth Street Baptist Church in Birmingham for Sunday services. Only months earlier, the church had been the rallying point for the marches against [Sheriff] Bull Connor's police dogs and fire hoses [A] group of young girls had just finished a Sunday school lesson and were in the basement changing into their choir robes. A few blocks away, but within sight of the church, a white man stood waiting on the sidewalk. He was Birmingham truck driver and one-time city employee Robert Edward Chambliss—the man whom friends in the Eastview 13 Klavern of the Alabama Klan called Dynamite Bob. At 10:19 a.m., fifteen sticks of explosives blew apart the church basement and the children in the changing room. The four who died were Addie Mae Collins, Carole Robertson, and Cynthia Wesley, all fourteen; and Denise McNair, eleven. Some twenty others were injured. (171–172)

In Walker's poem, this everyday quality of these girls' lives within the church is foregrounded by the title, "Winking at a Funeral," which connotes innocence or frivolity in the face of ever-present despair and depression. How many rituals are more somber in America than a funeral? How many acts are more subtle, or at times invasive, than a wink, especially if the setting is a funeral? And the last line of the stanza is immediately followed in the second stanza by a more sombre question as to the identity of the arsonist. This latter half of the poem leads the reader from a point of innocent "winking" and into a more grim, realistic realm of the event at hand; meaning, a funeral; meaning, someone's death is presently being mourned; meaning, more than a hint of foreshadowing/reflection is at work in these last three lines. Indeed, Walker's structural codes in this poem are entirely copacetic with the innocent act of four young African American ladies who had just finished a Sunday school lesson, only to eventually find themselves prey to a (lone?) Klansman and his explosives.

The bombing, supposedly a result of Klan resentment over school integration, went unpunished for fourteen years even though an eyewitness claimed to have seen Chambliss and three other men plant the bomb. Eventually, Chambliss alone was found guilty of murder, while no other charges were ever made. Immediately following the bombing, according to Bullard,

white supremacist leader Connie Lynch told a group of Klansmen that those responsible for the bombing deserved "medals." Lynch said the four young girls who died there "weren't children. Children are little people, little human beings, and that means white people. They're just little niggers and if there's four less niggers tonight, then I say, "Good for whoever planted the bomb." (63)

While these comments reinforce earlier statements and arguments, they are also difficult to digest without a certain sense of indignation. However, Walker, though obviously bothered by such historical events and comments, finds within herself (at least in this instance) the dignity or strength to turn the proverbial cheek. Evidence of this can be found in the poem "Torture" from *Horses Make a Landscape Look More Beautiful.* She writes,

When they torture your mother
plant a tree

When they torture your father
plant a tree
When they torture your brother
and your sister
plant a tree
When they assassinate
your leaders
and lovers
plant a tree
When they torture you
too bad
to talk
plant a tree.
When they begin to torture
the trees
and cut down the forest
they have made
start another. (1–20: 389)

In addition to being read as nonviolent social change, these lines also offer themselves to an interpretation of perseverance, resilience, and regeneration. The lines are also rooted in the ideology Walker sets forth in her introduction to *Revolutionary Petunias,* in which she states, "[T]he sincerest struggle to save the world must start from within. I was saved from despair countless times by the flowers and trees I planted" *(Her Blue Body* 153). This also points toward a need to remain creative and productive in the face of ever-present danger. Or, as Gloria Anzaldua puts it in *Making Face, Making Soul: Hacienda Caras,*

Art is a sneak attack while the giant sleeps, a sleight of hands when the giant is awake, moving so quick they can do their deed before the giant swats them. Our survival depends on being creative. Even when our bodies have been battered by life, these artistic "languages," spoken from the body, by the body, are still laden with aspirations, are still coded in hope. (xxv)

This sense/act of creative resistance is also echoed by Audre Lorde in the Foreword to *Wild Women in the Whirlwind: Afra-American Culture and the Contemporary Literary Renaissance* when she discusses the history and future of African American women. Lorde writes:

They will need to know that hatred destroys by silence, by civilization, by the pretense that nothing we have to say is worth anything simply because we are saying it. And of course there is the other side of that erasure so cleverly practiced against Black women and our words by all those establishments that presume hierarchy over us: the arrogant assumption that anyone knows better than we do which of our words should survive. (Braxton, McLauglin xiii)

The resistance and empowerment embedded in the metaphorical planting of trees and the literal planting of words by Walker, especially as they relate to African American women in Lorde's assertions, come into play again in the poem "Well" (*Horses Make a Landscape Look More Beautiful*). Walker insists,

> But what a pity
> that
> the poet
> the priest
> and the revolution
> never seem
> to arrive
> for the black woman,
> herself.

These lines and others directly confront the traditional patriarchal nature of poets, priests, and revolutions as they concern the Civil Rights movement. Without doubt, accounts of the Movement remain patriarchal for the most part, not fully incorporating the role of women or the Women's Movement. Barbara Melosh addresses this chasm in her essay "Historical Memory in Fiction: The Civil Rights Movement in Three Novels." While discussing Walker's *Meridian*, Rosellen Brown's *Civil Wars*, and Meredith Sue Willis's *Only Great Changes*, Melosh writes:

As a historian, I was intrigued by the authenticity of these writers' observations about the civil rights movement and by their recurring themes of history and memory. Their perspective reminds us again of the intimate connections between civil rights and feminism, a history not yet fully assimilated into scholarly accounts of postwar America and virtually absent from popular understandings of the women's movement. The best known of the three, Walker commands a wide audience through her writing and her political advocacy of civil rights and feminism; her work probes the consequences of racism and sexism in the lives of black Americans. (65-66)

And in the process of probing the "consequences of racism and sexism" in the African American experience, Walker has, according to Barbara Christian, "turned the *idea* of Art on its head." Christian, in "The Highs and the Lows of Black Feminist Criticism," continues by stating,

Instead of looking high, [Walker] suggested, we should look low. On that low ground she found a multitude of artist-mothers—the women who'd transformed the material to which they'd had access into their conception of Beauty: cooking, gardening, quilting, storytelling. In retrieving that low ground, Walker not only reclaimed her foremothers, she pointed to a critical approach. For she reminded us that Art, and the thought and sense of beauty on which it is based, is the province not only of those with a room of their own, or of those in libraries, universities and literary Renaissances—that *creating* is necessary to those who work in kitchens and factories, nurture children and adorn homes, sweep streets or harvest crops, type in offices and manage them. (44)

These reflections on Walker's work not only make clear the scope of her literary and cultural productions, but also delineate her far-reaching concerns for civil and human rights in America and those geographic regions outside the realm of the United States. Walker's poetic explorations of race, class, and gender manage to effectively articulate these issues in direct relation to such rights. In this sense, Walker and her work find themselves at the "focal point of cultural consciousness and social change," that Trinh T. Minh-ha speaks of (Minh-ha 6). Additionally, Walker's work often mirrors Carby's insistence that "[a] revision of contemporary feminist historiography should investigate the different ways in which racist ideologies have been constructed and made operative under different historical conditions" (Carby 18). A poem that definitely investigates these different historical conditions is "The Right to Life: What Can the White Man Say to the Black Woman?" Walker originally delivered this piece at a Pro-Choice/Keep Abortion Legal Rally in Washington, D.C., on April 8, 1989. I would like to conclude my analysis of Walker's often revolutionary stanzas by including the final portions of this poem, yielding the final words to Walker:

> And I will free your children from insultingly high infant
> mortality rates, short life spans, horrible housing, lack of
> food, rampant ill health. I will liberate them from the ghetto.
> I will open wide the doors of all the schools and the hospitals
> and businesses of society to your children. I will look at
> your children and see, not a threat, but joy.

WORKS CITED

Anzaldua, Gloria. *Making Face, Making Soul: Hacienda Caras: Creative and Critical Perspectives by Feminists of Color.* San Francisco: Aunt Lute Press, 1990.

Braxton, Joanne M., and Andree Nicola McLaughlin, eds. *Wild Women in the Whirlwind: Afra-American Culture and the Contemporary Literary Renaissance.* New Jersey: Rutgers University Press, 1990.

Bullard, Sara. *Free at Last: A History of the Civil Rights Movement and Those Who Died in the Struggle.* New York: Oxford University Press, 1993.

Butler, Judith. *Bodies that Matter: On the Discursive Limits of "Sex."* New York: Routledge, 1993.

Carby, Hazel. *Reconstructing Womanhood: The Emergence of the Afro-American Woman Novelist.* New York: Oxford University Press, 1987.

Carroll, Rebecca, ed. *Swing Low: Black Men Writing.* New York: Carol Southern Books, 1995.

Collins, Patricia Hill. *Black Feminist Thought: Knowledge, Consciousness, and the Politics of Empowerment.* New York: Routledge, 1991.

Fein, Rashi. "An Economic Status of the Negro." *Daedalus: Journal of the American Academy of Arts and Sciences* (Fall 1965).

Fidelman, Geoffrey Mark. *First Lady of Song: Ella Fitzgerald for the Record.* New York: Birch Lane Press, 1994.

Fuchs, Lawrence H. *The American Kaleidoscope: Race, Ethnicity, and the Civic Culture.* N.H.: University of New England Press, 1990.

Gates, Henry Louis, Jr. *"Race," Writing, and Difference.* Chicago: University of Chicago Press, 1986.

_____. *Reading Black, Reading Feminist: A Critical Anthology*. New York: Meridian Books, 1990.

Gates, Henry Louis, Jr. and Anthony Kwame Appiah. *Alice Walker: Critical Perspectives Past and Present*. New York: Amistad, 1993.

Hampton, Henry, and Steve Fayer. *Voices of Freedom: An Oral History of the Civil Rights Movement from the 1950s through the 1980s*. New York: Bantam Books, 1990.

Hewitt, Bill, Tom Nugent, and Bob Stewart. "Heat of Passion." *People*. 7 November, 1994: 89—90.

hooks, bell. "Eating the Other." *Black Looks*. 21.

Levine, Lawrence W. *Black Culture and Black Consciousness: Afro-American Folk Thought from Slavery to Freedom*. New York: Oxford University Press, 1977.

Lowe, John. *Jump at the Sun: Zora Neale Hurston's Cosmic Comedy*. Urbana and Chicago: University of Illinois Press, 1994.

Melosh, Barbara. "Historical Memory in Fiction: The Civil Rights Movement in Three Novels." *Radical History Review* 40 (1988).

Miller, Nancy K. *Getting Personal: Feminist Occasions and Other Autobiographical Acts*. New York: Routledge, 1991.

Minh-ha, Trinh T. *Woman Native Other: Writing Postcoloniality and Feminism*. Bloomington: Indiana University Press, 1989.

Morrison, Toni, ed. *To Die for the People: The Writings of Huey P. Newton*. New York: Writers and Readers Publishing, 1995.

Pieterse, Jan Nederveen. *White on Black: Images of Africa and Blacks in Western Popular Culture*. New Haven: Yale Press, 1992.

Rodney, Walter. *A History of the Upper Guinea Coast: 1545–1800*. New York: Monthly Review Press, 1970.

Turner, Patricia A. *I Heard It Through the Grapevine: Rumor in African-American Culture*. Berkeley: University of California Press, 1993.

Walker, Alice. *Her Blue Body Everything We Know: Earthling Poems 1965 1990*. San Diego: Harcourt Brace and Jovanovich, 1991.

_____. *In Search of Our Mothers' Gardens: Womanist Prose*. San Diego: Harcourt Brace and Jovanovich, 1983.

The Color Purple: An Existential Novel

Marc–A Christophe

Alice Walker's *The Color Purple* is a song of joy and of triumph: triumph of one woman's struggle against racism, sexism, and social determinism to ultimately blossom into the wholeness of her being. This epistolary novel evolves around Celie, a battered fourteen-year-old woman/child who, after having been raped by her stepfather, was married to a neighbor farmer who needed a mother/maid for his children from a previous marriage. The story unfolds through the many letters that the lonely and despairing Celie writes to God and later to her sister Nettie, who is a missionary in Africa. Thus, it is through Celie's eyes and consciousness that we learn of her tribulations, of Mr._____'s oppressive presence and of her friendship with Shug Avery, a blues singer whom Mr._____ brought into the house. Parallel to the main story, Walker introduces us to the gender conflict between Mr._____'s violent and sexist son, Harpo, and his wife, Sophia, an indomitable, amazon-like woman who dramatizes the plight of the female in rebellion.

Like a classical tragedy in which the fate of the hero/heroine unravels within a conventional locus which symbolizes the world, Alice Walker's story unfolds on a rural farm, a "microcosmic" domain complete unto itself with little or no interference from the outside world. However, it is the simplicity of this world which, as a creative device, allows Walker to emphasize her characters' traits and behavior in an almost caricature-like fashion. Thus, she is able to distill the oppressive brutality of Mr._____, to draw in vivid arabesques the complexity of Shug Avery's soul, and to present us in all its sorrow and beautiful epiphany the miracle of Celie's rebirth. It is this process of rebirth and self-realization which I will study through an analysis of Celie's alienation, her quest for the self, and her existential fight for recognition.

In *The Color Purple*, womanist[1] writer Alice Walker views oppression as an essentially masculine activity which springs from the male's aggressive need to dominate. In the novel, man is the *primum mobile*, the one by whom and through whom evil enters the world. Not unlike the great feminist Simone de Beauvoir, Alice Walker believes that human reality is such that there exists in each individual a consciousness of

a fundamental hostility toward every other consciousness; the subject can be posed only in being opposed—he sets himself up as the essential, as opposed to the other, the inessential, the object. (de Beauvoir xvii)

Accordingly, man expresses reality in terms of conflict and he perceives social relations and even nature itself as a series of dualistically opposed contrasts which create a dynamism of survival. These ideas form the core of the relationship between Mr._____ and Celie. *The Color Purple's* most daring and enduring quality is the novel's rejection of racial emotionalism and its emphasis on the main character's (Celie's) existential fight for recognition. This is not to say that Alice Walker is insensitive to the racial undercurrents of American society. However, as a militant writer who is engaged in liberation struggles, she feels that the cause of women can be best served if she focuses on the violent reality of what can be termed as the inhuman condition of woman. In an interview granted to *Sojourner*, she explains the reasons behind her emphasis on black male/female gender conflicts:

Of course, the [whites] oppress us; they oppress the world. Who's got his big white foot on the whole world? The white man, the rich white man. But we also oppress each other and we oppress ourselves. I think that one of the traditions we have in Black Women's literature is a tradition of trying to fight all the oppression. (Walker, *Sojourner* 14)

And then, she adds:

If someone is beating you up at home, you don't then just sit in the room afterwards and write a novel about the white man's rule. I mean to deal with the guy who beat you up in your house and then see who's beating you up on the street. (*Sojourner* 14)

For Alice Walker, racism does not fully explain the oppression of black women by black men. For whether it is an oppressive society (America) in which the emasculated black male feels the need to recapture his masculinity through the oppression of the female, or in a much "freer" society like the Olinkas (Africa) before the arrival of the British, the end result is similar: the male always oppresses the female. Thus, it may be concluded that in *The Color Purple* racial factors are irrelevant to the understanding of the existential fight between Mr._____ and Celie. The element to which the writer accords greater importance is not race but power, the power to be, to concretize one's self, as to mold others. As we saw in our discussion of reality as apprehended through existentialism, power as a concept and as a tool is more relevant to the interpretation of social mores and the understanding of the novel's thematic construction. The relationship between Harpo and Sophia is based on power, between Celie and Mr._____ on power, between the English settlers and the Olinkas on power, and between whites and blacks in America, on power. Accordingly, it can be argued that in a multiracial society like the United States, the dominant race uses its power to dictate the existential modalities of the minority races. This power is so intense that it controls the minorities' cultural and physical perception of self. This dynamic process explains why some blacks would want to borrow the external signs of whiteness by bleaching their skin, by straightening their hair, or by wearing colored contact lenses in order to move closer to white phenotypes, because white is synonymous with control, manhood, power. In reference to the social dynamism of American society, Walker had this to say:

They [Black men] never examine their relationship to Black women and rarely to Black children. Because their whole thing is to be manly. Not only to be men but to be white men. Their whole number is to be white men. (*Sojourner* 13)

From an existential standpoint, the white man is for the black man "the one who looks at," the one whose eyes give shape to and determine his existence, "the being for whom [he is] an object" (Sartre 360). The sociologist Hubert M. Blalock believes that oppression of one group by another results not when there is an inherent opposition to another race (racial, physical differences) but when "the majority group views discrimination as an effective tool for reducing the ability of the minority to act as a social competitor" (218). Furthermore, adds Blalock, prejudices (racial or social) arise when "the majority (dominant group) defines the minority's (the oppressed group's) variance from social norms (his norms) as a form of social deviance that threatens its sacred traditions" (218). In both examples, the dominant group yields power and unilaterally decides the modality of existence for the subgroup. Thus it can be stated that the one single fundamental difference between oppressor and oppressed, between subject and object, to use existential terminology, is the dominant group's freedom in dictating the social norms by which the minority group must abide. It is in this context that Jean-Paul Sartre declared that the subject possesses "pure and total freedom" (Sartre 362), because he is determined by none other than himself.

The above-mentioned social dynamism is highlighted in *The Color Purple* by the conflict between Celie and Mr._____. In Mr._____'s eyes, Celie is the ultimate object, someone who exists to satisfy his despotic whims and whose fate is determined by her very essence. He tells Celie, "You Black, you pore, you ugly, you a woman. Goddam, you nothing at all" (Walker, *The Color Purple* 176). For Mr._____, Celie is what *he* wants her to be; and to the extent that he interprets his wife's being and controls her existence, she exists only by and for him, not for herself. This observation is echoed in Sartre's statement on the relationship between subject and object: "Insofar as I am the object of values which come to qualify me without my being able to act on the qualification or even to know it, I am enslaved" (Sartre 358). In that respect, Celie is Mr._____'s slave, a being who derives her existence only through the goodwill of another being. Celie's subservience to Mr._____ was so complete that she could not bring herself to pronounce his name, for to name is to take possession, to project one's own perception on the Other. Celie could not call out Mr._____'s name until she regained control of her own existence.

The Color Purple's human dimensions reside in the successful coming into existence of Celie, who concretizes herself by revolting against Mr._____'s rule and determinism. In this most revealing quest, she will be helped and supported by Sophia and Shug, two independent women who become Celie's doors into a world of self-definition and self-fulfillment.

Gradually, as the novel unfolds, we witness Celie's metamorphosis——from a wretched woman who accepts her condition——into a free being who decides to take charge of her life. While threatening Mr._____ with a knife, Celie declares: "It's time to leave you and enter into the creation. And your dead body just the welcome mat I need" (22). This quote conveys both the extent to Celie's alienation as well as her understanding of the true existential meaning of power: power to decide for oneself, to decide for others, power to punish and to kill. The rapport between Mr._____ and Celie clearly exemplifies this creator-to-creature interplay:

He say, Celie git the belt. The children be outside the room peeking through the cracks. It all I can do not to cry. I make myself wood. I say to myself, Celie, you a tree. (22)

This depersonalization we witness in Celie (her wanting to turn into wood, to become inert) is standard clinical behavior of alienated people who, when facing seemingly insurmountable problems, pretend to be other than who they are and attempt to transcend their situation by transforming their reality. Often,

this depersonalization of the self results from the subject's impossibility to determine his/her life; it is a loss of feeling himself [herself] as an organic whole: an alienation from the real self. (Weiss 464)

Celie's alienation, the result of Mr._____'s oppression and objectification, is best illustrated by the following quote, which expresses for the reader the character's estrangement from the real self as well as Mr._____'s destructive and dehumanizing influence:

Buy Celie some clothes. She (Kate) say to Mr._____. She needs clothes? he ast. Well look at her. He look at me. It like he looking at the earth. It need something? his eyes say. (20)

And yet, it is within this emptiness, this absence of love, that she musters the will to survive. In that respect, it is interesting to note that Celie's quest started with her original "hatred" for Sophia. When she tells Harpo, Mr._____'s son, to beat his wife Sophia like she so often is beaten by Mr._____, she does so not out of meanness or simple evilness but because she envies Sophia's will and freedom. In response to Sophia, who asked her why she suggested such an action to Harpo, Celie replies,

I say it 'cause I'm a fool, I say. I say it 'cause I'm jealous of you. I say it 'cause you do what I can't. What that? she say. Fight, I say. (38)

By telling Harpo to beat Sophia, for perhaps the first time in her life, Celie expresses her own volition and, through Harpo, attempts to impress her will upon another being. And such is the paradox of existence; that one's redemption should emerge from another being's subjugation.

Again, it is easy to understand and accept Celie's attitude if we consider that before Shug's arrival, Sophia was Celie's only model of the indomitable woman. Sophia confesses to Celie:

all my life I had to fight. I had to fight my daddy. I had to fight my brothers. I had to fight my cousins and my uncles. A girl child ain't safe in a family of men. (38)

More than Shug, perhaps, Sophia's struggle against Harpo's will was the catalytic moment which made Celie aware of the existence of alternative rapport between male and female.

Even at this stage of her development, we find the origin of Celie's lesbianism in her contact with Sophia. Like the slave who perceives the master in any action or situation charged with power or violence, or like the attraction exerted by the dominant group over the dominated one, Celie comes to associate Sophia's freedom and Shug's detachment from social contingencies with their apparent masculinity, i.e., freedom. Actually, Celie's lesbianism is rooted more in the character's search for a role model, a kind of alternative reality rather than any "transsexual neurosis" symptomatic of post traumas or inner imbalance. Lesbianism in *The Color Purple* is for Celie and Shug the expression of a self directly in conflict with a man-made, man-dominated society. Interestingly, the two characters' behavior is echoed implicitly in one of Alice Walker's poems in *In Search of Our Mothers' Gardens* (39) where the author advocates her brand of radical individualism. Her candid injunction to women is to resist being cast as lovers' mates, but instead to take pride in being outcasts—social outcasts, that is—eager and happy to come to terms with the more negative aspects of their lives.

Alice Walker's own quest as well as her characters' in *The Color Purple* is a quest for authenticity. Her characters' lesbianism is not an end in itself but an expression of being, a philosophical attitude based on the individuals' rapport with their physical and moral environment. Many critics would argue, though, that by emulating man's social mores or behavior, Shug Avery lacks authenticity, that she in fact transvestites her "feminine essence" and borrows the trappings of man's power. However, in response to this argument, one may contend that the so-called feminine essence is more societal than inherent, that it is more a set of learned behaviors than predetermined ones, and that it is society which has created the myth of the "true woman" in its articulation of what a woman's existence should be. As Simone de Beauvoir expresses it, "she [the true woman] is an artificial product that civilization makes, as formerly eunuchs were made. Her presumed 'instincts' for coquetry, docility, are indoctrinated, as is phallic pride in man" (de Beauvoir 408). Shug Avery, in her bi-sexualism, may be symbolic of an absolute being—both subject and object in her feelings for Celie and in her rapport with Mr._____, who is struggling to resolve the gender and social limitations imposed upon her by society's definition of "normal," "natural" beings. The problem here, as we have previously noted, is less a sexual one than an existential one, for it deals with every human's perception of himself/herself or his/her perceptions by others. Simone de Beauvoir has clearly pinpointed the conflict existing between a woman's quest for self-accomplishment and her "role" as an object, a mere "tool" to be used to fulfill man's needs:

Woman is an existent who is called upon to make herself object; as subject she has an aggressive element in her sensuality which is not satisfied on the male body. Woman's homosexuality is one attempt among others to reconcile her autonomy with the passivity of her flesh. (de Beauvoir 406–7)

In Shug's lesbian embrace, Celie finds not only a refuge but also the crystallization of an otherwise unformulated wish: the wish to be other than what society (Mr._____) wants her to be. It is Shug who awakens Celie's body to love and the enjoyment of love's mystery. It is Shug who helps her transcend her objectification by Mr._____ and to finally accede to the rank of subject. Thus it can be concluded that Shug's feminine/masculine embrace, according to de Beauvoir's theory, allows Celie's own femininity to blossom in its full plenitude:

Between women love is contemplative; caresses are intended less to gain possession of the other than gradually to re-create the self through her; separateness is abolished, there is no struggle, no victory, no defeat; in exact reciprocity each is at once subject and object, sovereign and slave; duality becomes mutuality. (de Beauvoir 416)

The relationship between Shug and Celie is in direct opposition to the one between Celie and Mr._____ , for whereas Shug is bent on helping Celie discover her true self, Mr._____ thinks only about power, control, and self-realization through the oppression of others (Celie, Harpo).

This redefinition of human relationships, of human values as found in *The Color Purple*, is also encountered elsewhere in Alice Walker's work. In *In Search of Our Mothers' Gardens* (1983), she defines womanist as a serious, independent-minded woman intent on gaining possession of her own space in the world (xi–xii). This definition is echoed in *The Color Purple* in a conversation between Celie and Mr._____ in reference to Shug's and Sophia's "abnormal," "different" (we would say womanist) selves:

Mr._____ thinks all this is stuff men do. But Harpo not like this, I tell him. You not like this. What Shug got is *womanly* it seem like to me. Sophia and Shug not like men, he say, but they not like women either. (228)

These are indeed a new breed of women. They are in complete control of their lives and destiny. They are, to use Walker's declaration, "outrageous, audacious, courageous, responsible," and although they love women, they do not reject man's civilization, for they sometimes love "individual men," "sexually and non-sexually."

This womanist philosophy is a humanist one, for it is geared not only toward the full development of one gender but toward the recuperation of male and female, toward the "survival and wholeness of entire people, male and female." Within its parameters, it encompasses love, joy, music, artistic pleasure, and, above all, the reattachment of humankind to a cosmogonic worldview where everything is part of everything else, a world that would give importance to all living creatures, big and small, for they are expressions of the divine. To Celie, who objects to Shug's use of *It* in referring to God, Shug replies:

don't look like nothing, she say. It ain't something you can look at apart form anything else, including yourself. I believe God is everything. Everything that is or ever was or ever will be. (166-67)

It is Celie's conviction that she herself is part of God's design and forms one with all beings. This conviction will carry her in the final stage of her voyage of self-discovery. No longer a shadow in the light, she has rejoined the community of men and women; she has found herself, her own place in the great chain of being and is able to marvel at the creation, at life itself:

Now that my eyes are opening, I feels like a fool. Next to any little scrub of a bush in my yard, Mr._____'s evil shor shrink. (168)

Celie's final letter is a song of glory, the revelation of a newfound harmony between the heroine, the universe within and without: "Dear God. Dear stars, dear trees, dear sky, dear peoples. Dear Everything. Dear God," wrote Celie (242). And this is the true meaning of *The Color Purple*, which is a quest and a celebration, a song of sorrow and of joy, of birth, rebirth, and the redeeming power of love.

NOTE

1. Alice Walker prefers the term womanist over feminist. According to the writer, it expresses more completely the totality of her being.

WORKS CITED

Beauvoir, Simone de. *The Second Sex.* Trans. H. M. Parshely. New York: The Modern Library, 1968.
Blalock, Hubert M. *American Pluralism.* Ed. William M. Newman. New York: Harper, 1973.
Sartre, Jean-Paul. *Being and Nothingness.* Trans. Hazel E. Barnes. New York: Pocket Books, 1956.
Walker, Alice. "Alice Walker Is a Free Woman." *Sojourner*, January 1983: 13–14.
_____. *In Search of Our Mothers' Gardens*. New York: Harcourt Brace Jovanovich, 1983.
_____. *The Color Purple*. New York: Harcourt Brace Jovanovich, 1982.
Weiss, Frederick A. "Self-Alienation: Dynamism and Therapy." *Man Alone.* Ed. Eric and Mary Josephon. New York: Dell, 1962.

Alice Walker's Redemptive Art

Felipe Smith

The "saving" of lives is central to Alice Walker's art. This "redemptive" quality in her work goes beyond the thematic to the very heart of Walker's aesthetics, as she makes clear in her essay "Saving the Life That Is Your Own: The Importance of Models in the Artist's Life": "It is, in the end, the saving of lives that we writers are about. We do it because we care. We care because we know this: *the life we save is our own*" (*Gardens* 14). The urgency to "save lives" thus stems from Walker's acknowledgment of a spiritual bond connecting the writer to the lives she depicts: Artistic redemption "saves" the artist as well.

The most dramatic illustrations Walker provides of the saving power of art emphasize this mutual benefit to "saver" and "saved." In her essay "The Old Artist: Notes on Mr. Sweet," Walker tells how her career as a writer—her very life in fact—was "saved" by her art. She wrote her first published story "To Hell with Dying" instead of committing suicide. In the process, she saved for future generations the story of how the old guitar player Mr. Sweet "continued to share his troubles and insights [and] continued to sing." Simultaneously, through writing she gave herself the courage to "turn [her] back on the razor blade" (*Word* 39).

Mutual redemption is also the focus of Walker's discussion of her artistic debt to Zora Neale Hurston. In "Saving the Life That Is Your Own," she describes how crucial Hurston's *Mules and Men* (1935) was to her completion of a fictional version of her mother's remembrance from the Depression in a story called "The Revenge of Hannah Kemhuff." In this early Walker story, the narrator quotes a conjurer's curse directly from Hurston's book as part of her plan to secure justice for the wronged Hannah Kemhuff. Walker explains the effect of her "collaboration" with her esteemed literary ancestor in terms of an indescribable joy that comes from the auspicious knowledge of partaking in the ebullient community of historical personages and ancient spirits (*Gardens* 13).

The highly spiritualistic terms of this revelation are characteristic of Walker's discussions of the saving power of art. Walker secularizes such terms as *redemption* and *salvation* to encompass solutions to social problems such as racial and gender oppression. She models her redemptive strategy on writers such as Chopin, the Brontës, de Beauvoir, and Lessing, whom she describes as fully cognisant of their own oppressive condition and of the need to create a self-redemptive order (*Gardens* 251). One result of this is an implicit connection for Walker between "savers" and "saviors." She describes Anaïs Nin as "a recorder of everything, no matter how minute," a writer who "saves" in the sense of collecting and preserving. Tillie Olsen, though, "literally saves lives," in the sense of preventing danger or harm from befalling others. And by serving as a model for women, Virginia Woolf "has saved so many" from the terrible waste of unfulfilled lives (14).

Yet the key feature of Walker's redemptive art, in spite of the secular redemption that she envisions, is the feeling Walker gets from participating in the spiritual continuity of her people. At the heart of Walker's definition of the writer's social role is a cultivated awareness of the reciprocal saving potential of art, based on her sense of art as a means of keeping alive the connection between ancestral spirits and their living descendants. This multiple preservation of artist, subject, and communal spirit describes, I believe, the very core of Walker's artistic strategy.

In Walker's philosophy of redemptive art, *to save* means, first, to collect and thereby preserve the subject from loss by immortalizing it in art; by reclaiming the past the artist insures its availability to the future. The second meaning of *to save* involves providing the wisdom of the past both to ensure the continuity of the folk ethos and to serve as a blueprint for personal and communal survival for those who require artistic models. *To save* someone, in Walker's eyes, includes the obligation to liberate her/him from an oppressive cycle of violence. *To be saved* means to have achieved an "unselfconscious sense of collective oneness" (*Gardens* 264).

In certain ways, Walker's belief in the redemptive power of writing recalls Mark C. Taylor's description of textual interpretation as a form of "radical Christology." Taylor poses a theory of the text that views the act of interpretation as a reenactment of ritual sacrifice. For Taylor, the critic produces a text by victimizing the "host" text, dismembering and incorporating it in the process (63—69). The antecedent text, a victim of sacrifice, is for Taylor a "victimizer" as well because it cannot fulfill itself without the critic's participation. Like Christ, the text *requires* victimization in order to fulfill its destiny of becoming dismembered and disseminated to the multitudes. Identifying the central paradox that links textual and Christological functions, Taylor quotes Jeffrey Mehlman's assertion that "in order to be preserved the text must be interpreted, opened up, violated." Thus Taylor finds that textual interpretation is a process not unlike the commemoration of the crucifixion of Christ by the consumption of the Holy Eucharist in the Catholic mass: "Dismembering is, paradoxically, a condition of remembering, death the genesis of life." Taylor stresses that "incorporation is not mere destruction but is also reembodiment, reincarnation" (67).

Alice Walker has similarly iterated a theory of textual production that follows the process of incorporation, reembodiment, and reincarnation of anterior texts in the newly (re)created text. The spiritualistic terms in which Walker discusses her intertextual strategy show that she considers her approach not simply a form of rhetorical play, indirect critique, or homage to her literary ancestors (what Henry Louis Gates has termed "motivated and unmotivated Signification." [94, 121, 124, 255]) Walker, in summoning ancestral voices, seems to have bi-directional "salvation" in mind—redemptive "reincarnation." The process involves much more than acknowledging Zora Neale Hurston, to cite one example, as a literary "foremother"; it suggests instead a determined effort "literally" to reincarnate and redeem her as text-within-text.

Rather than focus on the "parasitic" relationship between host text and interpretive text that grounds Taylor's analysis, Walker sees her texts as eucharistic hosts in their ternary conjunction of spirit, word, and flesh. Simply put, Walker envisions her texts as redemptive sites which host the spiritual inclusion of words, reincarnating actual flesh-and-blood martyrs, saints, and sinners. Embodied in words, spirits "take flesh" in her texts. Her redemptive art, broadly imagined, is akin to the "radical Christology" which Taylor envisions the interpretive act to be. In Taylor's figuration, textuality is the state common to both the material and the immaterial. Everything nameable is a text: author and subject, body and spirit, the living and the dead. If living flesh can be converted into Word (text), then so can the dead. If existence within a text provides a kind of "life," then, by analogy, the generation of a text is a form of "transubstantiation," giving life to that which may in fact have no material existence. Textual inscription recalls, reincarnates, and reembodies ancestral spirits.

Here we can compare Taylor's "Embodied Word" to Alice Walker's description of the process by which the novel *The Color Purple* came into being. Walker explicitly addresses that novel's "invocation" "*To the Spirit*/Without whose assistance/ Neither this book/ Nor I/ Would have been/ Written." Assuming the "I" here is Walker herself, how do we account for her description of both the novel *and herself* as written texts? As Taylor points out, "When Incarnation is understood as Inscription, we discover Word. Embodied Word is Script(ure), the writing *in which we are inscribed and which we inscribe*" (71; emphasis added).[1]

Similarly, the novel's envoi ("I thank everybody in this book for coming./ A.W., author and medium") conceives the novel's characters as autonomous entities inhabiting Walker's newly created text, participating in the moral drama there enacted.[2] But as they are, like her, "Written" by the "Spirit," their claim to autonomy rests upon their priority as "texts." Walker acknowledges the anteriority and autonomy of these in-dwelling "texts" by describing her role as that of "author and medium." As "author," she participates in the inscription of ancestral voices into written text. As "medium," she invokes and "channels" the wisdom of ancestral "texts." Walker's own description of textual production relegates to herself a priestly role in the continuity of the textual chain, the site of gathering among ancestral presences, the living, and the unborn. Her strategy makes a place for the reader, too, conceiving the reader as a past, present, future potentiality whose presence and participation fulfill the text (and therefore part of the "everybody" thanked "for coming"). Despite the many interesting lines of inquiry that such a formulation raises, the importance of this collectivity of presences within the text to Walker's quest for a redemptive art has not been examined heretofore.[3]

Beyond thematic and structural considerations, Walker's "Signifying" gestures (in Gates's usage) signal her concern with rhetorical aspects of textual "salvation." To see clearly how the writer's power to "save lives" resides in rhetorical practices, we can look to Walker's description of the character Grange

Copeland in her 1973 self-interview. Walker explains that Grange's reason for kill-ing his son Brownfield in *The Third Life of Grange Copeland* (1970) and his subsequent death at the hands of the police are based on his desire to preserve what he valued in life: "To [Grange], the greatest value a person can attain is full humanity, which is a state of oneness with all things, and a willingness to die (or to live) so that the best that has been produced can continue to live in someone else." Grange does not acknowledge a spiritual authority, making his self-sacrifice an even greater gesture. For him, material continuity replaces spiritual value, giving urgency to his desire that "the best" continue in his absence. His act is a gesture of revolutionary theological revision, a skepticism comparable to Walker's added claim that she doesn't believe in "a God beyond nature. The world is God. Man is God. So is a leaf or a snake" (*Gardens* 265).

Walker's interest in communal continuity as an alternative to spiritual transcendence continues in *Meridian* (1976). Meridian Hill decides that, in the absence of spiritual value, existence itself should be revered above all: "'All those characters in all those novels that require death to end the book should refuse. All saints should walk away. Do their bit, then—just walk away'" (151). To her the only reason for self-sacrifice should be, as in the case of Grange, the preserving of another life: "she understood, finally, that the respect she owed her life was to continue, against whatever obstacles, to live it, and not to give up any particle of it without a fight to the death, preferably *not* her own." This heightened sense of existence extends "beyond herself to those around her because, in fact, the years in America had created them One Life" (204). Thus, the murder of the Civil Rights worker whose memorial she attends is "essentially a killing of herself, and approach[ing] the concept of retaliatory murder" (205) as a recognition of the need to preserve "the best that has been produced."[4]

But it is during the memorial ceremony that Meridian discovers the notion of preserving ancestral "spirits" as an extension of her obligation to One Life. The commemorative statement of the surviving parent of the slain worker provides a moment of existential clarity and economy: "My son died" (202). The response of the community is qualitatively different, however. In their ritual remembrance of the youth, they attempt to keep him "alive" by preserving in their memories the text of his liberation and reform philosophy. Meridian "hears" their covenant with the martyr as an unspoken communal "voice" addressing the aggrieved parent:

we are gathering ourselves to fight for and protect what your son fought for on behalf of us. If you will let us weave your story and your son's life and death into what we already know—into the songs, the sermons, the 'brother and sister'—we will soon be so angry we cannot help but move the church, the music, the form of worship that has always sustained us, these are the ways to transformation that we know. We want to take this with us as far as we can. (*Meridian* 204)

Not only is the youth's idealism textualized for communal preservation, but his "life and death" are also "woven" into that text—it is he who is repeatedly revived and sacrificed for the community. In order to see this "radical Christology" in its full rhetorical dimensions, we should recall Barthes's reminder that a text (from the Latin *textus*) is always "woven" from pre-existing materials (76). The unspoken "voice" of the communal One Life practices a distinct form of intertextuality ("'let us weave your story and your son's life and death into what we already know'" as a method of spiritual continuity and as a "way to transformation." That the text of the dead man does transform the community can be seen in the distinct departures in tone, content, and iconography of the church: The songs have a "martial" cadence and different, less conciliatory words; the church mission has been redefined as social activism; in the liturgy, God has been reduced to a "reference;" and the Lamb of God depiction of Christ has been replaced with a painting of a surrealistic, sword-wielding avenger (*Meridian* 199–203).

To the extent that she is certainly registering a critique through repetition and revision, Walker's "reformed" black church "Signifies" on traditional Christian ritual and doctrine. Further, Walker specifies through the unvoiced "voice" that the community is aware of "Signifying" as one of the primary "ways to transformation that [they] know" by highlighting the rhetorical nature of their attempt to keep the text of the worker "alive." His "life and death," as texts, are "woven" into the "songs," "sermons," and forms of address ("'brother and sister'") by which they identify themselves as a community. Walker underscores the significance of the process by describing another, more famous martyr being kept "alive" by the congregation:

The minister—in his thirties, dressed in a neat black suit and striped tie of an earlier fashion—spoke in a voice so dramatically like that of Martin Luther King's that at first Meridian thought his intention was to dupe or to mock. She glanced about to see if anyone else showed signs of astonishment or derision. (199)

Since signifying typically connotes disapproval, Meridian is immediately suspicious about the minister's intention and looks for clues in the reactions of the others to see if mockery is really the "message." The minister's youth and dress likewise semiotically "Signify" on Martin Luther King; the "text" of King—youth, voice, dress, sermon—has been "woven" into the ritual as one of the church's "ways of transformation," to enable the church to keep the past alive and to prepare for the future:

It struck Meridian that he was deliberately imitating King, that he and all of his congregation *knew* he was consciously keeping that voice alive. It was like a *play*. This startled Meridian; and the preacher's voice—not his own voice at all, but rather the voice of millions who could no longer speak—wound on and on. (200)

The preacher's voice is "not his own voice at all" because it is a "text" woven of many other texts, the ancestral "millions who could no longer speak." Mark Taylor notes the difficulty of ascribing authorship to any text: "Rather than *an author*, we discover a seemingly endless chain, an infinite proliferation of authors. Authors within authors, or as [Kierkegaard] puts it, 'one author seems to be enclosed in another, like the parts in a Chinese puzzle box'" (61). Meridian's discovery that the preacher's voice is a compendium of ancestral voices makes clear to her that the perpetuation of the "Signifying chain" of ancestral voices is the chief responsibility she owes to One Life: The "circle is unbroken" as long as someone remains alive to "speak" the texts. Her decision to kill before letting that "voice" become silent would not be possible except for her awareness that, beyond its implementation as a form of critique, "Signifying" is a culturally recognized vehicle of reincarnation and redemption—a "way of transformation." Significantly, Walker wrote "Saving the Life That Is Your Own" the same year that she wrote *Meridian*.

Thus, the invocation to the "Spirit" writer with which Walker foregrounds *The Color Purple* follows the question of authority to one of its several conclusions. Where there is no one "author" of the text of ancestral voices, the collectivity of authority may itself be named "the Spirit." Walker acknowledges that this authority "writes" her since its texts shape her and, through her, shape her texts. In *The Temple of My Familiar* (1989) Walker's idea of the corporeal text ("Embodied Word") is best exemplified in the character Lissie, "'the one who remembers everything'" (*Temple* 52). Lissie, whose spiritual reincarnations allow her to thumb through the texts of her lives back to the dawn of human history, achieves godhead through the saving of all of her "selves," even those which have been inimical to One Life. As Embodied Word she becomes a paradigm of redemptive intertextuality: She is Walker's spirit made text, many times over, each successive text a "repetition and revision" of past selves. Her authority derives from the unbroken chain of revisionary texts like Chinese puzzle boxes within her, herself the compendium of black female, of world experience.

II

We are a people. A people do not throw their geniuses away. And if they are thrown away, it is our duty *as artists and as witnesses for the future* to collect them again for the sake of our children, and, if necessary, bone by bone. (*Gardens* 92)

I will focus now on Walker's critique of the Christological model as a specific aspect of her redemptive art. Shug Avery's assertion in *The Color Purple* that "you have to git man off your eyeball, before you can see anything a'tall" (168) is an initial step in her ultimately successful campaign to teach Celie (and the reader) that religious observance is a matter of social convention. Since the characterization of Christ as male agent of salvation without whom the passive and powerless female cannot be saved serves, in Shug's estimation, to reinforce patriarchal and hierarchical social formations which perpetuate female oppression, that characterization is an obstacle to spiritual growth.[5] The notion of self-sacrifice and martyrdom runs counter to Walker's reformist impulses, since it valorizes victimhood as an index of spiritual progress. Walker's alternative to the Christ model, the result of many years of struggle with the implications of the entirely submissive role of the female and the otherwise oppressed, is a collective female agency (so-called "woman-bonding") that stresses self-help and group support.[6]

The supplanting of the Christ model by the collective redemption model in Walker's work, I will argue, is part of a complex intertextual strategy of redemptive art that involves Walker's two most cherished literary ancestors—Jean Toomer and Zora Neale Hurston. *"Cane and Their Eyes Were Watching God* are probably my favorite books by black American writers," Walker said in her 1973 self-interview, referring to the best known works by Toomer and Hurston, respectively. "*I love* [*Cane*] *passionately*; could not possibly exist without it" (*Gardens* 259). Her reverence for Hurston has also been well established. Through essays like "Looking for Zora," which recounts how Walker literally claimed kinship with Hurston in order to locate the writer's burial place, Walker herself became very instrumental in the "rescue" of Hurston from neglect by readers and scholars. Yet Walker's expressed reservations about each of these authors indicates that she would change things about their lives and about their writing, too, if it were in her power. As the epigraph to this section clearly demonstrates, Walker feels it is not only within her power, but it is her duty as a writer, to reclaim and restore ancestral geniuses.

Because Walker sees her texts as redemptive sites, the rehabilitation and preservation of her adopted ancestors, Toomer and Hurston, have been part of her creative practice almost from the start. Yet there is a clear distinction in the manner of Walker's textual reincarnations of the pair. Interestingly, while she strongly associates the Christological model with Toomer-like figures in her texts, Walker inscribes Hurston-like characters in her texts as innovators of the collective uplift model. Insofar as Walker characteristically associates Toomer with the discredited ideal of masculine agency, she must not simply reclaim him; she must (ironically) "redeem" him from his role as failed Christ. Walker must reclaim Hurston, on the other hand, in a fashion that compensates for the destitution and desperation that marked the writer's last years. In the process, Walker has become the catalyst for the current Hurston revival, "an act of literary bonding quite unlike anything that has ever happened within the Afro-American tradition" (Gates 244).

Walker's fascination with Toomer may be attributed in part to the fact that the site of his famous trip to the South immortalized in *Cane* is approximately an hour's drive from Walker's own hometown of Eatonton, Georgia. The women whose lives he sketched were women of Walker's own mother's time and circumstances. In "In Search of Our Mothers' Gardens," Walker describes Toomer's women as "our mothers and grandmothers, some of them: moving to music not yet written." (*Gardens* 232). Yet in explaining her attachment to Toomer, Walker acknowledges that her feelings for *Cane* come from a "perilous direction" (86). Despite her claim that she "could not possibly exist without" *Cane*, Walker says that she could indeed learn to do without Toomer himself: "I think Jean Toomer would want us to see; [the] beauty [of *Cane*], but let *him* go" (65, emphasis added). Apparently she allows Toomer to "go" based upon his choice "to live his own life as a white man," a "choice [which] undermined Toomer's moral judgment: there are things in American life [racism] and in his own [racial opportunism] that he simply refused to see" (62).

Examining Walker's valediction carefully shows it to be a more profound critique of Toomer than it might appear at first glance, for she lifts the phrasing of her dismissal of Toomer from Toomer himself. In "Theater," a sketch in the middle section of *Cane*, the story's central character, John, becomes transfixed by the earthy beauty and physical immediacy of the dangerous Dorris as she performs on the stage before him. John, however, decides against emotional or even physical involvement with the purple-stockinged chorine. He "desires her," but "holds off." This is but one instance in a pattern of ironized, self-conscious desire and denial that typifies Toomer's educated males (as well as some of his middle-class women), throwing into relief Toomer's own speculative relationship with black culture. Ultimately John's ambivalence about a black beauty whose vitality frightens him evolves into a passive aesthetic appropriation that provides him with the emotional distance he requires (and, in the process, produces the line that echoes in Walker's emotional separation from Toomer: "Keep her loveliness," he tells himself, but "let her go" [*Cane* 51]).

John, as the author's stand-in, embodies Toomer's tenuous relationship to *his* subject, "the rich dusk beauty" of black folk culture (*Cane* xvi). The aesthetic resolution to John's emotional dilemma is emphasized with a chiasmatic refrain, recalling the versification of Toomer's "Song of the Son": "Let her go," he repeats. "And keep her loveliness" (52). Walker's appropriation of Toomer's language is a classic example of "signifying'," identifying implicitly the aspects of Toomer's biography which most trouble her; his rejection of black women, compounded by his objectification and scopic appropriation of their pain and their beauty. In many of the sketches in *Cane*, the various Toomer surrogates, faced with the possibility of union with black women of the South, almost always choose to take the women's loveliness with them, but let their bodies go (or, rather, *stay*).

In "Fern," for example, the would-be savior who narrates the story is overcome by Fern's physical proximity, and, moving to exploit her vulnerability, he precipitates in her a fit of madness. Guiltily, he plans to do "some fine unnamed thing for her"(17)——something short, that is, of taking her with him as he leaves on the train. The narrator of "Avey" tries to interest Avey in an art that would articulate the black female soul, but as narrator and interpreter of the woman's life, it is *his* art, not hers, that he recites to her, putting her to sleep in the process. His art——in effect, the text of *Cane* writ small——repeats the pattern of the male observer who objectifies female existence, extracts its beauty, but leaves the woman herself behind. Ironically, the narrator's final comment on Avery "Orphan-woman" (47)——certifies this emotional abandonment.

In fact, Toomer's men are themselves the orphan——cultural orphans dislodged from the saving womb of their maternal culture by the stronger pull of a supersessive patriarchal embrace. Like Kabnis, they are figuratively Antaean, "suspended a few feet above the [culture] whose touch would resurrect [them]" (96). Like Dan Moore in "Box Seat" and Paul in "Bona and Paul," they are haunted by visions of earth mothers who would nurture them toward fulfillment of their potential destinies as "new-world Christs." Strikingly, Toomer's textual surrogates conjure a "new-world Christ" who is not a savior, but simply a martyr or, as Dan Moore puts it, "a slave of a woman who is a slave" (63). Committing themselves to black women signifies commitment to a black identity, a closing off of options that neither Toomer nor his surrogates seem willing to abide: "'God Almighty, dear God, dear Jesus, do not torture me with beauty,'" cries Kabnis. "Take it away Dear Jesus, do not chain me to myself' (83). Despite his prayer for deliverance, Kabnis becomes, however, a martyr—a Christ figuratively chained to the slow, tortuous wheel of racial antagonism in the South. When we read this event in light of Toomer's later disaffiliation with black culture and identity, it leaves the impression that Kabnis, who alone among Toomer's surrogates achieves physical union with the women and the soil of the South, exemplifies Toomer's horror at the prospect of "saving" the South's suffering black women at the expense of his own freedom.

The failure of the "new-world Christ" figures in Toomer's work is significant, given Toomer's professed desire to "save" the "plum"of black culture which had been "saved" for him in the folksongs he heard.[7] Unable to move beyond a model of redemption that requires their cultural "deaths" to "end the book," Toomer and his surrogates flee the South in tacit admission that those who stand apart from both the community and its culture cannot "redeem" either. What Toomer actually preserves is not the Southern black folk culture he set out to document, but the fact of his ambivalence toward it.

For her part, Walker not only critiques the proclivity of Christ figures to victimize those they have come to save, but she typically characterizes them as cultural voyeurs in the Toomer mold. Walker effectively encodes the "text" of Toomer as would-be-savior into her fiction, and there forces him to atone for the crimes of theft and abandonment. Toomer's appropriation of the stories of the women of the South, the real substance of *Cane*, followed by his abandonment of the race (and its women), is the "crime" which Walker redresses by her reappropriation of their lives and texts. She "redeems" the women of *Cane* in her own works—takes *back* their beauty, and lets the Toomer /Christ figure go. But she doesn't let him "off."

Among the earliest of the "Toomer archetypes" incarnated in Walker's fiction is Mordecai Rich, in the short story "Really, *Doesn't* Crime Pay?" The "crime" of the title is that of creative theft, a crime which Rich commits against a woman, Myrna, whose "madness" links her clearly to the women of Toomer's *Cane*. A Northern black man who goes to the South in search of literary material upon which to launch his career, Rich describes himself as an aesthete and a Romantic in the Toomer mold: "'A cold eye. An eye looking for Beauty. An eye looking for Truth.'" Myrna's suspicion of him stems from her belief that "nobody ought to look on other people's confusion with that cold an eye" (*In Love* 14), yet in the end, he seduces her and steals her stories—tales fittingly, of women victimized by men. His praise of her creative power masks his parasitical intent: "'You could be another Zora Hurston,'" he says archly (18). Sure—and *he* could be another Jean Toomer, for he appropriates Myrna's life and works and uses them to become a celebrated writer. To compound his crime, he replaces the black matriarch of Myrna's story "with a white cracker, with little slit-blue eyes" (21)—a commentary, perhaps on Toomer's aesthetic/romantic preferences—and announces his intention to write a book called "'The Black Woman's Resistance to Creativity in the Arts.'" Like the teller of "Avey," Rich becomes an "authority" on the inability of black women to appreciate "an art that would open the way for women the likes of her" (*Cane* 46), a trickster masked as savior.

Another such trickster/savior of Walker's is Truman Held in *Meridian*. Held, too, is a Northern black man who goes to the South during the Civil Rights Movement; leaves a local Southern girl (Meridian) behind physically, psychically, and emotionally violated; returns to the North to embark upon an artistic career built upon the representation of the black women of the South; and there marries, as Toomer did, a white woman. Similarly, Held's pretense of internationalism in clothing (African) and speech (French) "Signifies" upon Toomer's retreat into pan-culturalism to escape the onus of his black American identity. In naming Held, Walker also "Signifies" on Toomer's narrator in "Fern," who is "held" by Fern's eyes: "Her eyes, unusually weird and open, held me. Held God" (*Cane* 17).[8] Beyond these details, the interesting coincidence of Walker's heroine's having the same name as a favorite retreat of the young Toomer in Washington, D.C.— Meridian Hill—points to Walker's strategy of intertextual reference. It is on Meridian Hill that the Toomer surrogate in "Avey" tries to teach Avey the meaning of her life with a high-blown poetry also intended to seduce. If Truman Held stands in for Toomer in *Meridian*, Meridian certainly fills the role of the Aveys that have become "trapped in an evil honey" of Toomer's art (*Gardens* 232).[9]

In the end it is the very image which he exploits for profit, that of the Southern black earth mother, which "holds" Truman: "It was as if the voluptuous black bodies, with breasts like melons and hair like a crown of thorns, reached out—creatures of his own creation—and silenced his tongue. They began to claim him" (*Meridian* 170). Just as Fern haunts the would-be-seducer who abandons her, Meridian ("'The woman I should have married and didn't'") becomes "a constant reproach in [Truman's] thoughts" (138, 141). Since Truman surrounds himself with pictures of Meridian and with paintings and sculptures of the black women of the South, his torment poetically stems from the nature and source of his crime—the sin of reducing people to Art (128). Significantly, Truman, haunted by the image of the mother culture against which he has transgressed, must expiate his crimes by working as the "servant" to women who are "servants" in the South. Under Meridian's direction, he works out his "salvation" as a free-lance Civil Rights activist, assuming Meridian's role as communal sufferer after she decides to "just walk away."[10]

Male characters such as these and the white rock star Traynor in Walker's short story "Nineteen Fifty-five" share attributes which separate them from other victimizers of women in her works. Unlike the more typical male antagonist, they do not commit their crimes as a result of ignorance or simply as rough embodiments of a brutal patriarchy, but see themselves as saviors and liberators of women from emotional and physical violence, as men more sensitive to the plight of women due to their artistic temperaments. This Toomer-inspired figure of the "new-world Christ" who participates in the oppression of those he comes to liberate, and for whom "martyrdom" constitutes lifelong union with the culture and women of the black South, forms the core of Walker's "text" of the Christ model. The racial and cultural ambiguity of the figure, his outsider status to the culture, his "racial opportunism," and his career-defining cultural voyeurism and aesthetic banditry round out the cluster of discrete signifiers which typify this enduring Walker paradigm.

The fact that this violator suffers psychically from his crime echoes Toomer's summation of Fern's history of victimization: "When she was young, a few men took her, but got no joy from it. And then, once done, they felt bound to her" *(Cane* 14). Not only do these transgressors typically get no joy from their crimes in Walker's stories, but the very image of the violated "black madonna" (the nurturer in Toomer's work of the "new-world Christ") becomes the avenging ghost who drives the transgressor on a path toward purgation. Walker's textual appropriation of Toomer serves a purgatorial function then, becoming the theater for the passion, fall, and redemption of a particular, gender-focused Christology.

While Walker's redemptive efforts at textually reincarnating Toomer center on rehabilitating his history of racial and female exploitation, her effort at textual resuscitation of Zora Neale Hurston is redemptive in the sense that Walker attempts to reverse the catastrophic effects of poverty, isolation, and critical neglect. Noting Langston Hughes's description of Hurston as "a perfect book of entertainment in herself," Henry Louis Gates has also discovered the "presence" of Hurston in Walker's *The Color Purple*, but he attributes it to Walker's revisionary reconsideration of Hurston's heroine, Janie Woods, in *Their Eyes Were Watching God* (245). Gates compares Walker's description of a picture of Hurston which she owns to the picture of Shug Avery standing beside a motor car that Celie describes (Gates 254). He interprets this "Signifying'" gesture as evidence that Shug is a revision of Janie, a "letter of love to [Walker's] authority figure" (244). I think, however, that Walker's depiction of Shug Avery is meant to "Signify" on Hurston herself, especially since the picture of Hurston metamorphoses into the picture of Shug. Just as Walker "saves" the text of *Mules and Men* by transcribing it into "The Revenge of Hannah Kemhuff," Walker "saves" Hurston herself in *The Color Purple*. Shug Avery is Zora Neale Hurston reincarnated as "a perfect book of entertainment in herself."

Further, this inscription of Hurston serves the strategic purpose of "redeeming" the Christological model previously associated with Toomer. Toomer's outsider view of black women in the South falls just short, in Walker's estimation, of Hurston's insider view: "*There is no book more important to me than this one*," says Walker of *Their Eyes Were Watching God*," (including Toomer's *Cane*, which comes close, but from what I recognize is a more perilous direction)" (*Gardens* 86). The "ghost" of Hurston which dwells in Walker's works takes precedence over the "ghost" of Toomer, just as Hurston's text of black womanhood in the South authoritatively and chronologically supersedes Toomer's. Gates is correct, I think, to see *The Color Purple* as revisionary of both *Cane* and *Their Eyes* (194, 249). But Walker's novel seems, more appropriately, an attempt to "redeem" both parent texts by ensuring that "the best that has been produced" in *both* "can continue to live" in *The Color Purple*.

Not only does *The Color Purple* revise key tropes in Toomer's *Cane*, it owes its very title to the urgent chromatic display of Toomer's work, where we find the "purple haze" of dusk, the "purple" skin of the "Face" at sundown, lavender-tinted houses, and "pale purple shadows" contrasting with the "deep purple" of a woman's hair. Dusk tinges men with "purple pallor." The purple glow of the "Crimson Garden" signifies its transition from Eden to Gethsemane in "Bona and Paul," while women dress in "silk stockings" in the East. Nettie's discovery of the near-purple (i.e., "blue-black") skin of the Africans in *The Color Purple* tips off a further meaning of "the color purple" for Walker as well as Toomer: "The colored people." Toomer's memorable poem in *Cane*, "Song of the Son," shows his most striking use of the color in a figuration that captures the essence of *Cane*:

> O Negro slaves, dark purple ripened plums,
> Squeezed, and bursting in the pine-wood air,
> Passing, before they stripped the old tree bare
> One plum was saved for me, one seed becomes
> An everlasting song, a singing tree,
> Caroling softing souls of slavery,
> What they were, and what they are to me,
> Caroling softly souls of slavery (12)

For Toomer, the "Saved" plum is the essence of the slavery experience captured in the folksongs of the South which he believed were doomed to extinction. His text, then, has the redemptive purpose of preserving the souls of black folk, immortalizing them in "everlasting song"—but as *written*, not spoken, texts. As such, Toomer's saving gesture, a figurative "singing tree," represents the prototype of Walker's redemptive art.

"When reading Toomer's 'Song of the Sun' [sic] it is not unusual to comprehend—in a flash—what a dozen books on black people's history fail to illuminate," Walker has said. "I have embarrassed my classes occasionally by standing in front of them in tears as Toomer's poem about 'some genius from the south' [i.e., 'Georgia Dusk'] flew through my body like a swarm of golden butterflies on their way toward a destructive sun. Like du Bois, Toomer was capable of comprehending the black soul" (*Gardens* 258). Walker's particularly emotional response to this poem indicates her awareness of Toomer's characterization of "the colored people" as "the color purple" ("O Negro slaves, dark purple ripened plums"), and her depiction of Shug Avery in *The Color Purple* involves a redemptive gesture built on that figuration. Shug's nickname is an abbreviation for "Sugar," significantly, the chief product of the cane crop. On first seeing Shug, Celie notes, "Under all that powder her face black. She got a long pointed nose and big fleshy mouth. Lips look like black plum." (42) Later, Celie views Shug's disease-racked body in the tub: " Shug Avery long black body with it black plum nipples, look like her mouth." (45). In an interesting "Signifying" gesture, Walker transforms Toomer's "saved" plum into a real "singer" (and worshipper of trees). And, more importantly for Walker's redemptive strategy, by "saving" Shug, Celie performs the enabling action toward her own redemption for the kiss of those very black plum lips opens up to Celie her own sexuality, spirituality, and ultimately (through Shug's "saving" of Nettie's letters) her very identity.

In her most recent collection of essays, *Living By the Word* (1988), Walker claims that "there is no story more moving to me personally than one in which one woman saves the life of another, and saves herself", a feat that "black women wish they were able to do all the time" (19). In effect, what we see in *The Color Purple* is Walker's inscription of that very mutual saving gesture between herself and her literary ancestor, Hurston. Walker appropriates Toomer's figure of the "saved plum," which becomes the seed of the "singing tree" of his art. But significantly, the "voice" which comes through clearest is Hurston's, not Toomer's, and the song she sings is not of ineffectual male saviors who end up exploiting those they would redeem, but of women individually and collectively working toward their own and each other's salvation.

Moving Toomer "off her eyeball" allows Walker to see beyond the hierarchical Christological path, just as Shug opens up for Celie the route of mutual salvation. Toomer's singing tree is figuratively incorporated into Hurston's chorus of Nature. When, in *Their Eyes*, Janie's grandmother saves "de text" of her slave experience for Janie, the moment strikingly parallels Toomer's "saved plum" of the black slave experience. But Janie learns, as Walker does too, that saved "texts" are meant to be rewritten through the vantage of new experience. Janie revises, and therefore redeems, her grandmother's "text" of male-agent salvation (i.e., respectable marriage), passing on to Phoebe her own text of transformation from unvoiced cultural orphan to voiced and participating (yet determinedly autonomous) member of the folk community, a paradigm of redemptive agency which Walker appropriates and expands upon. Toomer's text of male-agent redemption—cognate with Nanny's, and therefore implicitly critiqued by Janie's experience in *Their Eyes*—becomes entirely obsolete in light of the manifold saving gestures of the women of *The Color Purple*.

At the heart of *The Color Purple* lies a complex redemptive artistry that encompasses saving gestures of various types. For example, Walker has acknowledged her grandmother as her source for Celie ("Characters" 67). Walker has also made much of the tale of the shared underwear as an influence (*Gardens* 355–56). But the ur-text of the redemptive fantasy at the heart of the novel appears in Walker's 1979 essay "Zora Neale Hurston," which concludes with the definitive statement of Walker's redemptive art that serves as the epigraph to this section of my essay: "*We are a people. A people do not throw their geniuses away.* And if they are thrown away, it is our duty *as artists and as witnesses for the future* to collect them again for the sake of our children, and, if necessary, bone by bone" (*Gardens* 92). In this concluding statement to an article on the cautionary aspects of Hurston's life and career, Walker signals her intent to reassemble the "text" of Hurston, "if necessary, bone by bone," and to reincarnate her as "Embodied Word." Equally revealing is what immediately precedes this declaration in the essay, a fantasy of mutually assisted salvation which includes not only Hurston but, significantly, the singers Billie Holiday and Bessie Smith too:

In my mind, Zora Neale Hurston, Billie Holiday, and Bessie Smith form a sort of unholy trinity. *It would have been nice if the three of them had had one another to turn to, in times of need. I close my eyes and imagine them.* [my emphasis] (*Gardens* 91–92)

Does this fantasy not represent the core of *The Color Purple*? Walker's assertion that Hurston "*belongs*" more among the singers than the writers grounds Shug Avery's incarnation as blues singer. Further, in Mary Agnes (Squeak), we can hear not only the words but also the "sort of meowing" voice of Billie Holiday. Both her drug use and tragic history with men relate her to Holiday, and the fact that she, like Celie (Hurston), benefits from an extended network of female strivers fulfills the fantasy's intent of rewriting and redeeming the lives of the ancestral voices Walker acknowledges. Physically and temperamentally, Sophia suggests Bessie Smith, the one who would keep the money. Walker's redemptive strategy works to empower each historical figure in a way that fictionally reverses the putative cause of her life's suffering. As Walker explains of her stepgrandmother's reincarnation in the novel as Celie: "I liberated her from her own history. I wanted her to be happy" ("Characters" 67).

Walker's various statements indicate her belief in the *actual, not figurative*, saving power of art—the ability of the artist to liberate people from their tragic histories—if necessary, to make them happy. In her poem "Each One, Pull One," Walker elevates this ability to an obligation. Addressing all who "write, paint, sculpt, dance/ or sing" as sharers in the "fate/of all our peoples" (i.e., One Life), she exhorts those standing with her on "the rim/of the grave" of the ancestors (including King, Malcolm X, Lorraine Hansberry, Hurston, Nella Larsen, and Toomer) to stop helping their enemies to "bury us":

> Look, I temporarily on the rim
> of the grave
> have grasped my mother's hand
> my father's leg.
> There is the hand of Robeson
> Langston's thigh
> Zora's arm and hair
> Each one, pull one back into the sun
> We who have stood over
> so many graves
> know that
> all of us must live
> or none. (*Horses* 50–53)

III

The story of Walker's redemptive effort on behalf of Toomer and Hurston has one additional chapter. In Walker's recent novel *The Temple of My Familiar*, the Toomer archetype reappears as the folk/pop singer Arveyda, a man of multi-racial background like Toomer. Arveyda's fame as a musician derives from his ability to "sing" the souls of his largely female audience, and as in Toomer's case, this talent feeds off his exploitative relationship with the women in his life. At the novel's end, Arveyda meets Fanny, the genetic descendant of Celie (through Olivia) and the spiritual descendent of Shug, having been raised in the household of the two women. The sexual union of these two, then, marks the "textual" bonding of the Toomer and Hurston archetypes in Walker's work. Their orgasm (in Shug's theology, the ecstatic achievement of god's presence) returns us to the key topological refiguration in *The Color Purple*. "Arveyda feels as if he has rushed to meet all the ancestors and they have welcomed him with job" (4–7). During this ancestral communion, they also share a vision which hints at their textual origins:

She is fearful of asking him what she must. Timidly she says: "And did you also see the yellow plum tree and all the little creatures, even the fish, in its branches?" But Arveyda says simply, "Yes. But best of all was the plum tree and everything and everybody in it, and the warmth of your breath and the taste in my mouth of the sweet yellow plums." (407–8)

This scene represents, I believe, Walker's reconciliation with the Toomer archetype—her attempt to lay to rest this ghost that has roamed her works in search of atonement. The yellow plums perhaps result from the cross-pollination of the two trees of Walker's ancestral gardens—Janie's pear and Toomer's plum. The sexual position of Fanny above Arveyda reflects the Toomer surrogate's abandonment of hierarchical sexual politics, while his achieved physical union with Fanny (a "space Cadet" in the mold of Toomer's Fern) indicates a fulfillment of both Toomer's quest for physical union with the spirit-maddened women of the race and the women's parallel discovery of a spiritual anchor. Thus their final salutes to each other attest to their success in mutually-assisted salvation:

"My spirit," says Fanny.
"My flesh," says Arveyda. (408)

NOTES

1. Wendy Wall (85) suggests that Walker ascribes a similar power to Celie, since Celie too is the author of a self which has only a textual existence.
2. See Walker's essay "Writing *The Color Purple*" (*Gardens* 355–60), in which she describes the "visitations" by the book's characters as crucial to the production of her text.
3. Henry Louis Gates (239–58) and Michael Awkward (135–64) have pursued other possibilities in interpreting Walker's spiritualistic stance, also with reference to Hurston and Toomer as literary ancestors.
4. In my forthcoming essay "Survival Whole: Redemptive Vengeance and Forbearance in Alice Walker's Novels," I consider Walker's continued interest in retaliatory violence as an alternative method of redemption.
5. Mary Daly points out that the Christological model leads inevitably toward sexism: "The underlying—and often explicit —assumption in the minds of theologians down through the centuries has been that divinity could not have deigned to 'become incarnate' in the 'inferior' sex, and the 'fact' that 'he' did not do so of course confirms male

superiority" (70). Daly goes on to insist that even the reform theologians who interpret Christ as a symbol miss the point that the historical use of the "symbol" to oppress indicates "some inherent deficiency in the symbol itself" (72).

6. Mary Daly's chapter "The Bonds of Freedom: Sisterhood as Antichurch" explains the rationale for such a reformist gesture: "The development of sisterhood is a unique threat, for it is directed against the basic social and psychic model of hierarchy and dominion upon which authoritarian religion as *authoritarian* depends for survival" (133).

7. See Darwin T. Turner's "Introduction" to *Cane* xxii–xxiii. For other aspects of Toomer's messianic self-image, see page xi of the "Introduction."

8. The eyes of Truman Held's own "judge," Meridian Hill, have a similar effect upon Truman: "There was something dark, Truman thought, a shadow that seemed to swing, like the pendulum of a clock, or like a blade, behind her open, candid eyes, that made one feel condemned. That made one think of the guillotine" (*Meridian* 139).

9. See Kerman and Eldridge (74) on Meridian Hill. When we consider the implications of the name Meridian, we should also note the central importance of the poem "Blue Meridian" as Toomer's attempt at racial and cultural self-definition. See Kerman and Eldridge (80–8) for a discussion of "Blue Meridian" (originally titled "The First American").

10. Martha J. McGowan points out that the working title for *Meridian* was *Atonement and Release* (29).

WORKS CITED

Awkward, Michael. *Inspiriting Influences: Tradition, Revision, and Afro-American Women's Novels.* New York: Columbia University Press, 1989.

Barthes, Roland. "From Work to Text." *Textual Strategies: Perspectives in Post-Structuralist Criticism.* Ed. Joshua V. Harari, Ithaca: Cornell University Press, 1979. 73–81.

"Characters in Search of a Book." *Newsweek* 21 June 1982: 67.

Daly, Mary. *Beyond God the Father: Toward a Philosophy of Women's Liberation.* Boston: Beacon, 1973.

Gates, Henry Louis, Jr. *The Signifying Monkey: A Theory of Afro-American Literary Criticism.* New York: Oxford University Press, 1988.

Kerman, Cynthia Earl, and Richard Eldridge. *The Lives of Jean Toomer: A Hunger for Wholeness.* Baton Rouge: Louisiana State University Press, 1987.

McGowan, Martha J. "Atonement and Release in Alice Walker's *Meridian.*" *Critique: Studies in Modern Fiction* 23.1 (1981): 25–36.

Taylor, Mark C. "Text as Victim." *Deconstruction and Theology.* Ed. Thomas J. J. Altizer. New York: Crossroad, 1982. 58–78.

Toomer, Jean. *Cane.* 1923. New York: Liveright, 1975.

Walker, Alice. *The Color Purple.* New York: Harcourt Brace Jovanovich, 1982.

_____. *Horses Make a Landscape Look More Beautiful: Poems.* San Diego: Harcourt Brace Jovanovich, 1986.

_____. *In Love & Trouble: Stories of Black Women.* New York: Harcourt Brace Jovanovich, 1973.

_____. *In Search of Our Mothers' Gardens: Womanist Prose.* San Diego: Harcourt Brace Jovanovich, 1983.

_____. *Living by the Word: Selected Writings,* 1973–1987. San Diego: Harcourt Brace Jovanovich, 1988.

_____. *Meridian.* New York: Harcourt Brace Jovanovich, 1976.

_____. *The Temple of My Familiar.* San Diego: Harcourt Brace Jovanovich, 1989.

Wall, Wendy. "Lettered Bodies and Corporeal Texts in *The Color Purple" Studies in American Fiction* 16 (1988): 83–97.

Walker's *The Temple of My Familiar*: Womanist as Monistic Idealist

Ikenna Dieke

It seems to me that even art is utterly dependent on philosophy: or if you prefer it, on a metaphysic. The metaphysic or philosophy may not be anywhere very accurately stated and may be quite unconscious, in the artist, yet it is a metaphysic that governs men at the time, and is by all men more or less comprehended, and lived.
——D. H. Lawrence, *Fantasia of the Unconscious*

In his groundbreaking study *The Signifying Monkey: A Theory of Afro-American Literary Criticism*, Henry Louis Gates suggests that part of the foundational essence of African American intertextual aesthetics lies in its exponential revisionism, involving two distinct but parallel processes. The first process comprises those African American texts that "Signify" (i.e., revise) on other African American texts that preceded them. The second involves those texts by African American authors whose primary goal is to revision either a given text or set of texts canonized within the Western tradition, or an idea or set of ideas that has been accepted as axiomatic truth or universal postulate. Of the latter process, Gates argues that when "black writers revise texts in the Western tradition, they do so 'authentically,' with a black difference, a compelling sense of difference based on the black vernacular" (xxii). Using Gates's assertion as a point of departure, I would posit that in her fourth novel *The Temple of My Familiar*, Alice Walker makes a conscious effort to signify on a worldview that has become the benchmark of traditional Western metaphysics—dualism.

Dualism, essentially, is a theory of knowing that represents reality in terms of an irreconcilable dyad—of two mutually irreducible elements or classes of elements. It manifests itself in such intellectual movements or epochs as the ancient Stoics' immanent cosmography, the Enlightenment Age, the theory of the Great Chain of Being, the medieval cosmological system—the basis of which was Ptolemaic astronomy, the Newtonian paradigm of rationalist empiriology, and finally, the Cartesian postulate of the mind/matter (res extensa) dichotomy. Dualistc philosophy (otherwise stylized as the "mechanistic worldview") postulates a world in which there is (and always will be) perpetual dissociation between rational intelligence and the affective domain of consciousness, between reason, on the one hand, and questions of faith and moral values, on the other—the former being paraded as the superior of the two. With time, the dangerous implications of this postulate begin to manifest in sexual, racial, and cultural politics. The male assumes a transcendent position in relationship to the female, since by the dualist's jaundiced account, he (the male) has become the sole inheritor of supraordinate reason; of course, to the exclusion of everyone and everything else. Josephine Donovan states it a little more succinctly:

The assertion of the primacy of human reason and of its right to rule all other aspects of reality led to a certain conceit or arrogance, indeed to a kind of "species," or male, chauvinism. For, inherent in the vaunting of human (male) reason is the idea that rational beings are the lords of creation and have the right to impose their "reason" on all who lack it—women, nonhuman creatures, and the earth itself. (3)

In other words, the danger of the dualistic worldview is that its rules are predicated on a conceptual paradigm unique to European culture that have no discernible analogues in African, African American, and other indigenous cultures. According to this paradigm, and as set forth by Donovan, "Man" is set above, and separate from "Nature," over which he retains total dominion. Men are assumed to be superior to women. And in a similar vein, Europeans and their cultures are assumed to have "divine" right of dominion over other cultures, notably African, which do not share this false and invidious hierarchical image of man over nature, and which are thus dubbed "savage" and "primitive."

     Against such a skewed worldview, and imbued with ecological thinking, womanist instincts, and multicultural vision, Walker goes beyond the intellective culture of binary opposition to construct a unique egalitarian womanist cosmology in *The Temple of My Familiar* in a calculated attempt to Signify on the sort of tosh and demonstrably false dichotomy inherent in the mechanistic worldview, to recycle the heritage of an alternate worldview—holism, and to somehow reclaim her own self-evident ecological insight that we are all a part of, and not apart from, each other, the other sex, and the Earth (Gaia) with its richly diverse denizens—human and nonhumans alike.[1]

     Thus for Alice Walker, artistic creativity is nothing but a deliberate act of giving form to a vision of the underlying or hidden links in the great universal chain of being. It is a vision deeply anchored in a traditional African worldview, one that neatly configures "the structure of phenomena from the perspective of interdependencey" (Schiele 27);[2] in other words, configures "the traditional mind's perception of reality [which] transcends the sensory and such levels of experience as could be regarded as empirical" (Obiechina 38). It is also a vision akin to that of the sixteenth-century Italian philosopher Giordano Bruno and the seventeenth-century English metaphysical poets, which is a way of suggesting "an aspect of rational order underlying surface diversity" (McNulty 79).[3] It is a vision that subserves a delicate interplay of continuity and change—*continuity* of the spirit of universal bond and sympathetic relatedness, what Walker once characterized as. "communal spirit; righteous convergence" (*Meridian* 199),[4] and *change* in terms of a deliberate break with the largely fragmented, fractured, and frustrated image of woman and her male-bedeviled world in the earlier novels. From the predominately Gothic vision in *The Third Life of Grange Copeland*, to the somewhat Camusian pastiche in *Meridian*, to the vision of the great gender divide-and-conquer in *The Color Purple*, Walker moves into *The Temple of My Familiar* and creates a salutary vision of reality, which points toward a monistic idealism in which humans, animals, and the whole ecological order coexist in a unique dynamic of pancosmic symbiosis.[5]

Evidently Walker must have been leery of the danger posed to her imagination by fragmentation—hence the urgency in the novel toward an ideal of unity, the unity of culture, moral truth, and imaginative thought and emotion. The best summation of this unity in *The Temple of My Familiar* is Lissie's long, moving story about the spirit of mutual dependence between humans and their animal cousins and Suwelo's reflections on its moral, agathological, and cultural implications, both for himself as well as for those with whom he has come in contact. Lissie says:

"When you knew every branch, every hollow, and every crevice of a tree there was nothing safer; you could quickly hide from whatever might be pursuing you. Besides, we shared the tree with other creatures, who, in raucous or stealthy fashion—there was a phython, for instance—looked out for us. They seemed nearly unable to comprehend separateness; they lived and breathed as a family, then as a clan, then as a forest, and so on. If I hurt myself and cried, they cried with me, as if my pain was magically transposed to their bodies." (84–86)

Suwelo, concurring, responds in a deeply philosophical, soul-searching reflection:

"What do human beings contribute, Suwelo was thinking morosely, as he waited one afternoon for Miss Lissie to appear. Her story about the animal cousins had moved him, and each day he found himself more conscious of his own nonhuman 'relatives' in the world" (89).

With this vision clearly set before her, Walker proceeds to construct *The Temple of My Familiar* into six major parts, each consisting of diverse vignettes that project iconographic narrative movement (iconographic because Alice Walker not only tells a story in each movement, but also conveys its underlying metaphysical meaning by a carefully selected mythico-iconic image, pretty much in the convention of African cosmological art and iconography).[6] Behind the insistent particularity of each individual story is a serious quest, albeit unconscious, for the demonstrable values of oneness, wholeness, and unity as opposed to dialectical tension, exclusivity, and separateness. Insistently and consistently, characters in the novel are in motion, even when it appears they are in conflict, toward an underlying kinship that binds them with one another and with forces beyond themselves. For Walker this act of seeking means a basic freedom, which only a bird can enjoy, to range over all time, to employ any subtheme, to consecrate a limitless range of subject matter, to begin where she pleases, and to stop where she wishes.

The basic intent is to trace human life in its pancosmic and mythical dimensions through all its protean turns and twists, all its recesses, all its races and peoples. The watchword throughout the novel is communion, a communion forged through three distinct metaphysical frames: time, nature, and self.

Communion with time translates in a unique sense into a kind of eucharistics of historical sentience. This sentience informs quite literally Alice Walker's creative resourcefulness. She herself has said: "I think my whole program as a writer is to deal with history just so I know where I am. I can't move through time in any other way, since I have strong feelings about history and the need to bring it along. One of the scary things is how much of the past, especially our past, gets forgotten" (Tate 185). In *The Temple of My Familiar*, time for Walker is a process of growth inseparable from the notion of the self and the self's ineradicable link to the world outside. Especially crucial to each character's quest for identity is the personal effort to recapture the past as a significant element in present experience. In other words, Walker, through the recollective monologues of her characters, develops creative uses of memory in order to express the feeling of duration and to recapture the sense of a unified self. Present in any moment of a character's life are not only the totality of personal experience but the cultural factors that have helped shape that experience. Walker peers not simply into the life of a single character but into the period of time which that character reflects. The characters have a unique quality of power, the power to remember. In remembering they explore cultural images and metaphors that guide and illuminate their lives. In fact, the whole novel, from start to finish, pulsates like a powerhouse of imaginal memory, constantly negotiating the copresence of memory and imagination in the psyche, engaging and making present whatever images most deeply stir characters' inner core.

Characters like Arveyda, the dandy rock star; his wife Carlotta, a Women's Studies scholar; Zede, Carlotta's mother and a latter-day shaman; Fanny, a literature teacher turned masseuse/massage guru; Olivia, Fanny's feisty mom, endowed with the power of cultural oratory; Suwelo, Fanny's erstwhile hubby and a rationalist, hard-nosed professor of history; Uncle Rafe, Suwelo's affable uncle and benefactor; Lissie, the genetrix of race memory and the reincarnational *shero* with a thousand faces; Hal, Lissie's lifelong and ebullient companion; Nzingha, Fanny's halfsister and look-alike, and a hardbitten feminist been-to; Ola, Fanny's and Nzingha's dad, a rebel/playright and a political/civil rights activist; and Mary Jane Briden, a white American liberal émigré married to Ola——all betray a peculiar passion to reconnect with their past, both personally and collectively. For them, without a principle of continuum, of the past merging with the present in a constantly shifting mélange, it becomes meaningless to speak of the self. A perfect example is Lissie's lecturing Suwelo on what amounts to as the quintessence of memorial consciousness:

"Hal and I feel you have closed a door, a very important door, against memory, against the pain. That just to say their names, "Marcia" and "Louis," is too heavy a key for your hand. And we urge you to open that door, to say their names. To speak of them, anything you can remember. To trace what you can recognize in yourself back to them; to find the connection of spirit and heart you share with them, who are, after all, your United Front. For really,

Suwelo, if our parents are not present in us, consciously present, there is much, very much about ourselves we can never know. It is as if our very flesh is blind and dumb and cannot truly feel itself. And, more important, the doors into the ancient past, the ancient self, the preancient current of life itself, remain closed. When this happens, crucial natural abilities are likely to be inaccessible to one: the ability to smile easily, to joke, to have fun, to be serious, to be thoughtful, to be limber of limb." (352–53)

The pith of Lissie's message is twofold: memory is eucharistic; it is also therapeutic/psychotherapeutic. It is eucharistic in that it forces us to acknowledge our sacred bond with our past and with those who might be regarded as the prime limbs of that past. It points up "the place of memory as ontological foundation of the experience of identity, continuity and relationship" (Perlman 34). The iconography of memory as a doorway to the eternity of the past and of those loved ones who have passed away subserves in an oblique kind of way a *participation mystique*, a certain normative value of fundamental human related-ness. Lissie maintains further:

"It is against blockage between ourselves and others—those who are alive and those who are dead—that we must work. In blocking off what hurts us, we think we are walling ourselves off from pain. But in the long run the wall, which prevents growth, hurts us more than the pain, which, if we will only bear it, soon passes over us." (353)

Memory is psychotherapeutic because it soothes a violently sundered heart and creates in its void what Reinhold Neibuhr might describe as "the inner life where the rational soul may cultivate equanimity in defiance of all outward circumstances" (*Webster* 767).

Thus, for Alice Walker, as for the post-Romantic French novelist Marcel Proust, recollective art is a rhetorical strategy of relocating the lost self, of seeking and uncovering an inner tapestry of identity, not mere psychological identity but the exterior contexts—social, political, and personal—that make up the human self in all its complexity. Recollective art uses what John McCormick says is "the impact, tragic in implication, of a virtually palpable past upon an impalpable present" (17). Recollective art builds historical consciousness into a mystique, very much as Faulkner did in the words of Baron Friedrich von Novalis, "We bear the burdens of our fathers, just as we have inherited their goods, and we actually live in the past and the future, and are nowhere less at home than in the present" (qtd. in McCormick 17).

In a way, each of the main characters in *The Temple of My Familiar* is like Huxley's archetypal historicist in *Those Barren Leaves*: Lilian Adwinkle, a woman who has literally purchased "history," searches for a durable source of value, and looks to the past to provide a means of interpreting the present. For example, the burdens of the past are an essential part of the personalities of Zedé—Carlotta's free-spirited mother turned shaman and her philanderer-boyfriend, Arveyda—the dandy rock star and Carlotta's cheating husband. The sea voyage that both undertake from San Francisco to the seashores of Zedé's South American home country represents a plunging into the depths of the sea of life in search of the lost fragments of her past:

> They traveled south.
> Under the open sky, the reflections of the turquoise water near her country's shoreline brightening her sad eyes, Zedé became a different woman. Gone the hesitant English that was a result of shyness, passionate excitement, or fear. Though her voice often cracked with the effort not to weep from the pain of relived experiences, she spoke with an eloquence that startled Arveyda, who held on to her as she talked, not as a lover, but as the ear that might at last reconnect her to her world. (45)

Zedé's world is that of the traditional setting. Her memory of where she came from originally, before emigrating to the United States—a small village in South America—is that of a child. The child memory motif neatly subserves a certain romantic agony with which Zedé now longs for the now-disappearing idyllic ambience of her traditional world. With a tremulous voice, she explains to Arveyda:

> "Of the way of my country you can have no comprehension," she said, "especially as it was when I was a child. Everything was changing, it is true, but still many of the old ways were everywhere on view. Our mothers taught us about lovemaking and babies when we became señoritas, of course, but all along also they taught us the history of our civilization." (45–46)

It is a uniquely rich civilization of a people who live close to the land, ever creative and omnificent, and proud of their heritage. Zedé's village environment is small-scale, and so people live in close compounds. And the proximity of the houses makes for intimate social relationships. Collective participation is the essence of communal activities. The village dancers, the musicians, the ritual priests and priestesses, the headdressers—all are appreciated for their individual talents. However, the richness of their individual capabilities is ultimately related to the well-being of the whole community. Through the elements of dance, ritual, headdressing, music, and sacerdotal calling, the people of Zedé's village express their individualism, but more important, their unique interrelatedness and a sense of organic responses shared with others. Like Zedé, Arveyda also was born in a small, rural setting, this time, a small midwestern town of Terre Haute, Indiana, where the idyllic sense of community and neighborly rapport is very strong. For Arveyda, the person who embodies this sense of sympathetic relatedness is Simon Isaac, or Uncle Isaac as he is fondly known around the neighborhood. The neighborhood greengrocer, a Palestinian immigrant, and a violinist, Uncle Isaac has served as a father figure to the adolescent Arveyda and has inspired the young Arveyda to take to singing. The community appreciates Uncle Isaac's success as a grocer, but it does so only within the context of his business helping to cement the bond among the people and promote their common well-being.

This communal sentiment epitomized by Uncle Isaac stays with Arveyda throughout his singing career. Thus when Arveyda sings, he sings about communal sentiments; he sings about the pride of a united country; he sings about his homeland, with its seawaters and marine life; and he sings about the primordial connection between man and the ecosystem. The truth is that when Arveyda sings, he does so within a recognizable musical, cultural, and ecological tradition, since the art of music making, like that of headdressing, is very much integral to a functional culture. Other characters in the novel profoundly affected by the mystique of community, culture, and lineal tradition include Fanny and Mary Jane Briden (formerly Mary Ann Haverstock).

Memory of the past also reveals psychological aspects and values in history, a kind of axiology of psychohistory. The legend of Chief John Horse, the black Native American chief among the Seminoles of Florida, serves as a lucid example. In the story of Chief John's numerous expeditions—his kindly reception of escaped black slaves into the Seminole nation, his leading his people on the incredible long march from Texas to Mexico, his long and selfless service to the Mexican government by fighting Mexican bandits, and his leading his people back to Texas after the abolition of slavery—we perceive the essential language, the language of myth, in which memory reveals the objective psyche of history. Behind his legend is a hallowed euhemerism—the interpretation of arcane myths as traditional accounts of historical personages and events. In other words, Chief John Horse's life subserves the euhemeristic argument that history becomes myth in imaginal memory.

A second important element in Walker's foregrounding of the interconnectedness of all life is nature. Walker's treatment of nature reminds us of two well-known writers—the novelist Thomas Hardy and the philosopher F. W. J. von Schelling. Walker uses Lissie's passionate interest in nature to reiterate the age-long truth palpable in Hardy's nature novels, especially *Far from the Madding Crowd*, that we are all part of the dynamic geology of natural scenery. In Carlotta's cavewalk, we sense Walker's reassertion of the Romantics' "interest in the unknown modes of being associated with the world of physical nature" (Alcorn 3). Lissie's and Hal's nature art and painting are significant ways of experiencing spiritual and imaginative growth, of feeling the immanentistic and vitalistic pulse of God evolving throughout the universe.

Lissie once told Hal, "Being a genius means you are connected to God" (335). Of course, being connected to God means that all of us are connected to nature, for behind nature is supernature. This is a theosophical and animistic conceptualization of the quintessential chiasma between man and cosmic intelligence. There is an almost lyric rapture surrounding their nature painting, nature appearing like a pure crystal mirror behind which is a deep metaphysical truth about the grandeur and majesty of the ecological order.

Lissie's and Hal's nature paintings make one feel close to the Spirit of the Universe, contemplating the deeper mysteries and the mighty invisible forms of the universe.[7] One of the best examples in the novel is the twin artwork ("Self-portrait, Lissie Lyles"/"Self-portrait, Harold D. Jenkins") that Lissie presents to Suwelo as a gift, in appreciation of the latter's visit with the couple in Baltimore. The paintings celebrate androgyny; they visualize a double birth—the bodily birth (God as Mother of the entire fabric of creation—Lissie) and the mental birth (God as Father of the creative mind—Hal) that must be spoken for ideas to be born. Moon and sun (lunar and solar consciousness); earth and sky; earth, wind, and fire; the eternal tree of life—all feature significantly here; all partake in the colossal mystery of wholeness and anagogic (i.e., mystical) valence, what C. G. Jung calls the *coniunctio oppositorum* (integration of duality). The metaphysical principle being played out in Lissie's and Hal's painting is the principle called *objective idealism*, which in the philosophy of Schelling means that nature is visible intelligence and intelligence invisible nature. For Alice Walker, creative intelligence is an instrument for promoting the acceptance of nature as ultimately ideal or spiritual and existing independently of any subjects.

In other words, the artist who paints nature visualizes a mystery—the symbolical dual being in whom the opposing energies are united (itself a sign of divine creative organismal kinesis), the energy born in the artist's mind and in the body of a divine biunity. Walker speculates that through nature painting each of us experiences this sexual sign of the mother-father (Lissie-Hal) creative symbiotic spirit within, and in each individual soul these energies appear to be uniquely reconciled. This is the spiritual dimension of womanist idealism. Lissie-Hal's images of nature may, in an indirect sense, dramatize Jung's concept of the animus (the inner male partner in a woman) and anima (the inner female partner in a man). Walker may be attempting to reinforce the kind of communion she idealizes—that which celebrates the coequal/coextensive power of man and woman. Each clearly compensates the other in a uniquely rich and visible way—a transpersonal concept of gender equalitarianism free from rancor and subjugation.

Another example of the mystical perception of nature is the story Zedé tells of a waterfall in her South American village, a magical abode of the goddess Ixtaphtaphahex, identifiable with the destiny of the community. In and around the waterfall, Zedé and her friends connect with one another and with their cultural heritage, the heritage of ancient deities whose pervasive presence is tied up inextricably with the destiny of the people.

But the most critical moment of mystical truth in the novel belongs to Carlotta, who, in discovering her true identity in nature—in the cave, under the tree, experiences a kind of rejuvenant enlightenment and inner peace. In her cave dream, she seems to find completeness and closure to inner strife. It is Carlotta who acknowledges psychical or metaphysical forces' coexistence with physical landscape. Carlotta's cave (as well as Lissie's temple) reflects personal awareness of myth and rite as predicate of vital continuity. Her dream in the cave is a powerful revelation of the archaic psyche and its primordial house—the cave. In this respect, Walker assimilates nature for the purposes of the psyche—discovering or projecting into the cave Carlotta's emotional concerns. In other words, Walker deliberately recreates by dint of active imagination this eternal link between mind and nature, and in so doing, clearly repudiates the languidity of Cartesian dualism.[8]

The symbiosis of memorial psyche and ecological ambience amplifies the construction of a unique sense of self. By *self*, I mean the innermost essence of each individual, within which he or she is attuned with the supreme, universal destinal order. In *The Temple of My Familiar*, Walker creates a unique self—which I will describe as the protean/metempsychean self. I am referring to Walker's preoccupation with the reincarnational topos—the belief that the human self is part of the infinite. Like Joyce's Anna Livia Plurabelle, Lissie goes through life knitting up relations that she believes to have originated in former existences. Her life seems like a tale that has no beginning and no end. Suwelo confirms what she already knows: "You are a spirit that has had many bodies, and you travel through time and space that way" (243). She responds, "Suwelo, in addition to being a man, and white, which I was many times after the time of which I just told you, I was also, at least once, myself a lion" (364).

Lissie's story reminds us of *Finnegans Wake*, in which Joyce paints the rotations of the wheel of life, rebuilds the city across the ages in Finn's multiple metamorphoses (Cranston and Williams 342). The cumulative effect of Lissie's story is that she achieves something resembling a universal soul, a transcendent harmony with the entire universe, as symbolized by the bird icon. Just as Christ represents for the Christian this principle of eternal harmonies, Buddha for the Buddhists, and Krishna for the Hindus, so Lissie represents for Walker this eternal spirit, a kind of womanist élan vital. Her hope is that some of us will some day become Lissies. In this sense, Alice Walker is a theosophist par excellence, and so can confidently be regarded as the latter-day Madame Blavatsky, or better still, in a conjurer's sense, Marie Laveau, of American belles lettres.

Walker also creates a second self, the totemic self. This self is a function of the protective familiar, usually an animal that indigenous people selected, each person for her/himself, generally through the monition of a dream during a kind of initiation. The character associated with this is again the indomitable Lissie. Here is how she describes her temple and her genie/familiar:

"Last night I dreamed I was showing you my temple," said Miss Lissie. "I don't know where it was, but it was a simple square one-room structure, very adobe or Southwestern-looking with poles jutting out at the ceiling line and the windows set in deep It was beautiful, though small, and I remembered going there for the ceremonies dressed in a long white cotton robe my familiar—what you might these days, unfortunately, call a 'pet'—was a small, incredibly beautiful creature that was part bird, for it was feathered, part fish, for it could swim and had a somewhat fish/bird shape, and part reptile, for it scooted about like geckoes do, and it was all over the place while I talked to you. Its movements were graceful and clever, its expression mischievous and full of humor. It was *alive!*" (118)

Lissie's dream is a journey into self. It is a metaphor of psychic development in which the dreamer—Lissie—recognizes the patterns of opposition in her life and attempts to synthesize them into some sort of self-healing totality.

Such a totality or wholeness is expressed in symbolic form, and the symbolic form is the icon. Here that icon is a temple, an archetypal image that represents aspects of the feminine psyche as united on a higher plane. In other words, it is a mandala of psychic totality. In feminist terms, it signifies the pyramidal or radial order of the woman. Like the Indian yantra, the temple motif is an instrument of invagination, of self-immersion, in which the female realizes inner peace, inner order, a communion with the angels of the soul that expresses the idea of a safe refuge. The temple is also a mandala of primal order whose purpose is to transform the chaos of gender into a kind of inner cosmic peace. Through the brilliance of the bird image of her familiar, Lissie's self-identity resounds with echoes of personal triumph, even if only momentarily. The sensuous and numinous qualities of her temple create a sense of place, in fact not just a sense of place, but a *topophilia*——love of place.

In short, the temple is equivalent to interior space; and the image of interior space is a symbol of reintegration and wholeness, "the wholeness of the female consciousness" (Fleenor 15). Furthermore, the temple is a loop, a functional circle, which helps Lissie's inner self transpose its own being, both on the subliminal plane and in the world of action——the phenomenal world. It transforms the woman/perceiver into a shared world of self/gender/racial identity, and thus helps her to illuminate the dark world outside.

Of crucial significance to the theme of monistic idealism, or the idealism of essential communion, in *The Temple of My Familiar* is the nature of language. In the novel every major narrative movement embodies a traditional convention of language, especially the art of conversation raised to a ritual act of phatic communion. Every movement is an exposé of one character's sharing his or her intimate thoughts, feelings, memories, and recollections with other characters, partly as a way of communicating ideas, but more important, as a means of establishing an atmosphere of sociability and rapport, of strengthening a sense of the unified whole and sympathetic relatedness. The recurrent use of conversational and recollective art, despite its banalities, provides part of the emotional and social matrix that holds the characters and their world together.[9] Recall Arveyda's and Zedé's use of Spanish sententious expressions, which reminds us of the vernacular characters of Leo Tolstoy (one of Alice Walker's favorite Russian novelists). When the characters use these fossilized expressions, they situate their individual utterances within a milieu of cultural continuity. Walker's aim is not so much to articulate her characters' uniqueness, as it is to demonstrate their kinship with the community in which they were born and bred; that is, with its psycholinguistic ethos.

The Temple of My Familiar can be read as a romance of the development of the human psyche in which the human ego strives consciously and unconsciously for wholeness. Man as separate from woman, humans as separate from animals, one race as separate from another, the old as separate from the young, the mind as separable from nature, the present as cut off from the past——all that foists a gribbled, self-destructive narcissism, a half-personality at best. But as C. G. Jung opines, "[S]ince everything living strives for wholeness, the inevitable one-sidedness of our conscious life is continually corrected and compensated by the universal human being in us whose goal is the ultimate integration of conscious and unconscious processes, or better, the assimilation of the [rational] ego to a wider personality" (Bickman 40) of becoming. As a romance of the psyche, *The Temple of My Familiar* follows three kinds of wholes that Proclus posits: the first, anterior to the parts——the human world of men and women; the second, composed of the parts——the earth of living organisms, including humans and animals; the third, knitting into one stuff the parts and the whole——the universe, the magic circle of reunion and integratation.

Alice Walker's concern with life is usually deep and metaphysical, full of fresh revelation of truth and beauty, and shows real depth of emotion and intensity of feeling. Like the prelogical and pristine Native Americans whom she adores dearly, Walker in *The Temple of My Familiar* plunges headlong into the wave that wafts her to her native shore—the eternal universe —where objects become symbols of the unique affections and ontological links in the catena of our endless being. Unraveling these eternal links is the metaphysician's way. In the novel, we see the aesthetic function of the imagination in its power of grasping in a single, firm vision the long course of African American history in all its tributaries and seemingly endless undulations. By enabling us to penetrate the magic circle of a past that is great in itself and vitally related to the confused present, Alice Walker invites us into her own magic temple for the ritual act of transforming the appliqués and racio-cultural intensives of her art into a quest for the metaphysical basis of reality. It is this metaphysical vision which relates *The Temple of My Familiar* to Ignazio Silone's *Bread and Wine*, "a novel that finds in the human relation the seeds of a truly sacramental sensibility" (McCormick 29). *The Temple of My Familiar* offers Alice Walker one more opportunity to consummate a momentary fusion of her own being with the souls of others, brought into a psychic intimacy by some magical affinity of creative intellect and cultural palingenesis.

NOTES

1. I am especially indebted for these ideas to Dr. Thomas I. Ellis, a former colleague of mine in the English Department at Hampton University. On numerous occasions, he and I had exchanged ideas about Alice Walker as a visionary writer. Dr. Ellis's interpretation of Walker as an artist is right on the mark—highly penetrating and illuminant.

2. Shirley Jackson offers a more elaborate exegesis of this vision: "Generally, traditional African beliefs focus on a world view that includes human beings, flora, fauna and nonhuman forces." According to traditional beliefs, "Africans consider themselves to be part of a universe which was complete upon creation. Everything in creation such as animals, plants and minerals is imbued, to one degree or another, with the power of God" (39).

3. This explains Alice Walker's persistent use of analogy or metaphysical conceit not only in her poetry, but also in much of her fiction. The sense one gets reading her works is the sense one gets reading the English metaphysical poets, which is to say that both Walker and the metaphysical poets recognize or "suggest underlying connections unifying things that on the surface [may] appear utterly unrelated. As J.A. Mazzeo puts it, the metaphysical poet is 'one who discovers and expresses the universal analogies binding the universe together.'" For more on this subject, see McNulty (79).

4. In a comment on the writing of her third novel, *The Color Purple*, Walker suggests that this communal spirit is the main springboard of her creative imagination: "I gathered up the historical and psychological threads of the life my ancestors lived, and in the writing of it I felt joy and strength and my own continuity: that wonderful feeling writers get sometimes, not very often, of being with a great many people, ancient spirits, all very happy to see me consulting and acknowledging them, and eager to let me know, through the

joy of their presence, that indeed, I am not alone" ("Writing" 453).

5. In this essay *idealism* is employed in relation to the theory of *metaphysical idealism*, which regards reality as essentially spiritual and which views the the intrinsic nature and essence of reality as consciousness. *Monistic* (which is here interchangeable with *holistic*) comes from the word *monism*; *monism* essentially relates to the metaphysical view that reality is a unitary organic whole. In sociological terms, it refers to the harmonious force which unites the laws of man and nature. Thus *monistic idealism*, as employed in this essay, is the consciousness of the intrinsic spiritual bond between humans, on the one hand, and between humans and the natural/ecological/destinal order, on the other.

6. Part I (1–141) contains 21 narrative movements; Part II (143–201) contains 11 narrative movements; Part III (203–34) contains 3 narrative movements; Part IV (235–83) contains 4 narrative movements; Part V (285–330) contains 8 narrative movements; and Part VI (331–416) contains 14 narrative movements. The total number of iconic narrative movements is 61.

7. In an interview with John O'Brien, Walker underscores the eternal, inextricable linkage between nature and the idea of deity: "Certainly I don't believe there is a God beyond nature. The world is God. Man is God. So is a leaf or a snake. So when Grange Copeland refuses to pray at the end of [*The Third Life of Grange Copeland*], he is refusing to be a hypocrite. He does, however, appreciate the humanity of man-womankind as a God worth embracing. To him, the greatest value a person can attain is full humanity, which is a state of oneness with all things, and a willingness to die (or to live) so that the best that has been produced can continue to live in someone else" (205).

8. Walker's ecofeminist activism is loudly proclaimed here. Zedé, Lissie, Fanny, and to some extent, Mary Jane Briden, seem like Walker's alter egos in the struggle to preserve the earth against man's desecrating madness.

9. This view of Walker's use of language in *The Temple of My Familiar*—the use of language for fostering ecumenical spirit among people—is borrowed from Emmanuel Obiechina's interpretation of similar use of language in the West African, tradition-oriented rural novel. And I hereby express my unreserved indebtedness. See especially chapter 7 in Obiechina.

WORKS CITED

Alcorn, John. *The Nature Novel from Hardy to Lawrence.* New York: Columbia University Press, 1977.

Bickman, Martin. *The Unsounded Centre: Jungian Studies in American Romanticism.* Chapel Hill: University of North Carolina Press, 1980.

Cranston, Sylvia, and Carey Williams. *Reincarnation: A New Horizon in Science, Religion, and Society.* New York: Julian, 1984.

Donovan, Josephine. *Feminist Theory.* New York: Frederick Ungar Publishing Company, 1985.

Fleenor, Juliann E., ed. *The Female Gothic.* Montreal: Eden Press, 1983.

Gates, Henry Louis, Jr. *The Signifying Monkey: A Theory of Afro-American Literary Criticism.* New York: Oxford University Press, 1988.

Jackson, Shirley. "African World View in Five Afro-Hispanic Novels." *Afro-Hispanic Review* 5 (1986): 37–42.

McCormick, John. *Fiction as Knowledge.* New Brunswick: Rutgers University Press, 1976.

McNulty, J. Bard. *Modes of Literature.* Boston: Houghton, 1977.

Obiechina, Emmanuel. *Culture, Tradition and Society in the West African Novel.*
    Cambridge: Cambridge University Press, 1975.
O'Brien, John, ed. "Alice Walker." *Interviews with Black Writers.* New York: Liveright,
    1973. 185–211.
Perlman, Michael. *Imaginal Memory and the Place of Hiroshima.* Albany: State University
    of New York Press, 1988.
Schiele, Jerome H. "Afrocentricity for all." *Black Issues in Higher Education,* 26 Sept.
    1991: 27.
Tate, Claudia. "Alice Walker." *Black Women Writers at Work.* New York: Continuum,
    1983. 175–87.
Walker, Alice. *The Temple of My Familiar.* San Diego: Harcourt Brace Jovanovich, 1989.
    _____. "Writing *The Color Purple.*" *Black Women Writers* (1950–1980): *A Critical
    Evaluation.* Ed. Mari Evans. Garden City, N.Y.: Anchor, 1983. 453–56.
Webster's Third New International Dictionary. Ed. Philip Babcock Gove. Springfield:
    Merriam, 1976.

Alice Walker's American Quilt: *The Color Purple* and American Literary Tradition

Priscilla Leder

Quilts and quilting play a key role in *The Color Purple*. Both the product and the process provide an outlet for thwarted energies, record a family's history by incorporating its discarded garments, and effect reconciliations between characters. Even more importantly, they embody the ideal of unity in diversity which permeates Walker's writings.[1] The pieces of a quilt, like individuals in a pluralistic society, retain their original identities while functioning as parts of something else—just as the star-like pieces in the "Sister's Choice" pattern remain recognizable as Shug Avery's yellow dress.

This pluralism, as symbolized by the quilt, suggests a way of reading *The Color Purple*. Like a skillfully crafted quilt, *The Color Purple* incorporates recognizable pieces of American literary traditions into its own pattern. This essay will identify some of those pieces and suggest how they have been cut to fit a pattern that incorporates competing literary traditions—the "domestic" tradition once damned by Hawthorne and more recently explored by Nina Baym and Jane Tompkins, and the "wilderness" tradition created in the late 1950s and early sixties by a group of critics, notably Richard Chase and Leslie Fiedler, who attempted to characterize "the American novel" and "the American tradition" (Chase, Fiedler).

The domestic novel, sometimes called the "sentimental" novel, came to prominence in the nineteenth century. As Nina Baym explains in *Women's Fictions: A Guide to Novels By and About Women in America, 1820–1870*, the author of such a novel, almost always a woman, told "the story of a young girl who is deprived of the supports she has rightly or wrongly depended on to sustain her throughout life and is faced with the necessity of winning her own way in the world" (11). Such a heroine wins out by self-discipline, forbearance, and loving-kindness rather than by aggression, and often religious faith helps her develop and maintain those virtues. Her victory usually brings her peace, security, and the love and respect of those around her, including some who have been responsible for her sufferings in the first place.

In the wilderness novel as described by Chase, Fiedler, and others, the (male) protagonist feels cramped and stifled by the strictures of "civilization," usually embodied by city, town, and/or home. He responds to his dilemma by fleeing to an unstructured landscape beyond those strictures. There, he finds freedom, but he also confronts a lack of structure which threatens identity. He may also find a male companion of another race whom he grows to love but from whom he must part. The writers who developed this tradition refer most often to Cooper, Hawthorne, Melville, Poe, and Twain. In choosing these writers, the critic assumed that the important American writers were those who expressed some quintessential American theme, such as conflict between individual and society.

In her article "Melodramas of Beset Manhood," Baym describes the myth which expresses that theme:

The myth narrates a confrontation of the American individual, the pure American self divorced from specific social circumstances, with the promise offered by the idea of America. The myth also holds that, as something artificial and secondary to human nature, society exerts an unmitigatedly destructive pressure on individuality. To depict it at any length would be a waste of artistic time; and there is only one way to relate it to the individual—as an adversary. (132)

In other words, the novelist, like his protagonist, is in flight from the constrictions of "civilization," and writers who concern themselves with everyday social reality and its problems do not belong among the classic American novelists.

For Chase and other writers, the American novel's reluctance to depict everyday social realities entails a refusal to reconcile contradictions. For example, Chase contrasts the English novel, which is notable for "its powerful, engrossing composition of wide ranges of experience into a moral centrality and equability of judgment" with the American novel, which "has been stirred, rather, by the aesthetic possibilities of radical forms of alienation, contradiction, and disorder" (2). Those everyday compromises between individual and group, ideal and reality, which are essential to social life often remain unresolved in the classic American novel.

The works included in the wilderness tradition, along with those in the domestic tradition, have evoked varying responses from readers and writers over the years. In the nineteenth century, the domestic novel enjoyed popularity, especially with the women readers who made up most of the audiences for literature. On the other hand, the writers whom we now venerate as "classic American novelists" often struggled—and sometimes failed—to earn their livings by their pens. Melville provides the most spectacular and best-known example, but even Hawthorne, who did sell, once complained bitterly that "America is now given wholly to a "d****d mob of scribbling women, and I should have no chance of success while the public taste is occupied with their trash." (qtd. Cowley 685).

The eclipse of the domestic novel began in the early decades of this century as readers came to crave more sophisticated, less didactic fare; certainly its descendants survive between pink and purple covers in supermarkets and chain bookstores. In contrast, the scholars who created the wilderness tradition helped to canonize the works of the writers they studied, and Twain, Hawthorne, Melville, and Poe were established as required reading for millions of students. In canonizing a group of works which emphasized conflict between the individual and society, critics either implicitly or explicitly disparaged the domestic novel, with its attention to the details of everyday life, as trivial.

When the feminist resurgence of the late sixties and early seventies reached the universities, feminist scholars began to call attention to the fact that the canon of American literature was almost exclusively white and male. Baym argues that, by taking conflict between the individual and society as the quintessential American theme, male critics had excluded women writers, whose works deal more often with the individual *in* society ("Melodramas" 132).

Though the question of canons and the bases for canon formation are still being argued, a glance at the panels proposed for the 1989 convention of the Modern Language Association reveals that the number and variety of works studied (and presumably taught) by American literary scholars has indeed expanded to include more women, as well as minority writers of both genders. As might be expected, this expansion encompasses writers in the domestic tradition. Baym, for example, published *Women's Fictions: A Guide to Novels By and About Women in America, 1820–1870*, in 1978. However, because of the role of the heroine, these novels remain problematic for some feminist critics. Since the heroine must often renounce her own desires and even efface herself in order to compromise and be reconciled, the domestic novels perpetuated the restricted status of nineteenth-century American women. Thus, according to Ann Douglas, such novels reinforced a status quo which deprived women of all economic power except as consumers:

Middle-class women became in a very real sense consumers of literature. The stories they read and wrote were themselves courses in the shopping mentality, exercises in euphemism essential to the system of flattery which served as the rationale for the American woman's economic position. (62)

Specifically, the example of the forebearing heroine's triumph cajoled the reader into a passive acceptance of her own lot.

Some readers of *The Color Purple* have placed it in the domestic tradition and have seen Walker's heroine as similarly problematic. Celie, the heroine of *The Color Purple*, does bear a strong resemblance to her domestic counterpart. She begins her story raped, beaten, orphaned, without emotional support, and with only minimal economic support. After years of suffering, enduring, and caring for others, she ends up with a house, a business, and a crowd of loving friends and relatives. However, in creating Cecile, Walker does not merely reiterate the past. Rather, much like the scholars engaged in revising and expanding the canon, she incorporates and reinterprets the past to serve a contemporary ideal of unity in diversity. Walker pursues this end not only by assimilating literary traditions but also by setting *The Color Purple* in the past.

Though set in rural Georgia in the twenties, thirties, and forties, Walker's novel provides little of the minute, realistic period detail that characterizes most historical novels. She aims not to re-create the period but to help today's readers, especially black women readers, come to terms with contemporary issues. For example, *The Color Purple* deals extensively with domestic violence in the black family. Setting the novel in the past enables Walker to locate the source of such violence in attitudes fostered by slavery and sharecropping.

Through the setting, Walker also addresses the issue she explores in the title essay of *In Search of Our Mothers' Gardens*—the black woman artist's search for role in a past where black women's creativity was neglected, stifled, or even forbidden. She concludes that, although few black women were able to leave behind books, symphonies, or paintings, their creativity nevertheless found expression in less tangible forms such as songs, quilts, and gardens. In *The Color Purple*, Walker celebrates that creativity by placing the seamstress Celie and the blues singer Shug in the south of the twenties, thirties, and forties.

The following pages will discuss both of these issues in more detail, but their primary purpose is to show how *The Color Purple* incorporates elements of both the wilderness and the domestic tradition. On the one hand, its vision of inclusiveness avoids the alienation and unresolved contradiction of the wilderness tradition. On the other hand, though its reconciliations and compromises place it more in the domestic tradition, Walker spares her characters the self-effacement which is demanded of the domestic heroine.

In the domestic novel, the most important change is redemption or salvation—the renunciation of sin and the acknowledgment of a commitment to God and to others. Tompkins documents a famous example of redemption in *Uncle Tom's Cabin*:

By giving Topsy her love, Eva initiates a process of redemption whose power, transmitted from heart to heart, can change the entire world. And indeed the process has begun. From that time on, Topsy is "different from what she used to be" and Miss Ophelia, who overhears the conversation is different, too. (Stowe 131)

In *The Color Purple*, most of the characters experience redemption: Celie, Shug, Harpo, Mary Agnes, Corrine, and Eleanor Jane are all "Different from that they used to be" at the novel's end. After undergoing such a change, the character not only attains a sense of personal autonomy which makes all her/his actions authentic but also recognizes this autonomy in others and thus treats them with respect. Thus Albert, who seems primarily a sinner against others, comes to feel differently towards himself as well as towards others. "I'm satisfied this the first time I ever lived on Earth as a natural man. It feels like a new experience" (221). This emphasis on personal autonomy varies the pattern of the domestic novel, where the self must often be subsumed by the needs of others.

Celie's redemption begins with her letters. First of all, they are a form of prayer, the force which strengthens the heroines of domestic novels. "Never mind," Celie writes, "as long as I can spell G-o-o-d I got somebody along." Because she writes her prayers, Celie effects God's presence. Since her letters constitute a kind of autobiography, they also enable her to imagine herself as well as God. Having imaged a self, she can begin to change it. Furthermore, her letters reflect her development: they begin as simple narrations of events, then include astute comments about other people, eventually incorporate analyses of Celie's own feelings and motives, and finally provide insights into the feelings and motives of others, as in the novel's final paragraph when Celie discusses the older and young characters' perceptions of themselves and each other.

In making the act of writing an element in the process of Celie's redemption, Walker incorporates issues from Afro-American culture as well as from the domestic tradition. For slaves, who were forbidden to learn to read and write, literacy seemed to hold special power. Frederick Douglass, hearing his master forbid further reading lessons, resolved to become literate at all costs: "that very determination which [my master] expressed to keep me in ignorance, only rendered me the more resolute in seeking intelligence" (147). Celie, the descendant of slaves, displays similar resolve. She and her sister Nettie are zealous students "cause us know we got to be smart to git away" (11). Perhaps in choosing to *write* to god, Celie is attempting to assert and maintain a skill which may someday enable her to "git away."

For Celie, writing forms part of the difficult process of achieving personal autonomy. Yet, according to Henry Louis Gates, Jr., the acquisition of literacy and the development of autonomous identity may conflict for black writers. He asks, "How can the black subject posit a full and sufficient self in a language in which blackness is a sign of absence?" (12). Gates partially answers his own question by calling upon black writers and critics to draw upon "the black tradition itself" for their literary forms and critical theories. In *The Color Purple*, Walker draws upon the black tradition by having Celie write in dialect, thereby asserting both her literacy and her blackness. In "Finding Celie's Voice," Walker writes that Celie "has not accepted an alien description of who she is, neither has she accepted an alien tongue completely to tell us about it" (72). Celie confronts the "alien tongue" when Darlene, the seamstress who assists her with her pants-making business, tries to teach her standard English. Celie largely rejects Darlene's lessons in proper speech, especially her suggestion that Celie stop substituting "us" for "we." That particular substitution epitomizes the function of dialect in *The Color Purple*: "us," a word which in white discourse denotes an object, takes on a new function as subject in Celie's dialect.

According to the critics who characterized the wilderness, writers in that tradition also sought to reject the forms of the majority—they looked for forms which would distinguish them from their literary predecessors. For Twain in *Huckleberry Finn*, as for Walker, dialect served as the distinguishing form. Both Huck and Celie speak dialect in ways that seem to revitalize the language and to give authentic expression to their experiences. Change the pronoun, and what Walker says of Celie could apply to Huck: "Her being is formed by the language in which she is revealed, and like everything about her it is characteristic hard-won, and authentic" ("Finding Celie's Voice" 72).

Celie's language forms only one part of the gradual affirmation of her being, however. The example and influence of others is equally important. Celie's relationship with Shug Avery is crucial to her redemption, and that relationship resembles key relationships between characters in both the wilderness and domestic traditions. In the domestic novel, according to Baym, "as her kin fail her, the heroine meets people in the community who support, advise, and befriend her" (*Women's Fictions* 38). Such friends and counselors often help the heroine to develop the Christian virtues which she needs to endure the trials of her existence. In the wilderness novel, the protagonist sometimes acquires a companion of another race who may advise and instruct but who also possesses a profound significance. According to Leslie Fiedler, such a companion represents nature, not only the living environment which surrounds the protagonist but also "the unconscious mind, what the age used to call the heart" (196). The "high natured" Shug Avery possesses the assertiveness and sexuality which are latent in Celie.

Celie's attachment to Shug begins with an image—a photograph of Shug—which embodies multiple possibilities for Celie.

The first [picture] of a real person I ever seen. Shug Avery was a woman. The most beautiful woman I ever saw. She more pretty than my mama. She bout ten thousand times more prettier than me. I see her there in furs. Her face rouge. Her hair like something tall. She grinning with her foot up on somebody motorcar. Her eyes serious tho. Sad some. (8)

Shug's furs and hair suggest her animal energy and sexuality and associate her with the active, even predatory aspect of nature. Celie, in contrast, associates herself with passive nature: when Albert beats her, she makes herself wood. "I say to myself, Celie, you a tree" (22). Celie views herself as powerless. Thus, for her Shug's dress and pose signify power—both economic and sexual power, for the pose is at once proprietary and flirtatious. Celie also sees the beauty which is absent in her life and, she believes, in her self. Although she sees in Shug qualities which she lacks, Celie also sees a counterpart of herself, as her emphasis on Shug's gender reveals. In Shug, Celie sees a *woman* who embodies everything she lacks, but she also sees the image of her own suffering in Shug's serious, sad eyes. Years later, Celie tells Albert that she loves Shug for what she's been through; that love begins with the photograph.

This vision of Shug as the embodiment of possibility motivates Celie's kindness to Shug. Thus, although Celie closely resembles the self-abasing heroine of the domestic novel when she feeds, bathes, and otherwise nurtures Shug, who is after all her husband's mistress and who initially rewards Celie's kindness with abuse, her motive is not the same. Domestic heroines nurture their oppressors because to do otherwise would be a willful assertion of pride; Celie nurtures Shug because Shug represents her own potential for assertiveness.

Although Celie's motives differ from the domestic heroine's, the relationship she develops with Shug has much in common with some friendships in domestic novels. First of all, Celie's love softens Shug's heart, just as Eva's softens Topsy's. In both works, loving touch proves the crucial ingredient. Topsy, acutely conscious that Miss Ophelia wishes to save her soul but cannot touch her body, responds to Eva's hand on her shoulder. Shug responds to Celie's combing out her hair: "that feel just right, she say. That feel like mama used to do" (48). Celie's gift of affection returns to her multiplied, as in a biblical parable: Shug becomes Celie's friend, teacher, counselor, and lover.

Though some aspects of Celie and Shug's friendship resemble such wilderness companions as Jim and Buck or Ishmael and Queequeg, their relationship lasts longer and affects each more strongly. The male companions, divided by race and culture, cannot live together or adapt each other's behavior to any great extent. Celie and Shug, on the other hand, take on each other's attributes: Celie becomes more sexual and more aggressive; Shug becomes more gentle and nurturing. Rather than parting, the two become like family. As Shug explains to Celie. "Us each other peoples now" (156). Such kinship characterizes the domestic novel, according to Baym:

In novel after novel, a network of surrogate kin gradually defines itself around the heroine, making hers the story not only that of a self-made woman but that of a self-made or surrogate family. (*Women's Fictions* 38)

Just as characters in the domestic novel work to create families, they work to create homes. Writers who have described the domestic novel agree that "home" constitutes its central value. According to Tompkins, home in the domestic novel is "an all-sufficient basis for satisfaction and fulfillment in the present" (168) and "the basis of a religious faith that has unmistakably worldly dimensions" (165). The home that Shug and Celie create in Memphis serves as a source of strength whose influence is felt beyond its confines. For example, it provides a headquarters for the pants-making business which eventually enables Celie to earn her living.

Since home is so important, its rituals take on special significance. Tompkins writes that in the domestic novel "the faithful performance of household tasks constitutes a reflection or expression of celestial love" (165). Thus, such tasks are often described in minute, loving detail—as is Shug's daily ritual when she's home:

She get up early in the morning and go to market. Buy only stuff that's fresh. Then she come home and sit on the back step humming and shelling peas or cleaning collards or fish or whatever she bought. When she git all her pots going and turn on the radio. By one o'clock everything ready and she call us to the table. Ham and greens and chicken and cornbread. Chitlins and blackeyed pease and souse. Pickled okra and watermelon rind. Caramel cake and blackberry pie. (178)

The rhythmical repetitions in this passage—"she get," "she come," "she git," "she call," and "humming," "shelling," "cleaning"—correspond to the music which accompanies the ritual and reinforce its lyrical quality.

Walker's treatment of home and household ritual in *The Color Purple* has its closest counterparts in the domestic tradition, but it also has parallels in the wilderness tradition. Although the protagonist of the wilderness tradition is in flight from the confines of civilization, he and his companion may create their own temporary shelter and there enjoy the sweetness of domestic intimacy. Ishmael and Queequeg in bed, Huck and Jim on the raft have their own lovingly detailed routines and rituals. Perhaps the wilderness and domestic traditions are complementary rather than antithetical, and the "anti-family of two" which Huck and Jim form on the raft are relatives of the "network of surrogate kin" which surrounds the domestic heroine.

In *The Color Purple*, as in some of its wilderness predecessors, the newly created family generates its own world view. On the raft, Jim and Huck engage in cosmic speculations:

we used to discuss about whether [the stars] was made, or only just happened—Jim allowed they was made, but I allowed they happened: I judged it would have took too long to *make* so many. Jim said the moon could a *laid* them; well, that looked kind of reasonable, because I've seen a frog lay most as many, so of course it could be done. (97)

In this conversation, Jim and Huck implicitly resolve the question of a supreme being through compromise by imagining an organic cosmos consistent with their own experience. Similarly, Shug and Celie discuss the nature of God and the cosmos, and Celie begins to accept Shug's belief that God dwells in everything. Though the visions may be similar, they do not have the same power. Huck and Jim's cosmology develops in one of those brief, peaceful interludes on the raft which occupy so much space in the reader's memory and so little in the actual text. Shug's vision, on the other hand, develops Walker's central themes: the God who dwells in everything is surely present in all people; therefore, each individual must be respected and cherished. Though she provides her own theology rather than simply assuming a traditional Christian faith, Walker's treatment of individual moral dilemmas has much in common with the domestic novel, where "the heart must be set right before life can be" (qtd. Tompkins 178). For Walker, sin grows out of the circumstances of the sinner, but it can always be overcome. When Shug condemns Albert for beating Celie, she articulates a crucial aspect of Walker's conception of sin: taking out one's own frustrations upon another is never justified and only spreads suffering. In Walker's works, black men's position in the world often urges them to do just such a sin: dominated and abused by racist whites, they in turn dominate and abuse their wives and children. Walker's earlier work, *The Third Life of Grange Copeland*, makes this causal sequence explicit by placing Grange's abuse of his wife and children in the context of the abuse he endures at the hands of his white bosses. However, because *The Color Purple* places less emphasis on racism and more on domestic violence between blacks, critics have condemned the novel as an unjust, indiscriminate attack on black men and/or all men. One of the most extreme of these critics, George Stade, insists that, for Walker, "masculinity is radical evil, irreducible, the causeless cause of what is wrong with the world" (266).

On the contrary, for Walker the real "cause of what is wrong with the world" is the human temptation to possess and dominate others—a temptation to which anyone might be subject—not a particular state of gender or race. Although almost all the characters in *The Color Purple* yield to this temptation at one time or another, the male characters do seem especially prone to the desire to "rule over" others. However, Walker clearly locates this tendency not in their masculinity but in a distorted conception of ownership to which their circumstances dispose them.

Perhaps the most disturbing masculine sin in *The Color Purple* is the incestuous rape of Celie by her father. Walker has been criticized for almost magically mitigating this sin by revealing later in the story that "Pa not pa" (151)—that the man is Celie's stepfather rather than her biological father. However, this revelation actually serves to locate the source of the "incest" in "Pa's" obsession with ownership. Although Pa tells Celie that he has concealed her true father's identity because "White-folks lynch him. Too sad a story to tell pitiful little growing girls" (155), his real motives come out after his death when his widow tells Celie: "Your real daddy owned the house and the land and the store. He left it to your Mama. When your Mama died, it passed on to you and your sister Nettie" (206). Clearly, Alphonso has maintained the fiction that he is Celie's father in order to retain her true father's property. He has bartered with Celie's identity and sense of self-worth just as he brags of bartering with whites: "But the fact is, you got to give 'em something. Either your money, your land, your woman, or your ass" (155). Alphonso's corruption grows out of his relationship with whites and his emulation of their grasping ways. Walker makes both Alphonso and Celie's husband Albert landowners, contrary to the norm for rural blacks in the south in 1930.[2] In doing so, she underscores the connection between proprietorship and exploitation. In this context, the black men in *The Color Purple* are especially susceptible to the temptation to dominate others. Nevertheless, through the influence of other characters, most of them overcome this temptation and begin to respect the autonomy of others. Albert learns that Celie is "such good company" and even develops a special relationship with "ole evil Henrietta," his bad-tempered step-grandchild. Like some characters in domestic novels, he exchanges cruelty for compassion.

There are those who fault *The Color Purple* precisely because they feel that such changes are unrealistically swift and its heroine unrealistically forbearing. Trudier Harris finds Celie's change abrupt and implausible. She writes: "I am not opposed to triumph, but I do have objections to the unrealistic presentation of the path, the *process* that leads to such a triumph." (156). What seems most unrealistic to Harris is Celie's failure to "fight" through most of the novel. However, just as Celie's change seems logical rather than arbitrary when viewed as a variation on the domestic theme of redemption, her attitude towards conflict makes sense in the context of Walker's vision of every individual as a manifestation of God.

Since every individual manifests God, encroaching upon another's autonomy, even under provocation, constitutes sin. The victim who becomes the aggressor may become indistinguishable from the oppressor, another link in a chain of abuse and violence. Significantly, the redeemed characters in *The Color Purple* strike (physically or verbally) only in self-defense. When they do, they deliver their own kinds of blows in their own individual styles. Sophia's ready fist expresses her powerful physique; Celie's curse reflects her contemplative nature and the role language plays in her self-assertion.

That curse, which finally brings about a profound change in Albert, provides the clearest example of the manifestation of God in and through individual(s). Celie delivers it in response to Albert's verbal abuse of her as she departs for Memphis with Shug:

I curse you, I say.
What that mean? he say.
I say, Until you do right by me, everything you touch will crumble.
He laugh. Who you think you is? he say. You black, you pore, you ugly, you a woman.
Goddam, he say, you nothing at all.
Until you do right by me, I say, everything you dream of will fail. I give it to him straight,
just like it come to me. And it seem to come from the trees.
Whoever heard of such a thing, say Mr._____ I probably didn't whup your ass enough.
Every lick you hit me you will suffer twice, I say. Then I say, You better stop talk-ing
because I'm telling you ain't coming just from me. Look like when I open my mouth the air
rush in and shape words. (175–176)

Celie can stand up to Albert at last partly because she has learned to value herself
not only as an individual but also as a manifestation of the God that dwells in all
things. In abusing her, Albert has assaulted God's creation, and thus the very trees
and air seem to speak his condemnation. But God dwells in Albert, too. Celie's
curse does not damn him irrevocably; instead, his punishment grows out of his own
actions and can be controlled by his own will. If he does right by Celie, he
appeases the God in her and permits the God in him to bless him. After considerable
suffering, Albert does do right; he learns to "live on Earth as a natural man."

     In documenting the process of redemption for Albert, Celie, and other
characters, Walker encompasses and transcends the essential concerns of the
domestic tradition. Like their domestic counterparts, Walker's characters undergo
a process of redemption which enables them to live in harmony with others; but this
process helps realize their individuality rather than effacing it. That process
sometimes recalls the struggles of the protagonists of wilderness novels; but, while
the wilderness characters fight clear of social constrictions only to find themselves
alone, orphaned on the waves, or lighting out for the territory, Walker's characters
create a community which allows for individual expression as well as mutual
support and protection. In creating her novel, Walker adapts the past and revises
literary traditions to envision such a community for the reader. Perhaps no
American ideals carry more force than those of individual liberty and unity from
diversity. *The Color Purple* weaves both into the pattern of an All-American quilt.

NOTES

     1. In *In Search of Our Mothers' Gardens* (New York: Harcourt Brace Jovanovich,
1984), for example, she criticizes feminist groups that exclude lesbians or straight women
and black groups that exclude dark or light-skinned blacks. See "Breaking Chains and
Encouraging Life" (278) and "If the Present Looks Like the Past, What Does the Future
Look Like?" (290). In two of her recent poems in *Horses Make a Landscape Look More
Beautiful* (New York: Harcourt Brace Jovanovich, 1984), she includes whites among
"people of color." See "Song" (68) and "These Days" (71). In an interview with Claudia
Tate she explained: "I know this sounds very strange, but I had been working very hard, not

consciously really, to let into myself all of what being an American means, and not to exclude any part of it." Claudia Tate, ed. *Black Women Writers at Work* (New York: Continuum, 1983), 78.

2. According to George B. Tindall, 1930 black landowners made up only 13.1 percent of black agricultural workers; see his *The Emergence of the New South, 1913 1945* (Baton Rouge: Louisiana State University Press, 1967), 161.

WORKS CITED

Baym, Nina. "Melodramas of Beset Manhood: How Theories of American Fiction Exclude Women Authors." *American Quarterly* 33 (Summer 1981): 132.

_____. *Women's Fictions: A Guide to Novels by and about Women in America, 1820–1870.* Ithaca: Cornell University Press, 1978.

Chase, Richard. *The American Novel and Its Tradition.* Garden City: Doubleday, 1957.

Clemens, Samuel Langhorne (Mark Twain). *Adventures of Huckleberry Finn.* New York: Norton, 1971.

Douglas, Ann. *The Feminization of American Culture.* New York: Knopf, 1969.

Douglass, Frederick. *My Bondage and My Freedom.* New York: Dover, 1969.

Fiedler, Leslie. *Love and Death in the American Novel.* New York: Stein and Day, 1960.

Gates, Henry Louis. "Writing 'Race' and the Difference It Makes." *Critical Inquiry* 12 (1985): 12.

Harris, Trudier. "On *The Color Purple,* Stereotypes, and Silence." *Black American Literature Forum* 18 (1984): 156.

Hawthorne, Nathaniel. Letter to William D. Ticknor. January 19, 1855. Quoted in Malcolm Cowley, ed. *The Portable Hawthorne.* New York: The Viking Press, 1977.

Stade, George. "Womanist Fiction and Male Characters." *Partisan Review* 52 (1985): 266.

Stowe, Harriet Beecher. *Uncle Tom's Cabin.* New York: Penguin, 1986.

Tompkins, Jane. *Sensational Designs: The Cultural Work of American Fiction, 1790 1860.* New York: Oxford University Press, 1986.

Walker, Alice. *The Color Purple.* New York: Harcourt Brace Jovanovich, 1982.

_____. "Finding Celie's Voice." *Ms.* 14 December, 1985: 72.

_____. *In Search of Our Mothers' Gardens: Womanist Prose.* New York: Harcourt Brace Jovanovich, 1984.

Who Touches This Touches a Woman: The Naked Self in Alice Walker

Ruth D. Weston

In *The New York Times Book Review* for March 9, 1986, Alicia Ostriker celebrates American women poets who refuse to be limited by the masculine ideal of "universal," meaning nonfemale, poetry. Ostriker believes that the writing of these women poets during the last twenty-five years constitutes a shaping force in American poetry. Their passionate, intimate poems "defy divisions between emotion and intellect, private and public, life and art, writer and reader," reminding us, she says, of the frank sexuality of Walt Whitman's poems, so aptly characterized by his own words: "Camerado, this is no book,/Who touches this touches a man." Such an impulse is alive today in both the poems and the stories of Alice Walker. Her work has been previously linked to Whitman's because of both poets' celebration of the common problems that unite and divide people (Gernes 93–94), yet hers is a uniquely feminist—Walker would say "womanist" (*In Search* xii)—perspective.

Whitman assumed his personal experience to be the universal experience, but it was more precisely the masculine universal. Walker writes about black women with the authority of the universal female experience, an experience made complex and contradictory by the phenomenon of love. Although some black critics, like Ishmael Reed, charge that white feminists' interest in black women's writing constitutes "intellectual fraud" (qtd. in Watkins 36), which exploits black women and undermines the black community (Watkins 36; qtd. in Sharpe et al. 149), Patricia Sharpe and her colleagues explain white feminists' ability for cross-racial identity. Initially recognizing the basis of such identity in anthropological theories of female "liminality" as a locus of power (See Mascia-Lees et al.), they have recently refined their analysis by pointing out women's common experience of victimization. These critics argue that:

[W]e, as white feminists, are drawn to black women's visions because they concretize and make vivid a system of oppression [and] abuse. [And further that] it has not been unusual for white women writers to seek to understand their oppression through reference to the atrocities experienced by other oppressed groups. Sylvia Plath, for example, likened her feelings of rejection by her father to the treatment of Jews under Nazism. (Sharpe et al. 146)

Alice Walker's song of the self, although ultimately a celebration (Davis

38–53), differs from Whitman's not only in expected ways due to their respective genders, races, and eras. It differs more basically in the fact that, in Walker's fiction and poetry of the Black experience, many women are almost entirely ignorant of love, never having been allowed to share it. What is more, they do not know, much less celebrate, themselves. When they are abused—and they often are—they do not know the value of the self that has been violated. Celebrations, in such circumstances, are necessarily infused with an irony completely alien to Whitman's *Leaves of Grass* period, when he envisioned an ideal equality between men and women.

Even in relationships between women, Walker often shows the undervalued selves of women. In the story "Everyday Use," Maggie suffers psychological scars long after physical healing from burns in a fire set by Dee, her older sister. When the citified and condescending Dee comes to visit, Maggie feels ugly and hides behind the door, providing a graphic symbol of the physical and psychological disfigurement of women that is an important theme in Walker's writing. Similarly, low self-esteem also leads Roselily, in the story that bears her name, to marry the Muslim who will take her away from her home, promising her rest and freedom from the hard work she has always known. But Walker's narrative is laced with images of the new bondage that awaits Roselily in a culture which undervalues women, images which reveal the irony of her hope to be "Free! In robe and veil" (*In Love* 7).

Walker does not ignore the black man's search for self-worth, a theme she explores in *The Third Life of Grange Copeland*; but the casualties of that search are the wives of Grange and Brownfield Copeland. Not only because they are influenced by a macho male white culture (Wallace; qtd. in Sharpe et al. 147), but because they are also frustrated in their own claim to manhood, Grange and Brownfield in turn deny their women's every assertion of self-worth. Thus, when Mem raises the family's standard of living, Brownfield systematically destroys first her health and then her spirit. Finally, he blows her face away with a shotgun (172), literally effacing her identity. That Walker intends the scene as an affirmation of the universality of female cultural effacement is clear from her statement in the "Afterword" to the novel that Mem, "after the French *la meme*, meaning 'the same,'" was so named because the actual murder victim Walker based the story on "in relation to men was symbolic of all women" (344).

The theme of regressive violence within black families is seen even earlier in the poems that reveal how the exigencies of the Civil Rights Movement of the 1960s helped Alice Walker to come to terms with personal wounds. An example that she herself has pointed to is that of her poem "The Democratic Order: Such Things in Twenty Years I Understood":

> My father
> (back blistered)
> beat me
> because I
> could not
> stop crying.

He'd had
enough 'fuss'
he said
for one damn
voting day. (*Once* 43)

Although Walker's relationship with her father was not good, the matter of the poem is not strictly autobiographical (Walker *Living* 11), yet it creates an idealized father character that allows her to displace her anxiety about her own father while the poem speaks to the general cultural frustrations that are vented upon women.

In the novel *Meridian*, however, the field of anxiety is broadened to include anxiety about men as sexual "partners." The adolescent Meridian, like many of Walker's female protagonists, becomes afraid of males as soon as she is seen as fair game by boys at school. She submits to Eddie's sexual needs not because they respond to her own but because they

saved her from the strain of responding to other boys or even noting the whole category of Men. This was probably what sex meant to her; not pleasure but a sanctuary. It was resting from pursuit. (54–55)

These women are ignorant of the joy of offering themselves as inherently valuable gifts, perhaps, because, as Barbara Christian points out, for such abused women "the body can become the tomb of the mind, [and similarly] the mind's anguish can diminish the body;" thus, Christian continues, Meridian's own guilt for "not living up to her mother's expectations about motherhood," combined with frustration at her sense of powerlessness, results in progressively more serious physical problems: "blue spells," then loss of sight, then temporary paralysis (*Black Women* 216). The world has touched women who have suffered similar experiences, perhaps indelibly marked them, but they are out of touch with themselves.

Celie, in *The Color Purple*, learns both psychological and literal touching of the self. Through her relationships with other women in the novel, she gets in touch with her moral and physical self. Jealous of Sophia's physical strength and sense of authority, and frustrated at her own lack of either quality, Celie strikes out at her by repeating to Harpo the advice his father had given him about how to make his wife obey him: "Beat her" (43). Celie rationalizes:

I like Sophia, but she don't act like me at all. If she talking when Harpo and Mr. _____ come in the room, she keep right on. If they ast her where something at, she say she don't know. Keep talking.

I think bout this when Harpo ast me what he ought to do to her to make her mind. I don't mention how happy he is now. How three years pass and he still whistle and sing, I think bout how every time I jump when Mr. _____ call me, she look surprise. And like she pity me.

Beat her. I say. (43)

When Harpo tries to beat Sophia and gets beaten himself, Celie realizes her culpability but can only turn her guilt inward. When she is abused by her husband,

Celie again internalizes her anger. She can't sleep, she feels like throwing up, and finally she feels nothing. Ironically, it is Sophia who calls her to moral responsibility, not only for allowing herself to encourage male brutality to women, but ultimately to responsibility for her own life. Celie's usual response to a beating from the man she calls only Mr. _____ has been, "But he my husband. I shrug my shoulders. This life soon be over, I say. Heaven last all ways." Sophia advises, "You ought to bash Mr. _____ head open. Think bout heaven later" (47). It is only when Celie can externalize her anger, can dare to express herself in spite of the fact that her father has forbidden her to speak, that she begins her journey toward selfhood by writing a revised self, by literally touching pen to paper to release her creative energy.

But the rite of passage comes through a different sort of literal touching of the self, in Celie's sexual awakening by Shug Avery. Although Celie has been raped repeatedly by her father and has given birth to two children by him, and although she is now married to Mr. _____, she is, according to Shug, still a virgin (79). In other words, she has never known, or even realized there could be, sexual pleasure for a woman. Thus her most significant initiation into human sexuality is by her husband's mistress, and the lesbian lovemaking that follows is Celie's first experience of erotic love. To Celie, "it feel like heaven is what it feel like, not like sleeping with Mr. _____ at all" (110). At last she is put in touch with her own body and her own needs. She learns to associate pleasure, not pain, with human touch. Thus, although women's relationships with men have impeded female self-development, their bonds with women, even literary bonds (Sadoff 4–26) *can* provide positive correctives. And certainly Celie's rite of passage provides the kind of cultural deconstruction that is a symbol of "emotive power" like those used by African women "mythmakers creating viable and meaningful new images of and for women" (Sharpe et al. 145–46).

Even in the face of the painful disjunctions of life, Walker's emphasis is always on the inherent yearning for unity in all life—of body and mind, of flesh and spirit, and especially of male and female. Thus in the title poem of *Horses Make a Landscape Look More Beautiful*, the most important element in the poem is the "s" in "Horses," a fact which is evident from the incident that provided the impetus for the poem. Walker tells the tale of a horse's wild suffering when deprived of his mate, and of his look that was "piercing, full of grief, [and] *human*" (*Living* 7). And the cruelty Walker sees in the humans who took away the mare after stud service seems an ironic reflection on the frequency of cruelty she notes *among* humans, who continually rupture their own intimate relationships. In the "Introduction" to her volume of poems entitled *Good Night Willie Lee, I'll See You in The Morning*, she states the basic need for human touch, a need which will, she says, "call out [one's] own heart for review" (vi). The complex theme common to the poems in this book is that of the perennial conflict of woman's two basic needs, which have historically been mutually exclusive: the need for intimacy with a man but also the need for mental and physical integrity. By "call[ing] out [one's] heart for review" in these poems, Walker shows us the state of the heart of woman. We see the continuing vulnerability of heart and body, but we also see hints of an emerging awareness of woman's equal need, and increasing ability, to resist abuse. It is as though Walker's book, published in 1979, is her answer to Adrienne Rich's call to action in her 1972 essay "When We Dead Awaken": a call not only for women writers to express anger at their victimization by men, but also a call for women to stop permitting the abuse, to take responsibility for their lives, to exchange the imposition of pain for what Rich calls the self-actuated "birth-pains [of] bearing ourselves" (25). And indeed, as Barbara Christian has shown, Walker's work contributes to, and perhaps represents the epitome of, a rapidly-developing theme in Afro-American women's writing: that of female self-development and self-definition ("Trajectories" 233–248).

The destructive results of a woman's need for a love relationship with a man are seen in Walker's poems through images of pain and death, suggesting the physical and mental stress on a woman in this double bind. Her conflicting needs cause a severe back pain, or as in the poem, "Good Night, Willie Lee, I'll See You in the Morning" (from *Good Night, Willie Lee, I'll See You in the Morning*), "they come up like weeds."

A reviewer of Walker's first volume of poems, entitled *Once* (1968), noticed the juxtaposition of images of the world's brutality with images of great tenderness (Walsh 20). In that book, however, the contrasting expressions were not often identified with sex; and sometimes they did not even appear in the same poem. Compare, for example, the soft eroticism of "The Smell of Lebanon," from the sequence of "impossible love" poems, with the following bitter passage from the long title poem "Once":

> I remember
> seeing
> a little girl,
> dreaming—perhaps,
> hit by
>   a
> van truck
> "That nigger was
> in the way!" the
> man
> said
> to
> understanding cops (*Once* 35)

Perhaps the volume's most emphatic ironic contrast comes in "Karamojans," where the poet suggests the inherent native African beauty and dignity, which has been spoiled by poverty and disease. Throughout the poem, images of the fineness of human beings are undercut by those of the world's brutal realities, as stanzas two and eight will suffice to show:

> The Noble Savage
> Erect
> no shoes on his feet

> His pierced ears
> Infected.
> How bright the little
> girl's
> Eyes were!
> a first sign of
> Glaucoma. (*Once* 20, 22)

The simple, perhaps even clichéd, vocabulary is elevated by the poem's sustained technique of ironic negation, a technique that also occurs in the title poem "Once," where the reality of the Southern jailer "in grey" negates, for the Civil Rights demonstrators, the "green lawn/ picket fence/flowers—/[and] the blue sky" (*Once* 23). The continual juxtaposition of positive and negative images produces an overriding antiphonal style in both the poems and the prose, a style apparent, for example, in the title poem of *Revolutionary Petunias*, in the structure of the stories "Roselily" and "The Child Who Favored Daughter" (*In Love*); and in the alternating voices of Celie and Nettie, which "encompass and interconnect all the characters" in *The Color Purple* (Fifer 156).

This ironic antiphony underlies what are perhaps Walker's most striking images of negation: those which occur in poems which express love's mental anguish in terms of physical pain or danger. Loving a man is analogous to bearing a "knife that presses / without ceasing/against [a woman's] heart" (*Good Night* 10); to being "in limbo" (11), to being "afflicted" to the point of "murder[ing] the man" (13); to having one's life "shredded/by an expert" (15). Often, however, a woman endures sexual pain that has nothing to do with love. A recurring reference in Walker's poems is to the rape her great-great-grandmother suffered at age eleven. A poem entitled "The Thing Itself," from the volume *Horses Make a Landscape Look More Beautiful*, is the poet's version of that experience. It includes these lines:

> There was no
> pornography
> in her world
> from which to learn
> to relish the pain.
> (She was the thing
> itself.) (62)

Nowhere is the body of the poem more at one with the female body than in Walker's "Early Losses: A Requiem," in which the poet, in the persona of a nine-year-old African girl sold into slavery, mourns the loss of her childhood friend but also the loss of her own childhood:

> Omunu vanished
> down a hole that
> smelled of blood and
> excrement and death
> and I was "saved"

for sport among
the sailors of the crew.
Only nine, upon a ship. My mouth
my body a mystery
that opened with each tearing
lunge. (*Good Night* 28)

In this volume of poems we touch a woman in pain.

But mitigating the pain expressed are also flashes of the spirited woman
that is Alice Walker. For example, in "Janie Crawford":

I love the way Janie Crawford
left her husbands the one who wanted
to change her into a mule
and the other who tried to interest her
in being a queen
a woman unless she submits is neither a mule
nor a queen
though like a mule she may suffer
and like a queen pace
the floor. (*Good Night* 18)

We also see a "moody woman/[with] temper as black as [her] brows/as sharp as
[her] nails" (19). We see her trying to survive with a dream different from that of
her grandmother, who longed only for some comfort in her poor life, and yet trying
to maintain some connection with her heritage, as she says in "Talking to my grandmother . . .,"

I must train myself to want
not one bit more
than what i need to keep me alive
working
and recognizing beauty
in your
so nearly
undefeated face.   (*Good Night* 46–47)

And there is the resurgent good humor in poems such as "Every Morning," the
poet's rebuke to a sleepy, complaining body:

"Don't you see that person
staring at you?" I ask my breasts,
which are still capable
of staring back.
"If I don't exercise
you couldn't look up
that far. (*Horses Make* 16)

Although the volume *Horses Make a Landscape Look More Beautiful* received mixed reviews, some readers alleging its "pathos" ("Private Voices" 19), banality (*Publishers'* 71), "forced" quality (*Virginia Quarterly* 57), or even racism (Disch 6), such poems as "Every Morning" speak—both for Walker and her readers—to the subject that Adrienne Rich said she herself addressed in writing "Planetarium": "the relief of the body/and the reconstruction of the mind" (30).

Contrary to charges of her insensitivity to black men, typified by the comments of Tony Brown (2), of her sexist polemic, according to Charles Johnson (107), or of both and more (Cheatwood; qtd. in Walker *Living* 88), Walker, as she herself has reminded us (*Living* 80), extends that same opportunity for relief and reconstruction to her male characters—to Grange Copeland, to Harpo, to Albert, and even to Mister. Yet there is no more false (that is, sexless) "universality" in Alice Walker's writing than there was false modesty in Walt Whitman's frankly sexual poems, notwithstanding even Walker's own cogent claim that all races suffered (and by implication still suffer) from the experience of slavery: "We are the African and the trader. We are the Indian and the settler, the slaver and the enslaved" (*Living* 89). To admit these common human afflictions is not to deny Chikwenye Okonjo Ogunyemi's claim that "black womanist writers are committed to the survival and wholeness of their entire people, female and male" (qtd. in Sharpe et al. 143). Yet in her fiction and poems, it is nevertheless the nerves and bodies and minds of Walker's *female* characters that are laid bare—to each other, to themselves, and to the reader. On the page in black and white (pun intended, in the spirit of Walker's own use in "African Images" [*Once* 71], the complex self of woman is naked and exposed, in the misery of its pain or the celebration of its worth. Alice Walker's writing will never be mistaken for that of Whitman; for who touches this touches a woman.

WORKS CITED

Brown, Tony. "Tony Brown's Comments: The Color of Purple Is White." *The Herald*, 1 Jan. 1986: 2.

Christian, Barbara. *Black Women Novelists: The Development of a Tradition, 1892—1976*. Westport, CT: Greenwood Press, 1980.

_____. "Trajectories of Self-Definition: Placing Contemporary Afro-American Women's Fiction." *Conjuring: Black Women, Fiction, and Literary Tradition*. Ed. Marjorie Pryse and Hortense Spillars. Bloomington: Indiana University Press 1985. 233–248.

Davis, Thadious M. "Alice Walker's Celebration of Self in Southern Generations." *Women Writers of the Contemporary South*. Ed. Peggy Whitman Prenshaw. Jackson: University Press of Mississippi, 1984. 38–53.

Disch, Tom. "The Perils of Poesy." *Book World*, 30 Dec. 1984: 6.

Fifer, Elizabeth. "Alice Walker: The Dialect & Letters of *The Color Purple*." *Contemporary American Women Writers: Narrative Strategies*. Ed. Catherine Rainwater and William J. Scheick. Lexington: University Press of Kentucky, 1985. 155–71.

Gernes, Sonia. *America* 152. 4 (2 Feb. 1985): 93–94; qtd. in Pratt, Louis H. and Darnell D.

Pratt, *Alice Malsenior Walker: An Annotated Bibliography: 1968—1986.* Westport, CT: Meckler, 1988.

Johnson, Charles. *Being & Race: Black Writing Since 1970.* Bloomington: Indiana University Press, 1988.

Mascia-Lees, Frances E., Pat Sharpe, and Colleen B. Cohen. "Double Liminality and the Black Woman Writer." *American Behavioral Scientist* 31 (Sept—Oct. 1987): 101—14.

Ostriker, Alicia. "American Poetry, Now Shaped by Women.," *New York Times Book Review*, 9 Mar. 1986: 1, 28—30.

"Private Voices." *Books and Bookmen,* Sept. 1985: 19.*Publisher's Weekly* 24 Aug. 1984: 71.

Reed, Ishmael. *Reckless Eyeballing.* New York: St. Martin's, 1986.

Rich, Adrienne. "When We Dead Awaken: Writing as Re-Vision." *College English* 34.1 (Oct. 1972): 18—25.

Sadoff, Dianne F. "Black Matrilineage: The Case of Alice Walker and Zora Neale Hurston." *Signs* 11.1 (Autumn 1985): 4—26.

Sharpe, Patricia, F. E. Mascia-Lees, and C. B. Cohen. "White Women and Black Men: Differential Responses to Reading Black Women's Texts." *College English* 52.2 (Feb. 1990): 142—53.

Virginia Quarterly Review 61.2 (Spring 1985): 57.

Walker, Alice, *The Color Purple.* 1982. New York: Washington Square, 1983.

_____. *Good Night Willie Lee, I'll See You in The Morning.* 1979. New York: Harcourt Brace Jovanovich, 1984.

_____. *Horses Make a Landscape Look More Beautiful.* New York: Harcourt Brace Jovanovich, 1984.

_____. *In Love and Trouble: Stories of Black Women.* New York: Harcourt Brace Jovanovich, 1974.

_____. *In Search of Our Mothers' Gardens.* New York: Harcourt Brace Jovanovich, 1984.

_____. *Living By the Word: Selected Writings, 1973—1987.* New York: Harcourt Brace Jovanovich, 1988.

_____. *Meridian.* New York: Harcourt, 1976.

_____. *Once.* New York: Harcourt Brace World, 1968.

_____. *Revolutionary Petunias and Other Poems.* New York: Harcourt Brace Jovanovich, 1973.

_____. *The Third Life of Grange Copeland.* 1970. Rpt. New York: Pocket Books, 1988.

Wallace, Michele. *Black Macho and the Myth of the Superwoman.* New York: Warner, 1979.

Walsh, Chad. "A Present Rooted in the Past." *Book World,* 3 Nov. 1968: 20.

Watkins, Mel. "Sexism, Racism and Black Women Writers." *New York Times Book Review*, 15 June 1986: 1, 35—37.

Whitman, Walt. "So Long." *Leaves of Grass*, 1860. Rpt. *Eight American Writers: An Anthropology of American Literature.* Ed. Norman Foerster and Robert P. Falk. New York: Norton, 1963. 1137—38.

"Nothing can be sole or whole that has not been rent": Fragmentation in the Quilt and *The Color Purple*

Judy Elsley

In W. B. Yeats's poem "Crazy Jane Talks with the Bishop," the speaker is a wild old woman, a culturally marginal figure, who meets the epitome of respectability in the form of the Bishop. The Bishop reacts predictably to Jane, despising her broken body and exhorting her to turn his way toward "a heavenly mansion." But social respectability means little to her. She answers his reproof in her strong, life-affirming voice, unintimidated by him or the patriarchal law he represents. Her reply refuses the epistemology of opposition, showing the Bishop that what seems opposed is, in fact interdependent:

> "Fast and foul are near of kin,
> And fair needs foul," I cried
> "For nothing can be sole or whole
> That has not been rent."

Her aphorisms seem like nonsequiturs to the Bishop and his ilk. Yet they make sense in an untraditional way by asserting that wholeness is composed of that which it is not fragments.

"Crazy" is just one label attached to women who don't fit in, or who refuse to play the patriarchal game. But Jane is not so crazy. She speaks a wild wisdom which does not coincide with linear reasoning. Jane shows a profound under-standing of a way of being for women marginalized by a culture that uses them for its own convenience. Nothing can be sole or whole that has not been rent.

A woman makes the world her own by taking apart the patriarchal ways of being to create a space for herself. That space allows her to accept her own fragmentation, embrace those fragments, and thus validate herself. Recognizing rather than denying her pieces is often a woman's way to become "sole or whole" in a more feminocentric way. In effect, she makes a patchwork quilt of her life.

Elaine Showalter, in her essay "Piecing and Writing," connects patchwork quilts and writing in North American short stories. She asserts that

A knowledge of piecing, the technique of assembling fragments into an intricate design, can provide the contexts in which we can interpret and understand the forms, meanings, and narrative traditions of American women's writing. (227)

Alice Walker's use of the quilt metaphor in *The Color Purple* illustrates just such a connection.

Walker is herself a quilter who integrates quilting and writing naturally into her daily routine, a mixture of activities that suggest cohesive fragmentation (*In Search*, 36–83) Walker speaks specifically of the interdependence of writing and quilting in her essay "Writing *The Color Purple*" (*In Search*, 355–60) After searching for a place where her characters would be comfortable enough to speak, Walker reports that as she waited for the characters and plot to take form in her mind, Walker worked on her quilt (*In Search*, 358). Quiltmaking, self-fashioning and the construction of a woman's text are all part of the same process, not only in the life of Alice Walker, but also within the text of *The Color Purple*.

Whether she uses old clothes or crisp new cottons, the quiltmaker begins work on her patchwork quilt by cutting or ripping her fabrics apart. Indeed, a patchwork quilt cannot come into existence without that rending. This deconstructive act is, paradoxically, also one of her most creative—an act of courage, necessity and faith. Tearing seems a singularly appropriate place to begin because *being torn* is so familiar an experience for women. We see this illustrated in the person of Celie.

Celie sees herself, both physically and emotionally, as living in irreconcilable fragments. She begins her narrative by writing "I am" which she then negates by crossing out (I), indicating her lack of self-confidence. We learn in the first few letters that her experience of life has been a series of tearings. She has been torn from childhood by Pa's incestuous rapes; torn from the two children she bears him when he takes them from her; and torn from the one person she loves, her sister Nettie, when she is forced into a marriage she doesn't want. Her life is a series of sacrifices—to Pa's destructive desires, to Nettie's safety, to Mister's needs and brutality. Each time the sacrifice is the same: herself. Celie has been fragmented into pieces which are given away to others, mostly at the insistence of the men who dominate her.

Celie's early experience illustrates Luce Irigaray's theory that patriarchal society puts value on women only to the degree that they serve the purpose of commodities of exchange between men. "For woman," says Irigaray, "is traditionally a use-value for man, an exchange value among men; in other words, a commodity" (31). "Celie's fragmentation is most strongly reinforced," says Daniel Ross in a 1988 article, "by the way her stepfather presents her as less than a whole woman to her future husband, convincing him to marry her because "God done fixed her. You can do everything just like you want to and she ain't gonna make you feed it or clothe it" (75). Celie's enforced hysterectomy has reduced her from person to commodity. Pa gives Celie to Mr. _____ as little more than a convenient labor-saving device. "Men make commerce of them [women], but they do not enter into any exchanges with them" (Irigaray 172).

Celie's negated "I am" is problematic in ways she can hardly imagine—there is deep wisdom in her early refusal of a sense of self as single and whole. That way of establishing her identity confirms her status in an order of rational dualism that already categorizes her as "other." The single "I" forces a woman to make choices, not only between self and other, but also between the different pieces of herself. A woman in Celie's position is damaged not strengthened by embracing one part of herself at the expense of denying other parts. She must choose, as Josephine Donovan points out in "Towards a Woman's Poetics," between bad and worse:

The harassed woman is forced into a schizophrenic response: either she can remain identified with her body which has been objectified as a tool for male purposes, in which case she denies her mind and her spiritual self; or she can deny the body and consider the mind the real self. The latter entails an autistic withdrawal from the everyday public world, a silent living thing. (101)

Celie is caught in just such a trap. She defends herself against the physical abuse of rape and beatings by withdrawing into autism, not only from Mr. _____, but also from a sense of herself as a person with feelings. "He beat me like he beat the children," she says of Mr._____ in an early letter. "It all I can do not to cry. I make myself wood. I say to myself, Celie, you a tree. That's how come I know trees fear man" (30). As a piece of wood, she has no voice of her own. She can only echo back the terms of her oppression, as we see in the same letter when Harpo asks her why she is stubborn. She replies, "Just born that way, I reckon" (30), accepting Mr. _____ 's estimation of her.

 As well as suppressing her feelings, she has disassociated herself from her body. After two children and years of marriage, she admits to Shug that she's never enjoyed sex. "I don't like it at all. He git up on you, heist your nightgown round your waist, plunge in. Most times I pretend I ain't there" (79). Shug responds that Celie is therefore still a virgin. In other words, she has not yet identified herself in any positive way with her body.

 Her way to a healthy sense of self comes neither from living as disjointed pieces nor forging a single "I," but in a route that lies between those alternatives. She begins to connect the fragments of herself by connecting with other women. Daniel Ross points to the incident in which Shug helps Celie look at her genitals for the first time as the starting place on that journey. Shug does indeed help Celie to recognize and accept her body, but before she is ready to do this she has taken an earlier step towards self-acceptance with another woman: Sofia. In the novel's first reference to quiltmaking, Celie and Sofia move through confrontation to reconciliation with each other. Their joint quiltmaking marks the beginning of Celie's journey to selfhood.

 By working together, Celie and Sofia break the power of a system of social exchange between men predicated on the use of women as commodities. In order for the system to work, women must remain separate from each other:

[W]omen no longer relate to each other except in terms of what they represent in men's desire, according to the forms this imposes on them. Among themselves, they are separated by his speculations. (Irigaray 188)

Celie has been separated from women all her life, but that changes when she quilts with Sofia. The scene, however, does not begin auspiciously. In an effort to control his powerful wife, Sofia, Harpo asks Celie for advice. She repeats the patriarchal attitude: "Beat her, I say" (43), thus participating in what Hélène Cixous calls men's "greatest crime against women":

Insidiously, violently, they [men] have led them [women] to hate women, to be their own enemies, to mobilize their immense strength against themselves. (310)

When Sofia discovers Celie's betrayal she storms over to Celie's house to confront her. The scene is set in rupture and violence, that between Harpo and Sofia, that between the two women, and that within Celie herself as she thinks with shame of the advice she gave Harpo. The honest communication that ensues, as Celie admits her guilt and asks Sofia's forgiveness, is the setting for the two of them to begin their quiltmaking. Putting together the fragments of "messed up curtains," torn in a fight between Sofia and Harpo, the two women reconfigure their bond. Guilt is transformed into quilt as discarded fabric and rejected women are sewn into something valuable and beautiful. As professional quilter Radka Donnell-Vogt says,

The quilt is first of all a speculum by which a woman looks into herself, and when she finds her unknown and disregarded beauty, she can find also the courage to prevail along with others for her share in the world. (56)

Ozzie Mayers, in "The Power of the Pin," argues that sewing is "a redemptive act" (671) for Celie. Sewing is important, but her quilting is the crucial initial act of redemption as Celie, working with pieces of fabric, begins to actively create herself out of the fragments of her life. Layers of fragments exist in that first quilt. Celie starts with curtains that function through their ability to both separate and come together, for the wholeness of curtains lies in their ability to also be fragments. The curtains come to her already torn in a fight between Sofia and Harpo, which makes a second layer of fragments. The fabric is further cut to make up the patchwork pattern, so that the quilt she makes is composed of at least three layers of fragments. Celie's quilt becomes a celebration of fragments, a recognition and reverence for pieces. The self she is creating, like the patchwork quilt she makes, is not so much an integrated whole as it is a vindication of fragments, a celebration of multiplicity.

Celie asserts her right to choose, for the first time, when she begins quilting with Sofia. She chooses a quilt pattern, the two women choose to be sisters, and they choose to work together. Those choices are signified in the quilt design Celie selects, a pattern called "Sister's Choice" (47). (This is a traditional pattern documented by Hall and Kretsinger in their 1935 classic survey of quilt patterns, *The Romance of the Patchwork Quilt in America*.) By asserting her right to choose, even in such small ways, Celie takes the first step toward living autonomously.

She is also connected with another woman through her choice of quilt pattern. Although she is not consciously aware of it, Celie is choosing connection with her beloved Nettie, for at the heart of the pattern "Sister's Choice" is a nine-square patch which is the design Corrine chooses to make her African quilt.

Celie and Sofia's quiltmaking is a process of healing because they are no longer passive victims who are torn. Quiltmaking turns being torn into tearing, turns object into subject. Active creation replaces passive victimization as the two women, their sisterhood reaffirmed, set about constructing a pattern of their choice out of the fragments of their lives. Celie's decision to make the quilt is thus the turning point in her life because it is the first step to her empowerment via connection with other women.

Sister's Choice

Nine-square block

Although Celie and her situation have not changed, her perception has. She is still Celie, the curtains are still messed up. But instead of rejecting them, and by extension herself, because they're in pieces, she accepts them by working with them. This change in perception is reflected in two images which embody both separation and wholeness in the way they function. The scissors Pa carries with him when he makes his sexual advances on the young Celie under the pretense of wanting his hair cut form the first image. Like the material cut by a pair of scissors, her sex has been sharply separated, cut into by Pa's rape and then forced open by the birth of her two babies.

The curtains from which Sofia and Celie make their quilt are the second, contrasting image. They also open and close, fulfilling their function, paradoxically, through their ability to find wholeness while also being fragments. They are complete in themselves as they draw together or softly separate, unlike the scissors which need an object to cut to do their work. Celie's choice to interact with the curtains is not accidental. Her association with the curtains is the beginning of her sexual identity in a way we see more explicitly set out by Luce Irigaray in *This Sex Which Is Not One*. Irigaray describes a woman's sex as two lips in continuous contact with each other so that a woman is "neither one or two" (26). Male oneness or wholeness is alien to woman. If she tries to attain that oneness, she is, like Celie, "put in the position of experiencing herself only fragmentarily, in the little-structured margins of a dominant ideology, a waste, or excess" (30). Irigaray warns women not to "renounce the pleasure that she gets from the non-suture of her lips" (30); in other words, to accept rather than reject her fragmentation.

The process of making fragments creates a necessary space, one that is often disruptive and destabilizing. From this place, a woman can begin her task of self-creation. "No woman can assume herself because she has yet to create herself" (593), says Myra Jehlen. In order to begin that process, Jehlen says, "all women must destroy in order to create" (583). The space between fragments gives her room to do that. Quilt artist Radka Donnell-Vogt expresses that same need for space in her creative process:

The double function of quilt-making, to help collect one's thoughts and provide an image of spatial integration that does not freeze one in one place as the observation of stationary paintings, was essential in giving me a base for exploring my situation as a woman and as an artist. (49)

Fragmentation is also an acknowledgment of that common condition of women's lives: interruption. Celie's life, her quilt, and her writing are all made up of discontinuous pieces. Her chosen form of self-expression, letter writing, consists of short, discrete units of discontinuous prose, broken off and interrupted by the demands on her life. Yet Walker makes that discontinuity into a shapely narrative. Celie works with fragments of text as well as textile.

As one who puts fragments together, Celie becomes what Lévi-Strauss designates a *bricoleur*; that is, a marginal figure who transforms the materials the world has rejected, turning

[B]ack to an already existent set made up of tools and materials, to consider or reconsider what it contains and, finally, and above all, to engage in a sort of dialogue with it, and, before choosing between them, to index possible answers which the whole set can offer to his problems. (18)

But rather than confine her to a structuralist masculine model, we can see Celie as one who practices what Miriam Schapiro calls *femmage*, the feminine equivalent of *bricolage*. This "process of collecting and creatively assembling, odd or seemingly disparate elements into a functional, integrated whole," is distinguished from *bricolage* in that, "Femmage denotes an aesthetic of connection and relationships" (Turner 7). Relationship is essential to *femmage* because it is essential to women. And appropriate relationship with herself and others is Celie's quest. Celie's quiltmaking gives her constant opportunities to make relationships—between herself and the fabric, between the pieces of fabric themselves, and between herself and other quilters. By the end of the novel her relationships have extended well beyond her quilting. She has successfully created friendships with her ex-husband, her lover, her children, and most importantly, with herself.

Quiltmaking, then, is a paradigm for the way Celie reinscribes her life.

What begins with quilting messed up curtains, culminates in facing up to Mr. _____. Celie takes all the pieces of her life with him, pulling them together in an assertion of her "I am" that adds up to "You a lowdown dog is what's wrong, I say. It's time to leave you and enter into the Creation" (180). Creation for Celie, of course, is self-creation. When she examines her life, her fragments parallel those messed up curtains: "I'm pore, I'm black, I may be ugly and can't cook, a voice say to everything, listening. But I'm here" (187). That last affirmation, "But I'm here,' is the thread that sews the rejected pieces together, transforming them from worthless to valuable. Cixous speaks of those same conjoined fragments, dancing in a heavenly consort in "The Laugh of the Medusa":

If she [woman] is a whole, it's a whole composed of parts that are wholes, not simple partial objects but a moving, limitlessly changing ensemble, a cosmos tirelessly traversed by Eros, an immense astral space not organized around any one sum that's any more of a star than the others. (317)

When the patchwork quilt is finished, the pattern and stitching continue to stand as a constant reminder that this "whole" is made up of many fragments. Wholeness is an illusion, an artificial construct, that has been replaced by the more viable cohesion of fragments.

The power of the quilt, then, is to transform lives from disparate fragments to a self-fashioned conjoining of pieces. This process becomes a way of life for Celie as the novel concludes:

Me and him and Shug sitting out on the porch after dinner. Talking. Not talking. Rocking and fanning flies. Shug mention she don't want to sing in public no more—well, maybe a night or two at Harpo's. Think maybe she retire. Albert say he want her to try on his new shirt. I talk about Henrietta. Sofia. My garden and the store. How things doing generally. So much in the habit of sewing something I stitch up a bunch of scraps, try to see what I can make. (249)

What she is making, along with the bunch of scraps, is her own life.

Celie's struggle is more dramatic than many women experience, but her journey is a familiar one. All of us in academia, especially those involved in feminist studies, are quiltmakers. We are creating a space for ourselves in order to gather up our fragments into the construction of a pattern to our own liking. Cheryl Torsney uses the quilt metaphor in a recent survey of the history and present status of feminist criticism:

Multipatterned and multicolored, stitched by women and men from various racial and national cultures from various critical predispositions, the feminist critical practice forms a sort of critical quilt, an alternative to the critical methods of the past. Moreover, like a pieced quilt, feminist literary criticism is clearly meant for everyday use, in readings of all genres in all periods. (191)

Fragmentation and diversity become not a limitation but a trademark, a strength, a defining characteristic of feminist critical theory. We have a lot in common with Celie.

WORKS CITED

Cixous, Hélène. "The Laugh of the Medusa." *Critical Theory Since 1965*, ed. Hazard Adams and Leroy Searle. Tallahassee: University of Florida Press, 1986. 309–321.

Donnell-Vogt, Radka. *Lives and Works: Talks with Women Artists*, ed. Lynn F. Miller and Sally S. Swenson. Metuchen, N.J.: Scarecrow Press, 1981. 37–56.

Donovan, Josephine. "Towards a Women's Poetics." *Feminist Issues in Literary Scholarship*, ed. Shari Benstock. Bloomington: Indiana University Press, 1987. 98–109.

Irigaray, Luce. *This Sex Which Is Not One*. Ithaca: Cornell University Press, 1985.

Jehlen, Myra. "Archimedes and the Paradox of Feminist Criticisms." *Signs* 6.4 (1984): 575–601.

Lévi-Strauss, Claude. *The Savage Mind*. Chicago: University of Chicago Press, 1972.

Mayers, Ozzie J. "The Power of the Pin: Sewing as an Act of Rootedness in American Literature." *College English* 50.6 (October 1988): 664–680.

Ross, Daniel. "Celie in the Looking Glass: The Desire for Selfhood in *The Color Purple*." *Modern Fiction Studies* 34.1 (Spring 1988): 69–84.

Showalter, Elaine. "Piecing and Writing." *Poetics of Gender*, ed. Nancy Miller. New York: Columbia University Press, 1986. 223–247.

Torsney, Cheryl B. "The Critical Quilt: Alternative Authority in Feminist Criticism." *Journal of Narrative Techniques* 16 (1986) 220–230.

Turner, Kay. "Mexican American Home Alters: Towards Their Interpretation." *Aztlan* 13.1 and 2 (Spring and Fall 1982): 310–323.

Walker, Alice. *The Color Purple*. New York: Washington Square Press, 1982.

_____. "One Child of One's Own: A Meaningful Digression Within the Work(s)." *In Search of Our Mothers' Gardens*. New York: Harcourt Brace Jovanovich, 1983. 361–383.

_____. "Writing *The Color Purple*." *In Search of our Mother's Garden*. New York: Harcourt Brace Jovanovich, 1983. 355–360.

Yeats, W. B. *Selected Poetry*, ed. A. Norman Jeffares. London: Macmillan, 1965.

A Matter of Focus: Men in the Margins of Alice Walker's Fiction

Erna Kelly

Alice Walker describes herself as a "womanist" and a "womanist" as "outrageous audacious, courageous, willful." Barbara Christian, in turn, has used Walker's definition of "womanist" to delineate the essential character of Walker's writing. What distinguishes Walker's writing, Christian says, is a "peculiar sound" that "seems to have to do with her contrariness, her willingness at all turns to challenge the fashionable belief of the day, to reexamine it in the light of her own experiences and of dearly won principles that she has previously challenged and/or absorbed . At the core of this contrariness is an unwavering honesty about what she sees" (82–83). What Walker sees, though, is not always something readers are necessarily inclined to see. The result is what might be called "reader resistance syndrome."

For example, when *You Can't Keep a Good Woman Down* first came out in 1981, like David Bradley, I found myself annoyed because I thought that some of the stories read too much like political tracts. Like Bradley, I thought this was particularly true of the story, "Coming Apart." However, after I reread the volume in 1990, my impression, especially of "Coming Apart," changed dramatically. What before had sounded like didactic tales now read like an integrated work of art. Because their social awareness is not sufficiently developed, some readers find it difficult initially to appreciate what a writer like Walker is doing. Resisting her text on their first reading, it sometimes takes them quite a while to embrace the "truth" as Walker perceives it.

Another example of reader resistance can be seen in the critical reception of *The Temple of My Familiar*. Although my initial response was positive, critical reception was mixed. Donna Winchell in her Twayne study of Alice Walker sums up the negative responses accurately: "The reviews indicate that critics like their characters a bit more particularized in time and space" and "favor a clash between characters as more dramatic than a clash of ideas" (131). However, the inference she drew—that Walker's fiction "is least successful when it is most polemical" (131)—was not warranted. Again, readers needed time to assimilate, perhaps even come to terms with, Walker's vision. Recent articles on *The Temple of My Familiar* show a more sympathetic grasp of and appreciation for the novel's subject and technique (see, for example, Dieke; Jablon; Juncker; Smith; Wisker). However, while initial annoyance with the "peculiar sound" of a new piece of Walker fiction usually subsides and even transforms itself into admiration, this sort of reception is not always the case. A more serious example of resistance to Walker's vision is the

criticism of male characters in *The Color Purple* and, through "guilt" by association, its extension to male characters in other works.

The sad truth is that in the United States, women of color are seen as
doubly "other"—they are neither white nor male. When viewed from the world
outside the short stories and novels, the term "other" applies doubly to most of
Alice Walker's female characters. In fact, for many it applies triply: not only are
they not white and not male, often they do not follow the script society has given
them. Both Margaret Bauer and Robert James Butler note that Walker's fiction
often exposes "the tendency the South has toward upholding abstract codes at the
expense of the human individual" (Bauer 151). Barbara Christian sees the
implications of this for Walker's female characters. The women of *In Love and
Trouble*, she says, "seek at all costs to be characteristically and spontaneously
themselves" and because they do so, they appear to conventional society as
"backward, contrary, mad" (88). I propose looking at the term "other," though, in
another way—that is, from within, rather than from without, the worlds of Walker's
fiction. Walker is well aware, in terms of the dominant culture in the United States,
that women of color are doubly other, but as an artist she has the power to fix the
focus on women, looking at what it is to be a woman of color and not only survive
but live a full life, learning to matter not only to others around her but also to
herself. In her fictive worlds, Walker often chooses to make black women—even
when, or especially when, they are contrary—the known, the norm. In other words,
her black male characters are cast as other, their actions and voices assigned to the
periphery. However, while Walker's fiction may marginalize men, contrary to what
some have maintained, it does not malign them.

At the opening of her first novel, *The Third Life of Grange Copeland*,
Walker presents a protagonist hurt by white America through the trap of
sharecropping, a protagonist as cruel and callous as Albert from *The Color Purple.*
Grange Copeland's transformation begins when he stops hating himself as white
America has taught him to do and begins to hate white people instead. Disrupting
church services, he cries, "Don't teach 'em to *love them*! Teach them to hate 'em.
We *have* loved them. We loves 'em now. And by God it *killing* us" (154). The next
stage of Copeland's transformation begins when he stops hating altogether and
decides to simply ignore white people: "He realized he could not fight all the whites
he met. Nor was he interested in it any longer. For the time being, he would
withdraw completely from them make a life that need not acknowledge them" (155).

Walker has done the same; that is, to a large extent in her fiction, she
ignores the white world. In her second novel, *Meridian*, she deals with the white
civil rights volunteers, but that is about all we see of the white world. In her third
novel, *The Color Purple*, we get a glimpse of the white world through Sofia's
encounters with the mayor and his wife, their daughter, and her son; Squeak's
encounter with the sheriff; and Celie's learning that her real father, a skillful
businessman, was lynched by the white community for his success. We get a similar
brief but hideous reminder of the white world in the short story "Flowers," when a
young girl walking in the woods finds evidence of a lynching. And on occasion
Walker makes the subject of the white world a larger part of a piece as she does in

"Communion Table," a story in which a white congregation rejects an old black woman. But even in this story, the focus is much more on the black woman, even though she is seen through the white congregation's eyes. The white community is always (or almost always) approached in a tangential way. In her fourth novel, *The Temple of My Familiar*, the white world is again in the far distance. For example, in describing his life in a white neighborhood in Baltimore, Hal tells Suwelo that he and Lissie and Rafe stayed to themselves, keeping their house and yard in very good shape in order to avoid trouble with their neighbors. We learn nothing about the white neighbors. They are just a vague presence to be avoided. Her most recent novel, *Possessing the Secret of Joy,* contains more interaction with the white world but still concentrates predominately on black communities.

As Loyle Hairston says in his article on *The Third Life of Grange Copeland*, Walker's fiction very clearly shows that "pernicious social relations imposed by the racial caste system corrode the sensibilities of men" (177). However, Walker is able to make this point without giving over large sections of her narratives to white characters. As she notes in an interview with Claudia Tate, twentieth-century black women writers "are much more interested in the black community" and consequently treat the "white world as a backdrop" (181).

In much of her fiction, Walker does something similar with black male characters. They are not pushed as far out in the margins as the white world is, but they are nevertheless out there in a ring somewhere between the outer white ring and the central female-of-color core.

For example, most of the stories in Walker's first collection, *In Love and Trouble*, leave men on the periphery. "Roselily" gives us the protagonist's thoughts during her wedding, revealing her marriage as an enclosing structure, one in which she will have to adapt to a new religion (he is a Black Muslim) in a new area (the urban North as opposed to the rural South). She has said yes to the marriage in hopes of finding a better life for her children, but the reader, even more than Roselily, sees how much she will have to give up: she will have to give up her identity. We are left wondering if Roselily, uprooted, will wither and die in Chicago. Yet, even though he is the story's moving force, we learn little about Roselily's husband. In "Really, *Doesn't* Crime Pay?" the protagonist is shown struggling against two male forces, her husband and her lover. Her husband tolerates her writing but thinks of it as something as trivial as polishing her nails, something to occupy her until she begins her real vocation, producing and raising his children. The other man in her life, a writer, at first encourages her to write but then leaves, having stolen and published one of her stories as his own. We never see these men except as forces against which she reacts—or tries to react—in an attempt to preserve her own voice. In "Her Sweet Jerome," the main character, an older woman of some means, buys herself a younger husband and then becomes jealous of his "mistress" (she is sure he has one, since he ignores her). We see her consumed with finding the woman; the protagonist is a funny, then pathetic, then tragic, figure, flailing and raging against the mysterious mistress, whom she never understands is not a person, but the revolution. Again, although a man is the motivating force, he is on the periphery. *Meridian* is the story of a woman finding a way to keep the Civil Rights Movement going after it seems to have died with the deaths of Kennedy, King, and so many others. *The Color Purple* is chiefly the story of Celie's struggle to acknowledge her own rights. And even though *The Third Life of Grange Copeland* is about a male, neither he nor the book finds resolution until he bonds with his granddaughter. It is she who teaches him how to be himself; the book ends looking forward to her future. She is, in a way, Copeland's third life.

Ironically, although Walker has chosen to focus primarily on women, many critics have chosen to focus on her treatment of men, accusing her of perpetuating stereotypes of brutality and neglect and/or presenting only weak men as alternatives. (See, for example, Barksdale 413; Bradley 34; Guy 8; Pinckney 17; Pratt 43; Royster 363–68; Stade 265–66; Towers 35–6). Initially, I was surprised that this criticism did not appear before *The Color Purple* was published. Grange Copeland and his son Brownfield are brutal to women and children much of the time; when they are not, they use women like Josie, Grange's mistress who is abandoned by Grange and taken up to be used again by Brownfield. Although we applaud Grange's acquiring a farm that affords him the space and means to nurture his granddaughter, we cannot forget that the money for the farm was taken from Josie. Nor do we forget that although Ruth has been given love and a future with promise, she has that love partly at the expense of Grange and Brownfield taking out their rage on their wives, her grandmother and mother, respectively. Grange merely debases and abandons his wife. Brownfield, after systematically taking away Mem's sources of strength (what he loved her for originally—her teaching, for example), finally kills her. And the short story, "The Child Who Favored Daughter" has the atmosphere of a nightmare. It is the first piece I read by Walker; I wondered if I could ever read anything more by her. This is the story of a man tangled in his rage against white men and in what he feels as his sister's abandoning him (she fell in love with a white man—one who owned the land on which he worked so hard). Seeing his own daughter (who looks like his sister) mature and, against his command, take on a lover, he lops off her breasts. I do not understand why those who fault Walker for being "hard on men" did not complain when these pieces were published.

Perhaps this silence exists because not so many people were reading Walker's fiction in the seventies, yet that does not provide enough of a rationale. Early assessments of *The Third Life* do not condemn Walker for portraying brutal males (see, for example, Callahan and Hairston). The reviews and articles that do criticize Walker's portrayals of males in early works were written after *The Color Purple* came out (Bradley; Royster; Pratt; Towers). Furthermore, Trudier Harris, who writes about the problems that she as well as some of her colleagues and students had with male characters in this novel ("On *The Color Purple*, Stereotypes, and Silence" 157–60), wrote two earlier articles that do not fault Walker for portraying violent men. Her 1982 article points out that black writers "tip-toe around the issue of incest," because they don't want to "air their dirty linen" in public ("Tiptoeing through Taboo: Incest in 'The Child Who Favored Daughter'"). She cites Ellison, Morrison, Walker, and others as examples of writers who deal with incest, albeit indirectly. Still, as she points out, while the father in "The Child Who

Favored Daughter" never does commit incest, his rage at his daughter and the violence he perpetrates on her can be attributed, in part, to unresolved wishes for his sister and perhaps his daughter. However, Harris does not condemn Walker for exposing this character to the public. Nor does she condemn Walker's portrayal of Grange or Brownfield in her 1975 article, "Violence in *The Third Life of Grange Copeland.*"

Perhaps Harris does not find fault with these narratives because in *The Third Life* and in "The Child Who Favored Daughter," Walker examines the forces that prompt the male protagonists' acts—shows us how the pain these men have experienced has twisted their thinking. But I do not think that is enough of an answer, either. The brutality I encountered in reading these two pieces is more graphic than that of *The Color Purple*; I find nothing in the latter so graphic as the scene in which a man amidst a field of yellow flowers in the heat of the day hacks off his daughter's breasts:

He can only strike her with his fist and send her sprawling once more into the dirt. She gazes up at him over her bruises and he sees her blouse, wet and slippery from the rain, has slipped completely off her shoulders and her high young breasts are bare. He gathers their fullness in his fingers and begins a slow twisting. The barking of the dogs creates a frenzy in his ears and he is suddenly burning with unnamable desire. In his agony he draws the girl away from him as one pulling off his own arm and with quick slashes of his knife leaves two bleeding craters the size of grapefruits on her bare bronze chest and flings what he finds in his hands to the yelping dogs. ("The Child Who Favored Daughter" 45)

In *Meridian* and *The Color Purple*, Walker seems to be moving away from seeing the world as hopelessly brutal. Although there is brutality in the latter, there is escape from it—healing, and forgiveness for more than just one character; there is some communal hope of transcending the violence. I think what triggered the reaction against Walker's portrayal of males is that in *The Color Purple*, she depicts male brutality but chooses not to focus on the pain that men are trying to escape through their violence. In earlier fiction when Walker put males on the periphery they were not violent; when men were violent, she devoted some time to demonstrating the source of that violence. Depicting some men as violent, but beyond that, to a great extent ignoring them, seems to have made critics notice what they had not objected to before in Walker's fiction: that she often puts male characters on the periphery. Darryl Pinckney complains, "The black men are seen at a distance that is, entirely from the point of view of the women" (17). Louis Pratt feels that Walker's men have "no legitimacy except that which is assigned them through the consciousness of her women" (55). Even Mel Watkins, in his overall favorable assessment of *The Color Purple*, notes that one of the novel's few weaknesses is its "somewhat pallid portraits of males" (7).

Another reason for *The Color Purple* triggering such a strong negative reaction may be that Walker's relegating men to the margins is underscored by a lesbian relationship, which, as J. Charles Washington notes, is very fulfilling for the central character. Certainly, this might increase the sense of being ignored. Washington, however, pushes this further: he thinks homophobia is at the root of much of the critical outcry, some critics equating lesbianism with hatred of males (26). Jacqueline Bobo thinks that the debate may, in part, be attributed to the popular press. After the film version of the novel came out, the press exacerbated what debate there was by depicting the difference between black male and female reactions as a wide rift, sensationalizing that difference by concentrating on angry male reactions to the film. Yet she points out that "although a predominant negative reading of the film was given dominant exposure, black women were able to extract meaning of their own" (341). While the film and novel are separate entities, some of the negative press given the film most likely spilled over to reviews of and articles on the novel. Finally, there is Richard Wesley's suggestion that critical anger at Walker's depiction of males in *The Color Purple* comes from "political concepts developed in the 1960s," concepts which include presenting a united front to the dominant culture (90). Trudier Harris's objections to the novel appear to stem from this source.

In her 1984 article "On *The Color Purple*, Stereotypes, and Silences," Harris says she is "caught in a love/hate relationship with *The Color Purple*" (161). She loves the language of the novel; it is Walker's characters that anger her. She feels they perpetuate racist stereotypes:

Black males and females form units without the benefit of marriage, or they easily dissolve marriages in order to form less structured, more promiscuous relationships. Black men beat their wives and neglect, ignore, or abuse their children. The only stereotype that is undercut in the book is that of the matriarch. Sofia is beaten, imprisoned, and nearly driven insane precisely because of her strength. (157)

It is interesting, though, that Harris objects to what she sees as negative portrayals of women as well as of men.

Much of her article deals with Celie's passivity. She notes early on: "I couldn't imagine a Celie existing in any black community I knew or any that I could conceive of. What sane black woman, I asked, would sit around and take that crock of shit from all those folks?" (157). Although I do not come from a black community, I have seen individuals from a variety of communities who, because they were abused and undermined so constantly from so early an age, were unable to stand up for themselves, precisely because the abuse came from "all those folks," that is, from so many people. Continuing to explain her discontent with Celie's passivity, Harris notes, "Even slave women who found themselves abused frequently found ways of responding to that—by running away, fighting back, poisoning their masters, or through more subtly defiant acts such as spitting into the food they cooked for their masters" (157). Harris, however, fails to note that Celie does spit into the water she has fetched for Albert's father, a man whom Celie rightly sees as more of an oppressor than Albert. Albert's father is, in part, the reason Albert acts as he does. But we also need to ask, Would passivity be likely to get recorded? It seems actions, not passivity, get told and passed on—eventually written down. Those who were bold enough to act, or act and tell us about it, leave records. Who speaks for the silent? Who has recorded their stories? These are eternally legitimate questions.

Finally, even if one believes that Celie's passivity gives black women poor press, must Walker give up her artistic freedom and not create a character like Celie or characters like her abuser in order not to air dirty linen in public?

Faith Pullin, in her article "Landscapes of Reality," is pleased that black women writers "do not feel the reassuring need to produce idealistic stereotypes to offset the destructive characterizations often found in the writing of other authors," that they "are beginning to provide their audience with the truth about themselves" (183). She then cites Mary Helen Washington, the editor of *Black-Eyed Susans.* In the preface to this collection of short stories, Washington commends the writers for portraying "black women who have nervous breakdowns, not just the ones who endure courageously; stories about women who are overwhelmed by sex; wives who are not faithful black women who abuse and neglect their children" (xxi–xxxii). Celie's passivity would seem to fit into this category. To allow black women to be human in narrative worlds is important. Likewise, to allow black men the full range of humanity—from the best to the worst behaviors—is also important, it would seem.

When David Bradley asked Walker for her response to those who criticized her portrayal of men, she answered:

I was brought up to try to see what was wrong and right. Since I am a writer, writing is how I right it. I was brought up to look at things that are out of joint, out of balance, and try to bring them into balance. And as a writer that's what I do. I just always expected people to understand. Black men, because of their oppression, I always thought, would understand. So the criticism that I have had from black men, especially, who don't want me to write about these things, I'm just amazed. (36)

But Trudier Harris is not. Her article cites male students' and acquaintances' reactions to the men in *The Color Purple*, and Harris seems to agree with them. At least, she does not critique statements like the following from a student: "Walker deliberately deprive[s] all the black male characters in the novel of any positive identity the only supportive males are young and potheads or middle-aged and henpecked [as is the husband of Sofia's sister, for whom Celie makes a pair of pants and whose only goal in life seems to be to please his wife]" (158). This student goes on to say that Harpo is too dumb to know when he has a good thing and Samuel is defective "because he must get down on his knees and ask a woman for permission to get married." Albert's lack of respectability comes from his being able to change only "in terms of doing things that are traditionally considered sissified, such as sewing" (159). It seems that the problems with males in this novel is that when they are not abusing women, they tend to treat them too well. David Bradley shares some points in common with Harris's student. Unlike the many who seem to have problems with the male characters only in *The Color Purple*, they look at male characters in earlier works as well. But like others who accuse Walker of being "hard on men," they did not write their articles until after *The Color Purple* came out. According to Bradley,

Black men in Alice Walker's fiction and poetry seem capable of goodness only when they become old like Grange Copeland, or paralyzed and feminized, like Truman Held. If they are not rendered symbolically impotent, they are figures of male violence like Ruth's murderous father, Brownfield. (34)

If it were only the brutal men in Walker's fiction who were cited as evidence, it would be easy enough to counter the charge that Walker maligns males. There are many examples of positive male characters. However, a number of critics agree with Bradley that the male characters who are not brutal are weak. Although most look at *The Color Purple* or earlier works for their evidence (Bradley 34; Guy 8; Hogue 61; Pinckney 17), James Wolcott even finds such characterization or attribution in *The Temple of My Familiar*: he describes the black men in this novel as "sheepish" and "ineffectual" (29). However, there are a good number of characters who are neither brutal nor weak. Samuel, despite the fact that he gets on his knees to make his marriage proposal, is not a weak man—simply a good man, and characters like Meridian's father and Suwelo's Uncle Rafe in *The Temple of My Familiar* are strong and still can respect others, those not like them—whether they be women or those of another culture. Meridian's father, for example, has a great deal of compassion and respect for Native Americans. Furthermore, there is no evidence that the husband of Sofia's sister is henpecked. It just may be that we are so unused to men who respect their wives that critics see Celie's words about him as evidence that he is henpecked. What Celie says about him is that "Jack is tall and kind and don't hardly say anything. Love children. Respect his wife" and that he quietly supports her in "anything she want to take on." There is no evidence that Odessa keeps him quiet. Celie intimates that there remains in Jack's character this warm sensitivity: The pants she makes for Jack have to be camel, soft and strong, like him (191–92). (Hal is another such character in *The Temple of My Familiar*.)

But even if we were to accept the view that all of Walker's male characters are either weak or brutal, what would we do with characters like Harpo, who, like all of us, sometimes is weak and makes bad choices, and sometimes is strong and does the right thing; or Grady or Germaine (two of Shug's lovers), who are simply somewhat shallow; or Roselily's new husband; or Jerome, the bought husband? They are not "weak," nor are they brutal—just humanly disappointing.

Finally, though, why do critics denigrate brutal characters who become nurturing? (See, for example, Stade 264; Bradley 34; Harris 159). Albert's cooking yams for Henrietta, collecting shells, sewing and chatting in the evenings with Celie, even expressing empathy for the way she must feel when Shug leaves her do not seem to me to be signs of weakness. These actions are a sign that he has once again joined the human race, after years of depression, years of just sitting on his porch; furthermore, they are signs that he no longer needs to inflict pain on others in order to feel alive. The same is true for Grange Copeland. His nurturing of Ruth is a strong and positive stance, and once again, is the very thing that connects him with himself and with humanity. Truman begins to rehabilitate himself, as Bradley puts it, by "mothering her (Meridian), accepting her illness and ignoring her sexuality" (31). Bradley says Truman, as he appears earlier in the novel, is "a weak skunk of a man" (31). Until he changes at the novel's end, Truman cannot see Meridian for who she is; he is just interested in how she can serve *his needs* (*Meridian*, 140-42). Why it is that these nurturing gestures—which not only balance what has been "out of joint" in the community as a whole but also rehabilitate the men who make them—are seen as emasculating is unclear to me. In fact, one could say that Walker is "easy on" the males in her novels: most of those who are in need of this nurturance are able to redeem themselves.

Although critics continue to find fault with Walker's portrayal of males (e.g., Pratt and Wolcott), much of the anger over this issue can be found in articles and reviews published between 1982 and 1986. More recently male critics have begun to see Walker's fiction as J. Charles Washington sees it:

Walker's works demonstrate her love for both men and women. She gives praise where praise is due; however, her strong moral sense, courage and commitment to truth and honesty will not allow her to shrink from criticizing in order that future improvement can be made. (48) (See also Awkward 161–64; Butler-Evans 35; Hernton 35–36, 158–59; Wesley 60, 90–92.)

I have said men become the "other" in Alice Walker's fiction because they are on the periphery of most of her fictive worlds. However, there is another way in which Walker's men become "other." Paradoxically, men can come back from the periphery, from being "other" when compared to the female core of Walker's narrative worlds, if they are willing to change, to become other than what they have been, other than dominators of women. Ironically, the dominating seems to be an imitation of white males, an effort to be less "other" to white society. As I said, Walker, in most of her fiction, with the exception of works like *The Third Life* and "The Child Who Favored Daughter," is not trying to understand the pain that drives men to brutalize their wives and daughters. She is trying to disentangle another problem: the problem of how black women deal with constraints, survive brutality, and beyond that, the problem of how the black community as a whole can heal the terrible wounds that have come from the pressures racism puts on their gender relations or, for that matter, from other sources, as her latest novel, *Possessing the Secret of Joy*, illustrates. To lose or diminish anyone is to diminish the whole. Near the end of Walker's latest novel, the protagonist asks, "Are you saying we should just let ourselves die out? And the hope of wholeness with us?" (279). She is answered just before her death when relatives and friends hold up a banner that reads, "*RESISTANCE* IS THE SECRET OF JOY."

An axiom from the 1960s says that if you are not part of the solution, you are part of the problem; in Alice Walker's fictive worlds those men who are part of the problem remain apart—other—unless they take on two qualities that Walker implies are necessary for any person to be whole and to be part of a whole or a community: vulnerability and responsibility. In the preface to one of her volumes of poetry, *Revolutionary Petunias*, Walker writes that "these poems are about the loss of compassion, trust, and the ability to expand in love that marks the end of a hopeful strategy." Many of Walker's female characters are associated with flowers. They have flower names, like "Roselily," or they plant flowers against a dry and hostile environment, like Mem; or they are intimately connected with flowers: the color purple is the color of flowers in a field and is Celie's color; the "child who favored daughter" is a flower cut off before fruition; Meridian is a revolutionary petunia, "Rebellious Living / Against the Elemental Crush" ("The Nature of This Flower Is to Bloom" 11. 1–2).

However, for a hopeful strategy to work, men, too, must allow themselves at times to be vulnerable. In *Revolutionary Petunias*, Walker has a poem she calls "Black Mail." Black mail keeps people from seeing the truth; what is the payoff for black men to keep themselves hard, invulnerable, and blind to the truth? It is the honorary title of male. Walker is, of course, playing with black mail/black male. But she is also talking of a coat of mail as part of an armor.

When men stop protecting themselves from feeling their own pain, then they may be able to see how others feel and stop their destructive behaviors. It is not just that men need to do this to become alive again themselves and to stop hurting women and children; without it their dreams of a strong community will remain just that——dreams.

The other quality the men in Walker's fiction need to embrace is responsibility——responsibility for their actions. It is Grange's granddaughter, Ruth, who teaches him to take on responsibility. After telling her of his hatred of white people, he confesses to her that he left her grandmother and her father, blaming Shipley, the man for whom he worked:

> "I worked for a old white man that would have stole the skin / right off my back, if black hides'd bring a good price."
> "Ah!" she said, taking a step away from him. He what was wrong. "Wait 'til you're grown. You'll see. They can be hated to the very bottom of your guts, can the white folks."
> "You put it *all* on them!" she said, starting up. "You just as bad as Him! He killed!"
> She could not go on. (142–43)

"Him" refers to Brownfield, her father, who killed her mother, blaming the white folks for his action. Later in a confrontation with Brownfield, Grange realizes how blame not only allows a person to continue to act outrageously, but makes a person weak:

"I *know* the danger of putting the blame on somebody else for the mess you make out of your life. I fell into the trap myself! You gits weak as water, no feeling of doing *nothing* yourself. Then you begins to think up evil and begins to destroy everybody around you, and you blames it on the crackers. *Shit*! Nobody's as powerful as we make them out to be." (207)

Men need to allow themselves to be vulnerable and, at the same time, become responsible: they need to get under the anger to the hurt at the bottom, to use it to help them see others besides themselves, prevent them from letting it out as brutality, and instead convert it to nurturing first themselves, and then others.

Women, too, need to take on responsibility, but in a different way. They need to become responsible for not letting the hurt they feel paralyze them. They must learn that it need not make them incapable of finding their own voice and acting on their own behalf. Unlike so many of the male characters who so readily embrace their anger, the female characters need to acknowledge the anger bound up with their hurt and use it to fuel their journey to independence and self-discovery. They must also be careful not to use their anger as men have: Celie almost kills Albert as she shaves him, and Fanny struggles for years to free herself of fantasies of killing white people. However, chiefly, they have to find a way to use themselves in service of themselves, not only in service of others. A few of Walker's women, like Celie, take a long time to learn this, and a few, like Mem and Margaret, never do, but many of Walker's women learn this relatively quickly, and a few even know it at the outset of a given story.

Walker recognizes the terrible pressures on gender relations in a subdominant group. She also notes that women do not often act out their oppression the way men do. When Bradley asks Walker why she is not as equally hard on black women as on black men, she answers,

Oh, I get to them. But I am really aware that they are under two layers of oppression and that even though everybody, the men and the women, get twisted terribly, the women have less choice than the men. And the things that they do, the bad choices that they make, are not done out of meanness, out of a need to take stuff out on people. (36)

Walker's "womanist" perspective makes her focus on the world of women imperative, because according to Walker a "womanist" perspective supports the "survival and wholeness of an entire people, male and female" (*In Search of Our Mothers' Gardens*, xi). Patterns and values from the dominant groups, patterns such as hierarchies, valuing "strength" that is possible only through loss of vulner-ability—haven't worked. I think Walker would argue that the community will not survive if it adheres to old patterns that allow the loudest and cruelest to survive at the expense of others. Walker is not espousing survival of the fittest; she is espousing "survival of an entire people." In a 1984 interview with Sharon Wilson, Walker said, "I'm always trying to give voice to specific people in hope that if I do that, then that specific kind of person will be better understood, really brought into the common fund" (39). She reiterates this five years later, explaining to Claudia Dreifus that through her writing, she is trying "to reconnect all of us." She adds that "an more or less equal and valid in order for the whole organism to feel healthy" (31). Her fiction works at clearing away old perceptions; in order to do that she must refocus. Men are pushed to the outside to make room for even the quietest and the most maimed members of the community and to hold up to view the variety of ways women can own their strength and the variety of ways men can learn a truer kind of strength—one without meanness—the strength of revolutionary petunias.

WORKS CITED

Awkward, Michael. *Inspiriting Influences*. New York: Columbia University Press, 1989.

Barksdale, Richard K. "Castration Symbolism in Recent Black American Fiction." *College Language Association Journal* 29 (1986): 400–13.

Bauer, Margaret. "Alice Walker: Another Southern Writer Criticizing Codes Not Put to 'Everyday Use.'" *Studies in Short Fiction* 29 (Spring 1992): 143–51.

Bobo, Jacqueline. "Sifting Through the Controversy: Reading *The Color Purple*." *Callaloo* 12 (Spring 1989): 332–42.

Bradley, David. "Novelist Alice Walker Telling the Black Woman's Story." *New York Times Magazine*, 8 Jan. 1984: 25–37.

Butler, Robert James. "Alice Walker's Vision of the South in *The Third Life of Grange Copeland*." *African American Review* 27.2 (Summer 1993): 195–204.

Butler-Evans, Elliott. *Race, Gender and Desire: Narrative Strategies in the Fiction of Toni Cade Bambara, Toni Morrison, and Alice Walker*. Philadelphia: Temple University Press, 1989.

Callahan, John. "Reconsideration: The Higher Ground of Alice Walker." *The New Republic*, 14 Sept. 1974: 21–22.

Christian, Barbara. *Black Feminist Criticism*. New York: Pergamon Press, 1985.

Dieke, Ikenna. "Toward a Monistic Idealism: The Thematics of Alice Walker's *The Temple of My Familiar*." *African American Review* 26 (1992): 507–14.

Dreifus, Claudia. "Alice Walker: Writing to Save My Life," *The Progressive*, August 1989: 29–31.

Guy, David. "A Correspondence of Hearts." *The Washington Post*, 25 July 1982.

Hairston, Loyle. "Work of Rare Beauty and Power." *Freedomways* 11 (1971): 170–77

Harris, Trudier. "On *The Color Purple*, Stereotypes, and Silence" Black American Literary Forum 18 (1984): 155–61.

_____. "Tiptoeing through Taboo: Incest in 'The Child Who Favored Daughter.'" *Modern Fiction Studies* 28 (1982): 495–505.

_____. "Violence in *The Third Life of Grange Copeland*." *College Language Association Journal* 19 (1975): 238–47.

Hernton, Calvin. *The Sexual Mountain and Black Women Writers*. New York: Doubleday, 1987.

Hougue, W. Lawrence. "History, the Feminist Discourse, and Alice Walker's *The Third Life of Grange Copeland*." *Multi-Ethnic Literature of the United States* 12: 2 (1985): 45–62.

Jablon, Madelyn. "Rememory, Dream History, and Revision in Toni Morrison's Beloved and Alice Walker's *The Temple of My Familiar*." *College Language Association Journal* 37 (1993): 136–44.

Juncker, Clara. "Black Magic: Woman(ist) as Artist in Alice Walker's *The Temple of My Familiar*." *American Studies in Scandinavia* 24 (1992): 37–49.

Pinckney, Darryl. "Black Victims, Black Villains." *New York Review of Books* 29 Jan 1987: 17–20.

Pratt, Louis H. "Alice Walker's Men: Profiles in the Quest for Love and Personal Values." *Studies in Popular Culture* 12 (Nov. 1989): 42–57.

Pullin, Faith. "Landscapes of Reality: The Fiction of Contemporary Afro-American Women." In *Black Fiction: New Studies in the Afro-American Novel since 1945*. Ed. Robert A. Lee. New York: Barnes and Noble, 1980. 173–203.

Royster, Philip. "In Search of Our Fathers' Arms: Alice Walker's Persona of the Alienated Darling." *Black American Literature Forum* 20 (1986): 347–70.

Smith, Felipe. "Alice Walker's Redemptive Art." *African American Review* 26 (1992): 437–51.

Stade, George. "Womanist Fiction and Male Characters." *Partisan Review* 52 (1985): 264–70.

Tate, Claudia, ed. *Black Women Writers at Work.* New York: Continuum, 1983.

Towers, Robert. "Good Men Are Hard to Find." *New York Review of Books,* 12 August 1982: 35–36.

Walker, Alice. *The Color Purple.* New York: Washington Square Press, 1982.

_____. *In Love and Trouble.* New York: Harcourt Brace Jovanovich, 1967.

_____. *In Search of Our Mothers' Gardens.* New York: Harcourt Brace Jovanovich, 1983.

_____. *Meridian.* New York: Washington Square Press, 1976.

_____. *Possessing the Secret of Joy.* New York: Harcourt Brace Jovanovich, 1992.

_____. *Revolutionary Petunias and Other Poems.* New York: Harcourt Brace Jovanovich, 1971.

_____. *The Temple of My Familiar.* New York: Washington Square Press, 1989.

_____. *The Third Life of Grange Copeland.* New York: Harcourt Brace Jovanovich, 1970.

_____. *You Can't Keep a Good Woman Down.* New York: Harcourt Brace Jovanovich, 1981.

Washington, J. Charles. "Positive Black Male Images in Alice Walker's Fiction." *Obsidian* II 3 (1988): 23–48.

Washington, Mary Helen, ed. *Black-Eyed Susans.* Garden City: Anchor Press-Doubleday, 1975.

Watkins, Mel. "Some Letters Went to God." *New York Times Book Review*, 25 July 1982: 7.

Wesley, Richard. "*The Color Purple* Debate." *Ms.* 15, Sept. 1986: 62, 90–92.

Wilson, Sharon. "A Conversation with Alice Walker." *Kalliope* 6 (1984): 37–45.

Winchell, Donna Haisty. *Alice Walker.* New York: Twayne, 1992.

Wisker, Gina. "'Disremembered and Unaccounted For': Reading Toni Morrison's *Beloved* and Alice Walker's *The Temple of My Familiar.*" In *Black Women's Writing.* Ed. Gina Wisker. New York: St. Martin's Press, 1993. 78–95.

Wolcott, James. "Party of Animals." *New Republic,* 29 May 1989: 28–30.

"What She Got to Sing About?":
Comedy and *The Color Purple*

Priscilla L. Walton

[Laughter] is a froth with a saline base. Like froth it sparkles. It is gaiety itself. But the philosopher who gathers a handful to taste may find that the substance is scanty and the aftertaste bitter.

———Henri Bergson, "Laughter"

This observation, written in 1900 by Henri Bergson, in the conclusion to his essay "Laughter," ironically anticipates the changes that occur in the comic mode of the succeeding century when laughter's "froth" virtually disappears and its "bitter after-taste"comes to predominate. After 1900, literature—comedy in particular—becomes more acrimonious and discordant, perhaps better to represent life in our century of "disorder and irrationalism" (Sypher 201). The comic novel ceases to ring with the "silvery laughter" that George Meredith applauds: rather it reverberates to the maniacal, paranoid laughter in which Thomas Pynchon revels. In short, comedy enters the realm of the absurd and begins to reflect the individual disorientation in a "senseless, chaotic" world.

Yet even within this context, it might seem anomalous to call Alice Walker's 1982 work, *The Color Purple*, a comedy. The novel is arguably bleaker than many of the others that are included in the mode, since it deals with rape, incest, and social prejudice; yet the ideal "womanist" world in which it culminates (Walker *Search* xi) is joyous and celebratory——a condition of the comic. Although its subject matter appears at times to counteract the levity expected of a comic novel and so to be at variance with the comic purpose, if we set aside our more traditional expectations of the mode and look rather at the intent of the comic, we see that *The Color Purple* rather closely adheres to its theoretical tenets.

While it is not my intention here to offer an absolute definition of comedy, some idea of what the comic signifies is necessary to come to an understanding of its relevance to *The Color Purple*. My discussion is selective: the characteristics I discuss relate more specifically to what theorists of the comic call "high comedy," or the "comedy of ideas," since Walker's novel is obviously not of the kind of comedy which elicits hearty guffaws from its readers. But this does not disqualify it from the mode, for theorists of the comic often note that laughter is a very deceptive criterion by which to assess it (Martin 74, Sypher 203). More often than not, high comedy concerns itself less with being "funny" than with dramatizing possibilities and exploring potentials. If it does provide laughter, it is because it mocks certain social conventions. Yet, it mocks because it devotes itself to social improvement and often provides a critique of societal limitations. James K. Feibleman suggests that comedy pursues the ideal:

A constant reminder of the existence of the logical order as the perfect goal of actuality, comedy continually insists upon the limitations of all experience and of all actuality. The business of comedy is to dramatize and thus make more vivid and immediate the fact that contradictions in actuality must prove insupportable. It thus admonishes against the easy acceptance of interim limitations and calls for the persistent advance toward the logical order and the final elimination of limitations. (82)

Comedy seeks improvement in a "negative way," for it asserts that if it is only the limitations of actuality which prevent it from achieving perfection, then the limitations should be eliminated (96). Therefore, in a period of social change (like the twentieth century), comedy often assumes an increasing importance because it is more subversive in nature than tragedy (96) and seeks to improve society: "Better to stress the fact that however much value any actual situation may have, it is prevented from having more only by its limitations. Why, then, be satisfied?" (96). Because comedy continually exposes the limitations of the actual to highlight the ideal, many comic theorists emphasize its potentially "dangerous" and even "revolutionary" nature. Indeed, Wylie Sypher goes so far as to suggest that the comedian

refuses to make concessions to actuality and serves, instead, as chief tactician in a permanent resistance movement, or rebellion, within the frontiers of human experience. By temperament, the comedian is often a fifth columnist in social life. (247)

All these criteria are relevant to *The Color Purple*, but of more specific interest at this point is the means by which comedy frequently displays its "revolutionary" tendency. If comedy is a subversive mode, it often succeeds in demonstrating the limitations of the social order through the incorporation of an excluded or marginalized individual. Northrop Frye perceives this as comedy's adaptation of the *"pharmakos"* or the victimized character who is "opposed to or excluded from the fictional society" and has "the sympathy of the audience" (*Anatomy* 48). The *"pharmakos"* generally appears in comedy in one of two ways and can be regarded as a "fool or worse by the fictional society, and yet impresses the real audience as having something more valuable than his [or her] society has" (48); or the *"pharmakos"* may choose to repudiate the society, and in doing so become "a kind of *pharmakos* in reverse" (48). The idea of the *"pharmakos"* also foregrounds what has been called comedy's "paradoxical nature," since in it frequently that which is "seemingly absurd [is] actually well-founded" (Martin 86) and therefore, in "the best sort of comedy," the "incongruous is finally seen to be congruent to a larger pattern than that which was originally perceived" (87).

While comedy seeks to improve society, often, particularly in its twentieth-century manifestations, it veers so close to tragedy that it is difficult to separate the comic from the tragic mode. But Frye suggests that this is because "tragedy is really implicit or uncompleted comedy [and] comedy contains a potential tragedy within itself" ("Argument" 455). If comedy completes itself, this completion is manifested in the new (or renewed) society which is evident in its conclusion. High comedy is not content to expose the limitations in a closed social order; once they have been exposed, it often offers what it perceives as the ideal, for in its aim for general improvement, it needs to provide an open society as an alternative to the closed or limited one it has dramatized. Comedy's theme, therefore, is often "the integration of society" (*Anatomy* 43) and this social integration "may emphasize the birth of an ideal society" ("Argument" 454). As a result, "that which gets born at the end of comedy" may "not impress us as true, but as desirable," since unlikely "conversions, miraculous transformations, and providential assistance are inseparable from comedy" (*Anatomy* 170).

High comedy forces its dramatized order to "open in many directions" (Sypher 249). It becomes "an achievement of man as a social being" (Sypher 252) because it compels us to recognize our potential by mocking what is less than ideal in our practice. Hence, while it exposes the limitations of our society, it either eliminates these limitations and so renews its fictional order or it posits a new, ideal order in its conclusions. Like tragedy, therefore, comedy too offers a "road to wisdom" (Sypher 154), and the comic protagonist often learns through suffering (Sypher 254); but the comic differs from the tragic in that it never "despairs of man" (Sypher 254).

And Alice Walker's novel, *The Color Purple*, does not despair of "man" either, for it incorporates these elements of comedy: it makes the incongruous congruent to a larger pattern; it refuses to accept the limitations imposed on its fictional society; and it posits atastrophic overthrow of the hero as he can get it, and then reverses the action as quickly as possible" (Frye, *Anatomy* 178).

However, if we are to apply these prescriptions to *The Color Purple*, we must first perceive it as a "high comedy," since it is only this mode which theoretically subscribes to the criteria discussed earlier. But "high comedy" invariably includes, and, in fact, culminates in the comedy of manners, and to characterize *The Color Purple* as such appears to be problematic, especially in light of M. H. Abrams's explanation that this mode

deals with the relations and intrigues of men and women living in a polished and sophisticated society, relying for comic effect in great part on the wit and sparkle of the dialogue—often in the form of *repartee*, a with conversational give-and-take which constitutes a kind of verbal fencing match—and to a lesser degree, on the ridiculous violations of social conventions and decorum by stupid characters such as would-be wits, jealous husbands, and foppish dandies. (26)

The male and female characters of *The Color Purple* do not live in a polished and sophisticated society, nor do they engage in what is traditionally considered sparkling and witty repartee. And the violations of social norms and decorum that occur are not perpetrated by foolish, stupid, or dandified characters but by female characters with whom we are expected to sympathize. However, the conventions of the comedy of manners are so clearly inverted in *The Color Purple* that we cannot but suspect it to be deliberate. Therefore, I would suggest that *The Color Purple* is a parodic inversion of the comedy of manners,[1] and so undercuts the form at the same time that it ironically adheres to its intentions—to improve and to open the closed social order it dramatizes.

Linda Hutcheon defines parody as "imitation with critical difference" (36). She also notes that parody too is potentially "revolutionary":

The presupposition of both a law and its transgression bifurcates the impulses to parody: it can be normative and conservative, or it can be provocative and revolutionary. [P]arody can, like the carnival, also challenge norms in order to renovate, to renew. (76)

In its parodic inversion of the comedy of manners, Walker's novel recalls the works of Jane Austen, who, as Sypher observes, "devastates our compromises and complacencies—especially male complacency" and "placidly undermines the bastions of middle-class propriety" (247). Austen too, of course, frequently parodies various literary modes, particularly "the popular romance fiction of her day" (Hutcheon 44), and through it "satirizes the traditional view of woman's role as the lover of men" (Hutcheon 44). But while she may call into question the social mores of her time, Austen presents, in the conclusions of her novels, a society in which women are integrated into the traditional order. Walker, on the other hand, recalls Austen's work with a "critical difference," since in her novel no compromises are brooked. She goes further than her predecessor and rejects the society which imposes the limitations and at the same time points out the exclusivity of literature, since traditionally few novels that have achieved significant "recognition" have dealt with anything other than a white social order or anything other than a patriarchal society. (To this end she also reworks to some extent Samuel Richardson's *Pamela* and the traditional endings of sexist fairy tales, specifically "The Frog Prince.")

By transposing the comedy of manners, Walker foregrounds the limitations she finds in it and so undercuts those social norms which it has incorporated and to which it ultimately contributes. Indeed, J. A. Cuddon suggests that the comedy of manners has "for its main subjects and themes the behavior and deportment of men and women living under specific social codes" (139). This definition takes on new significance in relation to a novel like *The Color Purple* because it subverts the form by parodically inverting its conventional notions of expected social codes.

Walker writes from the point of view of an outsider who is rebuffed by a closed social order; yet in her novel she transcends these social restrictions and envisions a world in which they cease to exist. *The Color Purple* is an intellectual comedy in that it is a comedy of ideas: it dramatizes possibilities and completes itself in a vision of an ideal world[2]—a world which is matriarchal, a parody of the boy-gets-girl endings of most comedies and fairy tales. This world is also an ideal one which is in direct opposition to the rigidly closed society that is in evidence in the opening pages of *The Color Purple*. However, the tragic elements so apparent here are necessary to Walker's idea, since she must work through the limitations of the closed order to give credence to the utopian possibilities of her open, womanist world.

Walker dramatizes the crippling strictures of this old order through her heroine, who is a social pariah. Celie is not just a woman, she is a black woman; but she is not just a black woman, she is—as she later learns—a lesbian, and is, therefore, thrice removed from the white male heterosexual norm. By writing from the point of view of this seemingly socially aberrant individual, Walker exposes the limitations that society imposes on anything outside the norm and the narrow, restrictive lifestyle that it upholds. The society in evidence at the beginning of the novel is a totally closed society, which would not open to include Celie even if she wished it, since she cannot change the color of her skin or her sex. Yet this social outcast is shown to be far wiser than the white patriarchy which excludes her. She is able to manifest at the conclusion of the work a society that "opens in many directions" (Sypher 249). And in doing so, she points up the limitations of life lived under the patriarchal norm by transcending them.

But before the ideal situation is reached, virtually every bastion of society is assaulted and little is left unscathed. Walker exposes the limitations in most social values and institutions and attacks the autonomy of the white male heterosexual norm which has generated them. It is difficult to pinpoint the prescriptions of this norm, primarily because they operate as the basis of our society and so seem self-evident to us. As Feibleman writes:

It is a notorious historical observation that customs and institutions rarely enjoy more than a comparatively brief life; and yet while they are the accepted fashion they come to be regarded as brute givens, as irreducible facts, which may be depended upon with perfect security. (81)

However, by extrapolating from the text, we can reconstruct those social mores that Walker questions.

The prescriptions are formulated in the nuclear family, which perpetuates the notion of male and female roles. The male role dictates that man perform "manly" work, such as field work and carpentry (*Purple* 22, 27), and that he act as the head of his household and the maker of its laws (36, 37). The female role demands that woman be domestic; she must clean her house, cook, tend to the children (20), and obey her husband (37). It is not thought proper for men and women to trade these positions, and, if they do, they are subject to criticism and mockery (36). Marriage, which begins on this restrictive basis, merely perpetuates the stereotyped roles that its members are expected to play and again does not allow for deviation from them. Both the family and marriage are shown to operate on the assumption of feminine inferiority. Religion, in support of this order, preaches platitudes and casts narrow moral judgments upon those who are different or who refuse to conform to the conventions of family life (46). The laws effected by the patriarchy in the name of "equality" and "justice for all" merely function as a support to the existing order by keeping those outside that order "in their place" through the use of force (90, 91). While the theory behind the institution of the patriarchal order may have been altruistic and idealistic, Walker's novel shows how far from the ideal it has strayed in its practice. She therefore dramatizes these social values and institutions as they function in actuality and then redramatizes them in terms of the possible and the desirable.

The novel begins by portraying the family as a social unit which subjects girl children to a life of rape and terror: "First he put his thing up against my hip and sort of wiggle it around. Then he grab hold my titties. Then he push his thing inside my pussy. When that hurt, I cry. He start to choke me saying You better shut up and git used to it" (1–2). The first three letters suggest that Celie's "father" kills her mother through abuse, at which point he ominously begins to eye her favorite sister, Nettie. Clearly, "a girl child ain't safe in a family of men" (42) and no woman in the household is inviolable. Nor is marriage a safe haven for Celie; it merely becomes an extension of her unhappy home life. Ironically, she is offered to Mr. _____ like a slave on an auction block, and Mr. _____ is more interested in her dowry than in her: "Mr. _____ say, That cow still coming? He say, Her cow" (12). In turn, Celie's wedding day is equally desolate, "I spend my wedding day running from the oldest boy. He twelve" (13). Marital sex is brutal and animalistic, and Celie later equates it with defecation, since it is hardly an act based on mutual fulfillment: "He git up on you, heist your nightgown round your waist, plunge in. Most times I pretend I ain't there. He never know the difference. Never ast me how I feel, nothing. Just do his business, get off, go to sleep" (81).

Celie's life is more death-in-life, a life without hope, joy, or any indication of improvement. Nettie comments on this before she leaves: "I sure hate to leave you here with these rotten children, she say. Not to mention with Mr. _____. It's like seeing your buried, she say. It's worse than that, I think. If I was buried, I wouldn't have to work" (18). But Celie does not despair, and her faith sustains her: "I just say, Never mine, never mine, long as I can spell G-o-d I got somebody along" (18).

While Celie may find a vent for her anguish in writing to God, religion itself is undercut when Shug Avery comes to town. Shug, who refuses to accept the limitations that society imposes on a woman's life, becomes the target for attack:

Even the preacher got his mouth on Shug Avery, now she down. He take her condition for his text. He talk about a strumpet in short skirts, smoking cigarettes, drinking gin. Singing for money and taking other women mens. Talk bout slut, hussy, heifer and streetcleaner. (46)

Not surprisingly, however, Celie does not hold with the virtues preached from the pulpit and repudiates conventional social behavior as prescribed by Mr. _____'s father. Independently, she rejects the "virtues" which society applauds, and takes the ill Shug in to nurse. Astutely noticing his refusal to acknowledge her as a person, Celie discounts Mr. _____'s father words: "Celie, he say, you have my sympathy. Not many women let thy husband whore lay up in they house. But be not saying to me, he saying to Mr. _____" (57). Celie chooses instead to champion Shug and responds: "Next time he come I put a little Shug Avery pee in his glass. See how he like that" (57).

Celie identifies with the rebellious Shug from the seventh page of the novel, when she finds her picture and begins to idolize the blues singer. Shug provides an ideal for Celie, since, unlike the other women in Celie's life, she is not broken through years of abuse. Pretty and different, she offers an alternative lifestyle:

Shug Avery was a woman. The most beautiful woman I ever say. I see her there in furs. Her face rouge. Her hair like somethin tail. She ginning with her foot up on somebody motorcar. Her eyes serious tho. Sad some. An now when I dream, I dream of Shug Avery. She be dress to kill, whirling and laughing. (7)

Celie is also attracted to her stepdaughter-in-law, Sofia, an Amazon who refuses to be dominated by her husband, Harpo. But an independent woman has a more difficult time than one who meekly accepts his meager lot in life. Ironically, Harpo wants Sofia to act like the submissive Celie: "I want her to do what I say, like you do for Pa. But not Sofia. She do what she want, don't pay me no mind at all. I try to beat her, she black my eyes. Oh, boo-hoo, he cry" (66). Even though he loves Sofia, Harpo's marriage is troubled because society has taught him that this is not the way a woman should behave. Celie tries to reason with him, but to no avail; social conventions are too deeply ingrained in his mind:

Sofia *love* you. You *love* Sofia. Mr. _____ marry me to take care of his children. I marry him cause my daddy made me. I don't love Mr._____ and he don't love me. But you his wife, he say, just like Sofia mine. The wife spose to mind. (66)

Sofia becomes a victim of social injustice when she refuses to respect authority in the person of the white mayor's wife, who wants Sofia to work as her maid. When Sofia responds with a "hell no" (90), a brawl ensues and the police are called. The dangers of fighting back are clear since Sofia's punishment is hardly "just" or merited by her crime:

when I see Sofia I don't know why she still alive. They crack her skull, they crack her ribs. They tear her nose loose on one side. They blind her in one eye. She swole from head to foot. Her tongue the size of my arm, it stick out tween her teef like a piece of rubber. She can't talk. And she just about the color of eggplant. (92)

Society's justice is again satirized when the astute women realize that the only way to get Sofia released from the prison that is killing her is to plead that "justice ought to be done" (99) and to assert that Sofia will only be sufficiently punished when she becomes "some white lady maid" (99). After raping Squeak, the sheriff promptly takes action to ensure that Sofia will be "properly punished," and she is released into the mayor's custody. We realize how correct the women's assessment of society's "compassion" is when the mayor's (white) wife wishes to be "kind" to her maid and drives her to visit the family she has not seen in five years, only to make her leave in fifteen minutes (110–111). She later berates Sofia for her in-gratitude.

The novel is often criticized for its melodramatic disposition, but I would suggest that this is a result of Walker's parodic inversion of Samuel Richardson's *Pamela*. Certainly the epistolary style of *The Color Purple* reminds us of Richardson's work, which, itself, is often melodramatic.[3] *The Color Purple* deliberately recalls *Pamela*, but ironically transposes it, for Pamela becomes reconciled to the world of men, and if she is accorded any stature within it, that stature is bestowed when Mr. B. learns to appreciate her, makes her his wife, and thus allows her entry into his world. Like Pamela, Celie too suffers at the hands of men, with the "critical difference" that she is never incorporated into their society. Rather, she overturns this order and instigates a new one, into which *she* allows Mr. _____ to enter when he rehabilitates himself.

Despite the almost overwhelming oppressiveness of Celie's life, she endures and finally begins to accept herself: "I'm pore, I'm black, I may be ugly and can't cook, a voice say to everything listening. But I'm here" (214). Yet, this self-acceptance is dearly bought, and Celie suffers extreme anguish when she learns that Mr. _____ has been hiding the letters which her sister, Nettie, has written. She is so angry that she nearly kills her husband and is saved only by Shug's replacing the destructive razor in her hand with a constructive needle——a symbolic act. However, Nettie's letters provide a further source of anguish for Celie, when, through them, she learns of her true parentage. At this point, her anger turns to despair, and she rejects God:

Yeah, I say, and he give me a lynched daddy, a crazy mama, and a lowdown dog of a step pa and a sister I probably won't ever see again. Anyhow, I say, the God I been praying and writing to is a man. And act just like all the other mens I know. Trifling, forgitful and lowdown. (199)

But a woman——Shug——teaches Celie to love and to trust again, and when she offers to take Celie to Memphis, Celie's world is rejuvenated. In the pivotal dinner scene, when Celie and Squeak announce that they have decided to forge new identities by leaving their husbands, they refuse to conform to the old patriarchal order. Celie stabs Mr. _____ when he tries to slap her (271) and Squeak demands that she be called by her proper name: "Listen Squeak, say Harpo. You can't go to Memphis. That's all there is to it. Mary Agnes, says Squeak. Squeak, Mary Agnes, what difference do it make? It makes a lot, say Squeak. When I was Mary Agnes I could sing in public" (210).[4] The final pages of the novel are spent in dramatizing the positive aspects of society, by incorporating and revitalizing the social values and institutions in light of the new order.

The family itself becomes a positive force when Sofia changes it into an entity that succors and helps its members. She extends the nuclear family when she welcomes Squeak's children into her home and heals the breach that had existed between the two women, both rivals for Harpo's affections: "Go on sing, say Sofia, I'll look after this one till you come back" (211). Family is, therefore, no longer

based on blood but on mutual love and respect. Shug and Celie form a new family
unit when Celie learns the truth of her parentage, and Shug's tenderness helps her
to overcome her despair: "Shug say, Us each other's peoples now, and kiss me"
(189). Further, Shug's relationship with Celie takes on the sanctity that Celie's
marriage with Mr._____ lacked and offers a positive view of "non-marriage"
as a union which proffers acceptance and concern: "Besides, she say, You not my
maid. I didn't bring you to Memphis to be that. I brought you here to love you and
help you get on your feet" (218).

Even religion is revitalized when it extends to encompass the segregated,
and God loses "Its" color and gender: "God ain't a he or a she, but a It ain't a
picture show. It ain't something you can look at apart from anything else, including
yourself" (202). When religion loses the limitations imposed on it by a white, male
hierarchy, faith "opens in many directions" (Sypher 249), and Celie's perception
of God becomes all-inclusive and whole. She comes to accept Shug's belief in a
God who is "everything" (202) and begins to understand "It" need not be restricted
to a church:

> God love everything you love—and a mess of stuff you don't. But more than
> anything else, God love admiration.
> You say God vain? I ast.
> Naw, she say. Not vain, just wanting to share a good thing. I think it pisses God
> off if you walk by the color purple in a field somewhere and don't notice it. (203)

Society itself can become more enlightened when its members are able to
repudiate the dictates of societal norms. Indeed, there is an attempt on the part of
the daughters to overcome the sins of the fathers when Eleanor Jane tries to make
reparation for her parents' treatment of Sofia by working for her: "Do her peoples
know? I ast. They know, say Sofia. They carrying on just like you know they would.
Whoever heard of a white woman working for niggers, they rave. She tell them,
Whoever heard of somebody like Sofia working for trash" (288). The new society
is not a closed order; it is open to all; even Mr._____ can be included when
he realizes the errors of his ways, rejects his old, narrow outlook, and learns the
meaning of love:

> he say something that really surprise me cause it so thoughtful and common sense. When
> it come to what folks do together with they bodies, he say, anybody's guess is as good as
> mine. But when you talk bout love I don't have to guess. I have love and I have been love.
> And I think God he let me gain understanding enough to know love can't be halted just
> cause some peoples moan and groan. It don't surprise me you love Shug Avery, he say, I
> have love Shug Avery all my life. (277)

The novel's major narrative symbol is associated with the act of sewing:
Celie literally sews her life back together when she begins to design pants, and Mr.
_____'s salvation is symbolized when he begins to make shirts to match them.
Indeed Mr._____ asks Celie to marry him again, "this time in the spirit as well
as in the flesh" (290), but she refuses him because, as she states, "I still don't like

frogs" (290). Celie's reference to frogs recalls the fairy tale, "The Frog Prince," which the novel parodically inverts. In this story, Mr. _____ may kiss the "princess," but he undergoes no miraculous transformation into a handsome prince; he remains a "frog." Celie, on the other hand, is still able to live "happily ever after" without him, which, as mentioned earlier, undercuts the traditional boy-gets-girl endings of most fairy tales and comedies. However, Celie does forgive Mr. _____ when she allows him to join in her creative process, and her forgiveness constitutes the basis for the new society, for men and even white women like Eleanor Jane, although viewed skeptically, are allowed a chance to atone.

Since the novel attacks those bastions of society—family, religion, and marriage—but also offers a rejuvenation of them in its final pages, it evidently suggests that society itself is not what Walker questions and rejects but rather the limitations that are imposed upon it and make it closed and restrictive. The womanist utopia of the conclusion signifies a renewal of the initial social order because it is more accessible and more humane. Walker's utopia is "humanist" as well as womanist in the sense that it offers a revivification of humanity as a whole. This concept is epitomized in Celie's sewing.[5] Her first pair of pants are made out of army fabric—hard, stiff to the touch—which she later rejects in favor of soft, pliable material: "Shug finger the pieces of cloth I got hanging on everything. It all soft, flowing, rich and catch the light. This a far cry from the stiff army shit us started with, she say" (219). The clothes that Celie designs out of the new fabric enhance the people who wear them; she creates pants that are comfortable and designed with their wearer in mind:

these pants are soft, hardly wrinkle at all, and the little figures in the cloth always look perky and bright. And they full round the ankle so if she want to sing in 'em and wear 'em sort of like a long dress, she can. (219)

Mr. _____'s shirts are also devised to become extensions of their wearer; they support life rather than stifle it: "Got to have pockets, he say. Got to have loose sleeves. And definitely you not spose to wear it with no tie. Folks wearing ties look like they being lynch" (290).

The clothes that Celie and Mr. _____ design celebrate rather than restrict people; they become a symbol of the humanist/ womanist utopia manifested at the end of the novel. Indeed, this utopia becomes an Edenic paradise, as Thadious M. Davis suggests, for the arrival of Celie's son, Adam Omatangu, and the rest of her family from Africa

signals the continuity of generations, the return (ironically perhaps) to the 'old, unalterable roots.' Their return is cause for a larger hope for the race, and for celebration within the family and community, because they have survived 'whole,' literally since they miraculously survive a shipwreck and symbolically since they have acquired definite life-affirming attitudes. (52)

This is precisely the note on which the novel ends, since the new order, the order that opens to the once segregated, is celebratory: "White people busy celebrating they independence from England July 4th, say Harpo, so most black folks don't have to work. Us can spend the day celebrating each other" (294). To paraphrase Martin, in Walker's comedy, the female/black incongruous is seen to be more congruous than the white patriarchy, which made them incongruous in the first place by denying them entry into its closed society.

Therefore, while it may seem "incongruous" to classify *The Color Purple* as a comedy, it cannot truly be called anything else, for it seeks to improve society by eliminating the limitations prescribed by the societal norms. Meredith stresses that where "the veil is over women's faces, you cannot have society, without which the senses are barbarous and the Comic Spirit is driven to the gutters to slake its thirst" (31). In *The Color Purple*, the "veil," of which Meredith speaks, is lifted, the barriers between the sexes are razed, and a new world is erected on the ruins, in which the sexes meet on an equal footing and celebrate each other, life, and humankind.

NOTES

1. I am indebted to Linda Hutcheon for showing me the significance of this aspect of the novel.

2. Romance too offers a utopia in its conclusion. However, romance offers idealized characters and incorporates other-worldly elements (Frye, *Anatomy* 186–95). To suggest that *The Color Purple* belongs to this genre, I think, would be to stretch a point. However, Frye does suggest that comedy will often overlap with romance in its conclusion (177) which seems to me to be the case here.

3. The similarity of the two male protagonists' names (Mr.and Mr. B.) further supports the idea that the novel plays on Richardson's text.

4. Names are very important in this novel. Walker dramatizes the idea that when we name we possess, and as a result, the women reject the names accorded them by the patriarchy. On the other hand, Mr. _____ is also transformed into Albert when he sees the "errors of his ways" and convinces Celie of his sincere repentance. He, therefore, must be renamed to signify his renewal and his incorporation into the new order. It is also interesting to note that he loses the title— Mr._____ which is used, to some extent, to subjugate Celie.

5. It is also symbolized in Celie's dialectal language which is preferred as natural and supportive of life. When she is given a chance to "improve" her speech, she says, "only a fool would want to talk in a way that feel peculiar to your mind" (223).

WORKS CITED

Abrams, M. H. *A Glossary of Literary Terms*, 4th ed. New York: Holt, 1981.

Bergson, Henri. "Laughter." *Comedy*. Ed. Wylie Sypher. New York: Doubleday, 1956.

Cuddon, J. A. *A Dictionary of Literary Terms*. Harmondsworth: Penguin, 1982.

Davis, Thadious M. "Alice Walker's Celebration of Self in Southern Generations." *The Southern Quarterly: A Journal of the Arts in the South*. 21.4 (1983): 39–53.

Feibleman, James K. "The Meaning of Comedy." *Aesthetics*. Toronto: Collins, 1949.

Frye, Northrop. *Anatomy of Criticism: Four Essays*. Princeton: Princeton University Press, 1973.

_____. "The Argument of Comedy." *Theories of Comedy*. Ed. Paul Lauter. New York: Doubleday, 1964.

Hutcheon, Linda. *A Theory of Parody: The Teachings of Twentieth Century Art Forms*. New York: Metheun, 1985.

Martin, Robert Bernard. "Notes Toward a Comic Fiction." *The Theory of the Novel*. Ed. John Halperin. New York: Oxford University Press, 1974.

Meredith, George. "An Essay on Comedy." *Comedy*. Ed. Wylie Sypher. New York: Doubleday, 1956.

Sypher, Wylie. "The Meanings of Comedy." *Comedy*. Ed. Wylie Sypher. New York: Doubleday, 1956.

Walker, Alice. *The Color Purple*. Pocket Books, 1982.

_____. *In Search of Our Mothers' Gardens*. New York: Harcourt, 1983.

Alice Walker: Poesy and the Earthling Psyche

Ikenna Dieke

In what has now become one of the most significant books of essays in the rich repertoire of African American critical hypotheses—*In Search of Our Mothers' Gardens*—Alice Walker enunciates what amounts to a thematic and quasi ideological preoccupation of an artistic imagination that might well be dubbed the earthling subjectivity. Firing back justifiably at a reader's disparaging remarks that the daughter of a farmer (such as Walker is) could not possibly become the material out of which great poets are made,[1] Walker insists that the grubstake out of which the poet constructs or entifies the world of her art must have its essential provenance in the humble affairs of the common people for whom she clearly writes. Contrasting her humble, indigent beginnings with that of the young John Keats, whom the reader apparently cited in his criticism, Walker dismisses as baseless reverie the presumption that the only good poet is the one who salivates and mimics Keats or those of his privileged background. She concludes by insisting, very much in the spirit and tradition of Langston Hughes, that poetry written for and about the common people, for and about one's own people, is infinitely more ennobling, and therefore more satisfying, than that gaudy stuff composed exclusively for and about the stiff upper lip royal court of England (*In Search*, 18).

If we put aside, for the moment, Walker's oblique and sardonic swipe at the English monarchy, the phrase "Queen of England" (royal court of England) should be construed as an intensive troping of the concept of art as the domain of the privileged aristocracy. By this phrase, Walker seeks to highlight the marked difference between some art, which grows out of an inspired response to the ordinary, the commonplace, the experiences of common people, and the other, which has as its primary donnée the high and mighty in society—the privileged elite. It is a distinction between the high mimetic art and that of the low mimetic.[2] In other words, at least as Ms. Walker sees it, the enduring aspect of art is the artist's uncanny ability to hallow the commonplace, to imagine the limitless possibility of the extraordinary in the common run of affairs—in the words of Ralph Waldo Emerson, to see the miraculous in the ordinary everyday reality (qtd. McNulty, 114—15). Barbara Christian explains what this means in terms of Walker's own "unique" populist conception of Art:

But Walker turned the idea of art on its head. Instead of looking high, she suggested, we should look low. On that low ground she found a multitude of artist-mothers—the women who'd transformed the material to which they'd had access into their conception of Beauty: cooking, gardening, quilting, storytelling. In retrieving that low ground, Walker not only reclaimed her foremothers, she pointed to a critical approach. For she reminded us that Art, and the thought and sense of beauty on which it is based, is the province not only of those with a room of their own, or of those in libraries, universities and literary Renaissances—that *creating* is necessary to those who work in kitchens and factories, nurture children and adorn homes, sweep streets or harvest crops, type in offices or manage them. ("Highs and Lows" 573)

This "low ground" sensibility is displayed at every level of her writing, but most particularly energetically in her poetry. In fact, her poetry, from *Once* to *Revolutionary Petunias*, and from *Good Night, Willie Lee, I'll See You in the Morning* to *Horses Make a Landscape Look More Beautiful*, reads like a grand pastoral metaphor of the earthling consciousness, which indeed is an attempt to redeem through the poetic medium a world thought to be of little worth or importance—what is commonly known in Anglo-American literature of the seventeenth, eighteenth, and nineteenth centuries as the low mimetic sensibility. It is very much like dining with Keats and being swept off one's feet by his doctrine of *negative capability*—"the abandoning of one's self to a selfless sympathy with common everyday things" (McNulty 109).

Walker's poetry, therefore, like the verse of John Greenleaf Whittier; Thomas Gray; Robert Burns; Oliver Goldsmith; the sage of Walden, Henry David Thoreau; Walt Whitman; and William Wordsworth, does significantly share in many of the essential motifs of the earthling subjectivity, motifs neatly jelled and goulashed in the unique cadences of the familiar and the commonplace in the experiences of a woman of color in America and beyond. The essential characteristic elements of this earthling subjectivity are expressed through a preoccupation with certain themes and concerns.

First, the imagination that informs the earthling psyche is an imagination that originates from the artist's/poet's concern with the affairs of common people. According to J. Bard McNulty, the earthling or low mimetic psyche is informed by a certain verisimilitude and mimetic power, since the experiences it seeks to construct, or in some cases reconstruct, strike us as being true to life (108). This quasi-populist realism intersects with feminism, or better yet, womanism, in that the focus of its subject now shifts from a concern with dominating powers and wills to an interest, in fact, a sympathy, with the lowly and the commonalty, their hopes and aspirations, their secret dreams and disappointments, their sadnesses and moments of incandescent joy, even personal triumphs. In fact, appealing to the common run of people and things is for Walker a measure of power, both in a personal and in a political sense.

In "Remember," the first poem in Walker's fourth poetry collection, *Horses Make a Landscape Look More Beautiful*, the poet assumes the persona of one who evokes and honors the memory of an unassuming, humble, almost self-effacing young girl "with dark skin/ whose shoes are thin." With characteristic modesty, the girl declares: "I am the girl /with rotted teeth/ I am the dark/ rotten-toothed girl/ with the wounded eye/ and the melted ear." Her nobility and her almost reticent dignity comes not from class or high birth, but rather from her humanness, in other words, her capacity to respond to and satisfy human needs and desires. She is the one on whom we always call to hold our babies, to cook our meals, to sweep our yards and to launder our clothes. But in spite of her meekness and lowly dispostion, or perhaps because of that, she achieves, at least in the eyes of the poet, the highest honor and distinction as the repository of hope for humanity—hope for regenerative healing and wholeness.

In "Ballad of the Brown Girl," the twenty-third poem in her first volume of poetry, *Once: Poems*, Walker writes about the tragic suicide of an ordinary girl of color. The reason for her suicide is that she lives in a society that does not tolerate interracial love relationships. The poet's sympathy is unquestionably with the girl. In fact, the last lines, a question, are meant to dramatize in bold relief the poet's anger and dismay, dismay at the fact that "here love fails to cross the racial barrier" (Winchell 11).

In the first movement/canto of *Revolutionary Petunias*, Walker's second poetry volume, the poems, "Burial" and "Women" continue this sympathetic interest in the affairs of common people. In "Burial," the occasion is a solemn one, the burial of the poet's father's grandmother, Sis Rachel Walker, alias "Oman." In a tone reminiscent of Thomas Gray's persona in "Elegy Written in a Country Churchyard," the speaker visits the gravesite of her immediate departed forebears and surveys the sense of neglect and desolation brought on by the passage of time. She grieves over the fact that alone she mourns amidst the crumbling tombstones that once "mark[ed] my family's graves." She is particularly distraught because what is supposed to be a final resting place of honor for the dead has now been turned into a place of near disuse and of obsolescence. The place where once stood the grieving mourners at the funeral ceremonies for her departed family members has become a weft of weedy pasture where the transhumant cattle now graze with ardent abandon. But the poet, despite all that, is still interested in renewing her contact with the cult of the dead, mindful of "the old, unalterable roots" that supply a large chunk of the emotional and social matrix that binds her to them.

In "Women," the poet turns historicist and pays homage to a generation of black women—contemporaries of her mother—ordinary women with tireless industry who have achieved extraordinarily. Their raw physical strength, their fortitude and endurance expressed metaphorically as "Headragged Generals," and their pioneering work in minority education—all are, for the poet, decisive terms of personal endearment. The politics of primogenitorial memory and the passionate intensity of remembering these otherwise ordinary womenfolk is consistent with Walker's avowal to keep the tradition and memory of African American women alive and to let that be a constant source of inner strength and personal wholeness (*In Search* 36).

In "Did This Happen to Your Mother? Did Your Sister Throw Up a Lot?," the first poem in Walker's third volume of poetry, *Good Night, Willie Lee, I'll See You in the Morning*, we have the simple tale of a colored woman forlon of love. Deserted by a man she thought she loved, she swears that "I love a man who is not worth/ my love," and that the same "love has made me sick." Love, that special sense of warm attachment and sympathetic tenderness, has become instead one long, woe-be-gone chapter of lies, deception, and cunning. As a result, she feels a gorgelike emptiness inside, an emptiness she compares to the massive depth of the Arizona Grand Canyon.

> My hand shakes before this killing
> My stomach sits jumpy in my chest
> My chest is the Grand Canyon
> sprawled empty
> over the world.

And yet her lovelornness is not hers alone. She shares the same fate with a host of other women, who at one point or another in their chequered lives have had to endure the unsettling disappointments and humiliations of unrequited love.

Aside from depicting the ordinary scheme of everyday reality and the people that loom in it, another way in which Walker exemplifies her earthling subjectivity is through the hallowing of the place of nature in the lives of ordinary people. For Walker, the creative mind that perceives nature is an attingent traditional mind that hallows and celebrates the reciprocal dependence of internal and external processes of natural ambience. In other words, part of Walker's earthling consciousness is focused on the sympathetic symbiosis between her creative intellect and the natural environment. In this symbiosis, the natural environment is not perceived as "other," but instead as an essential part in the expression of one's individuality (in this case the individuality of the poet) as well as one's reciprocal relation to other people, that is, other members of one's community.

The one place where Alice Walker reflects this coordinative and organic perception of nature is in "African Images, Glimpses from a Tiger's Back," one of the longest poems in *Once*. The poem begins:

> Beads around
> my neck
> Mt. Kenya away over pineappled hills
> kikuyu land.

The proximity of Mt. Kenya and the pineappled hills to Kikuyu land is hardly fortuitous. It speaks to as well as amplifies the interfusion of nature in the lives of the people of Kenya. The poet is acutely aware of how closely human life here is integrated with physical nature. The pineappled hills, which appear as interlacing arches that weave the lives and destinies of the people, suggest that the people autochtonous to the Kikuyu land are farmers whose contact with the earth is fixed, almost like an ineluctable fate or inexorable necessity. When the poet says:

> A book of poems
> Mt. Kenya's/ Bluish peaks
> "Wangari!"/ My new name,

she suggests that from nature the woman artist draws everything, even herself. Consequently, the poetry that she composes is, like nature itself, ultimately concerned with the generative forces of being. For Walker this affinity between benign nature and artistic self situates and defines the essential matrix of her ecofeminist sensibility. We would return to this point a little later.

Meanwhile, the imposing majesty of Mt. Kenya, strewn across the elongated ridge of "pineappled hills," parallels the graceful charm, the virid brilliance of the "beads around my neck," offering the visiting poet to East Africa her real conception of beauty as well as the language in which to express it. Besides, in an esemplastic imagination akin to Wordsworth's in "Tintern Abbey" and *The Prelude*, the conflation of "a book of poems" and the "bluish peaks" of Mt. Kenya suggests that nature is a creative force to which the human mind (but especially that of the earthling poet) is "exquisitely fitted."[3] It points up the manner in which nature goes about its kind of imaginative creation. According to McNulty, "the process is the 'express resemblance' of the process of imagination in the human mind" (112).

Furthermore, the act of taking on a new name suggests that nature provides the fundamental essence of the process of naming built into the consciousness of the indigenous people. The formal endowment of the praise/heroic epithet "Wangari" upon the visiting poet, apparently by the august assembly of the elders, and the cotangent and correlative processes of naming in the Kikuyu and Leopard clans underscore the unique ontological signification of nature in the thinking of traditional Africans, a thinking that Ernst Cassirer has described as "the myth-making consciousness" (qtd. Obiechina 82). This myth-making consciousness further demonstrates how traditional peoples like the Kikuyus assign names that bear the tutelary influence of primogenitor/ancestor and how the unique dimensions of clan psychology, which manifest in a variety of formal ritual inductions or initiation rites, all relate to the unique primitialization of nature.

The poet is so delighted, so enthralled by the majestic blossom, the almost enchanting comeliness of the East African topography, the distant peaks and virid vistas spread before her very eyes, that she cannot help but catalogue its manifold beauty with a flurry of images. Walker's poetic intelligence is able to transform the grandeur of the manifold objects of sense into an expression of an indissolvable unity of universal poetic thought. This expression reminds us of Plato, for whom "the world of Nature is the expression of an all-dissolving Unity of which the prevailing features are truth and beauty" (Bryan 2–3).

With a technique akin to cinematography, the poet-visitor takes the reader on a guided panoramic tour of the East African landforms. First, the poet, from the relative security and comfort of her safari, peers at "a green copse" and "a shy gazelle" and an elephant bulldozing her way through the shifting rents of the morning mists. Next she looks out on "the clear Nile" inside of which "a fat crocodile/ scratches his belly and yawns." Then the tropical evergreen woodland of the African rain forest comes clearly into view, lush with red orchids and the spinning cobra. From here, under the overarching blue sky, the poet sails gently through on "a placid lake" in "a small boat," then through another "silent lake" along "bone strewn banks/ Luminous/ In the sun." Earlier the poet had stroked the water buffalo and the two ears of the mammoth hippopotamus with his hand, seen a leopard zap effortlessly through the branches of trees, a giraffe "munching his dinner," while off yonder on a high rise are Uganda mountains with their black soil and white snow, "and in the valley/Zebra."

There is hardly any doubt from the foregoing that our earthling poet on an exhilarating African safari reserves deep appreciation of and respect for nature, its kaleidoscope of sights and sounds and colors, as well as the intense emotions they stir. The uniqueness of the verdant culture of an East African landscape is a source of incandescent joy for the poet. The safari itself amounts to a kind of initiatory rite. Besides, the topography, especially the verdure of the rain forest, reflects the culture of the indigenous people who occupy it and eke out their livelihood off it. All of that now unfolds before the travelling poet's eye in endless undulations of varying greens, all blending in a delightful, stark harmony of form and texture and color and atmosphere.

In "Torture," the thirty-eighth poem in *Horses Make a Landscape Look More Beautiful*, nature takes on the function of the healer, the regenerative anodyne, serving to assuage the pain and trauma of life, to soothe, to calm and comfort in a moment of grief or seemingly irreparable loss.

> When they torture your mother/ plant a tree
> When they torture your father/ plant a tree
> When they torture your brother/ and your sister
> plant a tree/ When they assassinate/ your leaders
> and lovers/ plant a tree/ When they torture you
> too bad/ to talk/ plant a tree.

The juxtaposition of dissimilar acts of torturing and soothing, of damage and reparation, in the process of self-renewal, intensifies the healing and restorative power of nature. The poet ends his moral admonition with these words:

> When they begin to torture
> the trees
> and cut down the forest
> they have made start another.

Here Walker's ecofeminist sympathies ring clear and loud. The speaker is enjoining us to feel the life of the "other"——the natural ambience. She is enjoining us to feel a compassion for nature of which the tree and the forest are but synecdochic symbols. According to Judith Plant in *Healing the Wounds: The Promise of Ecofeminism*, "this compassion is the essence of a new paradigm," of the moral necessity of grieving for the loss of our sisters and brothers who are the forests. "Our pain," continues Plant, "for the death of the forests is simply, and most fundamentally, compassion for the senseless destruction of life" (1).

The truth that the poet adduces with her injunction is that we are part of this earth, and that fact must predispose us to see "how relations with each other are reflected in our relations with the natural world." Here Walker's message, like that of the ecofeminist spiritualists, becomes "a praxis of hope," the hope "that like the forests we destroy, or the rivers we tame, we are Nature" (Griffin 10). In her prose work *Living by the Word*, Walker notes how, when she was residing in the northern hills of California, she had witnessed almost with helplessness the daily horror of the loggers' (she calls them "hearses") as they felled the trees and carried, in her own words, "the battered bodies of the old sisters and brothers" (qtd. Winchell 112). She also relates another incident at a national park during which she gazed at some gnarled, diseased old trees. "What the trees tell her," writes Winchell, "is that when it comes to human beings, trees do not discriminate; all people must share the guilt for the destruction being done to the planet and all its life forms" (Winchell 112). Again Walker writes in *Living by the Word*:

Our thoughts must be on how to restore to the Earth its dignity as a living being; how to stop raping and plundering it as a matter of course. We must begin to develop the consciousness that everything has equal rights because existence itself is equal. In other words, we are all here: trees, people, snakes, alike. (qtd. Winchell 112)

In fact, planting a tree, from the perspective of the poem "Torture," has become for the speaker a vehicle for, in the words of Joanna Macy, "awakening to the ecological self," in which "conventional, customary notions of self and self-interest are being shed like an old skin or confining shell" (201). And the person doing the planting itself has come into a new covenant that transcends separateness and fragmentation. By planting another tree or starting another forest, the planter is no longer just trying to secure it from mindless deforestation, but rather she herself has become a part of the forest protecting herself. She has become that part of nature recently emerged into human thinking.[4] The transition from the grisly scenarios of mindless sadists and assassins to the interdependent/symbiotic plane of regenerative nature is analogous to what Hazel Henderson has described as the shift in consciousness from "phenotype" to "genotype." Henderson writes:

We may be emerging from the "age of the phenotype," of separated ego awareness, which has now become amplified into untenable forms of dualism. The emerging view is rebalancing toward concern for the genotype, protection of species and gene pools and the new intergenerational risks being transferred to our progeny, about which economics says little. (qtd. Macy 210)

A third and final way in which Walker engages her earthling imagination is by a systematic attempt to understand her own personality, a kind of personalist idealism, beyond axiological or moral categories. She does that by asserting her own thoughts, feelings, perceptual experiences, and valuations. The attempt also involves the unique interplay of character, ego, and circumstance vis-à-vis the workings of the artistic intelligence evinceable within the processes of imaginative creation. In her essay "The Black Woman Artist as Wayward," Barbara Christian suggests that the main distinguishing mark between Walker's poetry and her prose is that the former is a graph of the Alice Walker self. She writes: "In her poetry, Walker the wayward child challenges us to accept her as she is. Perhaps it is the stripping of bark from herself that enables us to feel that sound of the genuine in her scrutiny of easy positions advocated by progressive blacks and women" (53).

There are many poems in which Walker shows this interest in self and introspective self-analysis. But six of them especially stand out as the most eloquent expression of the trinity of feeling, condition, and character of the poet's self. Each of them, by sheer eloquence of voice and candor, reveals an aspect of the poet's personality predominant at a given time and under certain definable conditions. That personality often is a unique mark of an individual who has grown, fashioned as it were by the processes of self-fertilization/self-pollination beyond easy categories of self-abasement and/or social adaptation.

For Walker the graph of self that Christian speaks about is the ideology of the experience of the self as the essential arbiter of reality. That ideology celebrates autonomy as a fundamental individual right that must not be violated or vitiated by a sentimental or even the most pious appeal to collective experience. It is the ideology of self that Professor Mihaly Csikszentmilhalyi has described as "the autotelic self"—a self that has self-contained goals" (207). It is a self that fiercely asserts and guards the validity and integrity of her own experience, a validity and integrity that requires no other validation either morally, socially, or culturally. The epitome of this self is revealed most trenchantly in Walker's "On Stripping Bark from Myself," one of the most significant poems in *Good Night, Willie Lee, I'll See You in the Morning.*

The sheer audacity of voice with which this self announces her presence on this earth is unmistakable. The announcement, which sounds almost bellicose, comes down like a peal of thunder. It is as if out of the nebulous depths of social conformism and conditioned selves, a new ego wrapped in sympathetic eros emerges to claim her place in the logos of the world. The speaker says:

> I find my own
> Small person
> a standing self
> against the world
> an equality of wills
> I finally understand.

But the audacity is somewhat weaned within the rhetoric of the underdog, which is intended not so much to elicit sentimental sympathy as it is to warn the world, which is traditionally accustomed to taking advantage of small people, that this time there is and must be a new deal. And the new deal, which in figuratively coextensive terms subserves the agonistic mythos of David and Goliath, is a bold vision of the world as a level playing field where small people and big people, rich people and poor people, the advantaged and the disadvantaged, live each their own space as they see fit without any of them ever assuming for one moment that what is good and right for one is necessarily good and right for another. It is an intensely relativistic world in which patterns of responses need not be the patterns of responses shared with others dictated by society or political correctness, but instead patterns of responses shared with others dictated solely by the individual's defined needs and desires. In this regard, the self becomes the critical medium through which collective responses and sentiments are distilled and/or crystallized.

Thus when the self swears direly:

No I am finished with living
for what my mother believes
for what my brother and father defend
for what my lover elevates
for what my sister, blushing, denies or rushes to embrace,

she is warning that often what is passed off as the collective outlook of conventional wisdom from which all reality must receive its legitimating authority is no longer tenable. Back in the days when women were "expected to keep silent about/ their close escapes," and felt content with living the lie that society's conditioning and customary sanctions had imposed on them, that might have sounded perfectly normal. Back in the days when women could not see themselves outside of the assigned roles and normative constructs in society, and others could not see them independently of those roles and constructs, the kind of deviation and subversion of "the common will" contemplated, even idealized, by the Walker self here might have seemed too indefinable, even dangerous. Other poems in which Walker explores the assertive will of the self include, but are not limited to, "So We've Come at Last to Freud and "Mornings/of an Impossible Love" (*Once*); "Sunday School, Circa 1950," "Will," "Rage," "Beyond What," and "Reassurance" (*Revolutionary Petunias*); and "On Stripping Bark from Myself" and "Early Losses: A Requiem" (*Good Night, Willie Lee, I'll See You in the Morning*). In each one of these poems, the capacity and freedom to launch out on a "ruthless" pursuit of one's inwardness is systematically vocalized and indulged. In other words, Walker's intent, as always, is to find her own personal turf and ultimately, this turf is in accord with the thoughts of Hermann Hesse as vocalized in *Demian*:

Each man had only one genuine vocation—to find the way to himself. He might end up as a poet or madman, as prophet or criminal—that was not his affair, ultimately it was of no concern. His task was to discover his own destiny—not an arbitrary one—and live it out wholly and resolutelywithin himself. Everything else was only a would-be existence, an attempt at evasion, a flight back to the ideas of the masses, conformity and fear of one's own inwardness. (qtd. Miller 112)

In closing, I want to return to the repartee with which I began this essay, namely Walker's verbal sally against the white northerner. It is not so much that John Keats was opposed to the earthling idealism. As a matter of fact, Keats, through his aesthetic doctrine of *negative capability*, not only preached about it, but in fact practiced it in much of his poetry. It is not so much that Keats was white, and Alice Walker black. Instead it is that Walker is making a point about the immanent necessities of poetic thought, in other words, the contingent phenomenality of earthly experience, which some people, like the white northerner, would rather ignore or relegate to the backyard. But Walker through her poetry reminds us of the ineluctability of poetic art as the immanent act of the mind and the relation of that mind to perceptual experience. What some people mistakenly call the transcendence with which they identify certain writings and writers is nothing but an epistemic category of a continuum involving a vital relationship with objects in the material universe and the transcendental universal forms or ideas of which they are mere embodiments.

Thus the earthling psyche can be appropriately defined as the immanent act of the artistic mind that celebrates immanent reality, a consciousness of the pursuits and interests of earthly life, including the consciousness of immaterial essences captured in the objective, as well as those elements such as emotions, sentiments, thoughts, and sensations that constitute the unique dimensions of the subjectivity and identity of a person. It embodies a somewhat primitivistic, quasi-theologic view of reality in which the earth as a whole is conceived as the primal or numinous source of terrestrial life. Its characteristic elements include, but are not limited to, a flair for the commonplace in the affairs of common people, an impassioned animist-ecologist celebration of nature, an exploration of the phenomenal self, and sometimes an engagement in a kind of mild, verbal satirical wit.[5]

NOTES

1. Walker identifies this reader as "a white Northerner." As the daughter of indigent sharecropper parents from rural Eatonton, Georgia, Walker, naturally, is offended by the reader's reckless insensitivity and elitist pose. See Donna Winchell's *Alice Walker* (Boston: Twayne, 1992), especially p. 15.

2. For a note on the differences between the two, see McNulty, pp. 108–9. And for a summary of the low mimetic characteristics, see p. 127. I would like to take the opportunity to acknowledge my indebtedness to McNulty's discussion of the low mimetic era in English and Anglo-American literature, and to categorically state that his discussion alone is the main inspiration for my theory of the earthling imagination.

3. For a fuller discussion of the technique employed by low mimetic authors such as Wordsworth to explain the creative essence of nature, see McNulty, especially pages 111–14, 118–25.

4. Joanna Macy characterizes the understanding of the significance of this relationship as an "ecological sense of selfhood" (202). Macy also recalls, in particular, a visit to and a walk through the jungle of eastern Australia:

One day, under the vine-strung jungle trees of eastern Australia, I was walking with my friend John Seed, director of the Rainforest Information Center. I asked him how he managed to overcome despair and sustain the struggle against the mammoth lumber interests. He said, "I try to remember that it's not me, John Seed, trying to protect the rainforest. Rather I am part of the rainforest protecting myself, I am that part of the rainforest recently emerged into human thinking." (202)

5. Some of the poems in which Walker displays her satirical wit include: "First, They Said," "Listen," "We Alone," "Killers," "Songless," "A Few Sirens," "SM," "Attentiveness," and "The Diamonds on Liz's Bosom" (*Horses Make a Landscape Look More Beautiful*); "Sunday School, Circa 1950" (*Revolutionary Petunias*); "Janie Crawford"

(*Good Night, Willie Lee, I'll See You in the Morning)*; and "On Being Asked to Leave a Place of Honor for One of Comfort" (*Once*).

WORKS CITED

Bloom, Harold, ed. *Alice Walker*. New York: Chelsea House, 1989.

Bryan, J. Ingram. *The Interpretation of Nature in English Poetry*. Tokyo: Folcroft Library, 1972.

Christian, Barbara. "The Black Woman Artist as Wayward." In *Alice Walker*. Ed. Harold Bloom. 39–58.

_____. "The Highs and Lows of Black Feminist Criticism." In *The Woman that I Am: The Literature and Culture of Contemporary Women of Color*. Ed. D. Soyini Madison. New York: St. Martin's, 1994. 573–78.

Csikszentmilhalyi, Mihaly. "The Autotelic Self." *Reading Critically, Writing Well*. 3rd edition. Ed. Rise B. Axelrod and Charles R. Cooper. New York: St Martin's, 1993. 207–10.

Griffin, Susan. "Split Culture." In *Healing the Wounds: The Promise of Ecofeminism*. Ed. Judith Plant. 7–17.

Macy, Joanna . "Awakening to the Ecological Self." In *Healing the Wounds: The Promise of Ecofeminism*. Ed. Judith Plant. 201–11.

McNulty, J. Bard. *Modes of Literature*. Boston: Houghton Mifflin, 1977.

Miller, James E. *Word, Self, Reality: The Rhetoric of Imagination*. New York: Dodd, Mead, 1974.

Obiechina, Emmanuel. *Culture, Tradition and Society in the West African Novel*. Cambridge: Cambridge University Press, 1975.

Plant, Judith, ed. *Healing the Wounds: The Promise of Ecofeminism*. Philadelphia: New Society Publishers, 1989.

Walker, Alice. *Good Night, Willie Lee, I'll See You in the Morning*. New York: Dial Press, 1979.

_____. *Her Blue Body Everything We Know: Earthling Poems 1965–1990 Complete*. New York: Harcourt Brace Jovanovich, 1991.

_____. *Horses Make a Landscape Look More Beautiful*. San Diego: Harcourt Brace Jovanovich, 1984.

_____. *In Search of Our Mothers' Gardens*. San Diego: Harcourt Brace Jovanovich, 1983.

_____. *Once: Poems*. New York: Harcourt, Brace and World, 1968.

_____. *Revolutionary Petunias and Other Poems*. New York: Harcourt Brace Jovanovich, 1973.

Winchell, Donna. *Alice Walker*. Boston: Twayne, 1992.

Appendix: Chronology

1944	Born to sharecropping parents Willie Lee and Minnie Tallula (Grant) Walker-February 9 in a small rural town of Eatonton, Georgia.
1952	Wounded in her right eye with a BB gun wielded by one of her brothers. This incident would later have a profound effect on Walker, leading to the kind of intense, inexorable self-consciousness discernible in all her writing.
1961	Matriculates at the prestigious Spelman College in Atlanta, GA.
1963-1965	Transfers from Spelman to Sarah Lawrence College. Takes a summer trip to Mother Africa. Goes through the harrowing trauma of an abortion following an unintended pregnancy. Composes two landmark pieces: "To Hell with Dying," her first ever published short story, and *Once: Poems*, her first volume of poetry.
1965-1966	Graduates from Sarah Lawrence. Participates in successful voter registration in Liberty County, GA. Becomes an active worker for the Civil Rights Movement in racist Mississippi.
1966	Becomes the Breadloaf Writer's Conference Scholar.
1967	Wins first prize in the American Scholar essay contest for her penetrating essay, "The Civil Rights Movement: What Good Was It?" Marries the Civil Rights attorney Melvyn Roseman Leventhal and together, they have one child, daughter Rebecca, now a Yale graduate.
1968	Publishes her first book of poems—*Once: Poems*. Takes up appointment as writer-in-residence and Black Studies professor at Jackson State University (then Jackson State College), Jackson, MS.
1969	Assumes a new teaching post at Tougaloo College, Tougaloo, MS.
1970	Commences work on her important short story, "The Revenge of Hannah Kemhuff." Begins her crucial search for Zora Neale Hurston. Publishes her first novel, *The Third Life of Grange Copeland*.
1971-1972	Becomes a Radcliffe Institute Fellow

1972   While still serving as Fellow at the Radcliffe Institute, takes up con-
                       current visiting professorship positions at both Wellesley College and
                       the Boston Campus of the University of Massachusetts.

1973   Publishes two important works *Revolutionary Petunias* her second
                       volume of poetry; and *In Love and Trouble: Stories of Black Women* her
                       first collection of short stories.
                       Wins two awards for *Revolutionary Petunias*-the National Book Award
                       and the Southern Regional Council Lillian Smith Award.
                       Mourns the loss of her dad Willie Lee.
                       Continues her personal crusade to salvage Zora Neale Hurston's name
                       from the ruins of critical neglect by visiting the dead writer's unmarked
                       grave in Eatonville, Florida.

1974-1975   Leaves Mississippi finally for New York where she lands a job as
                       contributing editor for *Ms.* magazine.
                       Publishes *Langston Hughes: American Poet*—a reader for minors.
                       Wins the American Academy of Arts & Letters Rosenthal Foundation
                       Award for *In Love and Trouble*.

1976   Publishes her second novel—*Meridian*.
                       Divorces Melvyn Leventhal.

1977   Receives a second McDowell Colony Fellowship.
                       Wins the Guggenheim Fellowship.

1978-1979   Relocates to San Francisco, thereby laying the ground for writing *The
                       Color Purple*.
                       Publishes her third volume of poetry—*Good Night, Willie Lee, I'll
                       See You in the Morning*.
                       Edits a reader—*I Love Myself When I Am Laughing . . . And Then
                       Again When I Am Looking Mean and Impressive: A Zora Neale
                       Hurston Reader*.

1981   Publishes her second collection of short stories—*You Can't Keep a
                       Good Woman Down*.

1982   Publishes her third and most polemical novel—*The Color Purple*.
                       Nominated for a National Book Critics Circle Award on account of *The
                       Color Purple*.
                       Named Distinguished Writer in Afro-American Studies at the University
                       of California Berkeley.
                       Becomes Fannie Hurst Professor of Literature at Brandeis University.

1983   Publishes her first volume of essays *In Search of Our Mothers'
                       Gardens: Womanist Prose*.
                       Wins the coveted Pulitzer Prize and the American Book Award for *The
                       Color Purple*.

1984   Publishes her fourth volume of poetry—*Horses Make a Landscape Look
                       More Beautiful*.
                       Wins the Townsend Prize for *The Color Purple*.
                       Sets up, in conjunction with former buddy Robert Allen, the Wild Trees
                       Press.

1988   Publishes two works—*To Hell With Dying*, and her second volume of essays *Living by the Word*.

1989   Publishes her fourth, ecofeminist novel—*The Temple of My Familiar*.

1991   Publishes her fifth volume of poetry—*Her Blue Body Everything We Know: Earthling Poems 1965-1990 Complete*.
                Publishes a children's story book—*Finding the Green Stone*-with Deeter Catherine.

1992   Publishes her fifth and unsettling novel—*Possessing the Secret of Joy*.

1993   Co-authors with Pratibha Parmar *Warrior Marks: Female Genital Mutilation and the Sexual Blinding of Women*.

1996   Publishes her soul-searching, confessional book—*The Same River Twice: Honoring the Difficult: A Meditation on Life, Spirit, Art, and the Making of the Film, The Color Purple, Ten Years Later*.

1997   Publishes a very candid, self-revealing book—*Anything We Love Can Be Saved: A Writer's Activism*.

1998   Publishes her sixth novel—*By the Light of My Father's Smile*.

Selected Bibliography

Abbandonato, Linda. "A View from 'Elsewhere': Subversive Sexuality and the Rewriting of the Heroine's Story in *The Color Purple.*" *PMLA* 6 (Oct 1991): 1106–1115.

Ajayi, Omofolabo. "Transcending the Boundaries of Power and Imperialism: Writing Gender, Constructing Knowlwdge." *African Women And Imperialism.* Ed. by Obi Nnaemeka and Ronke Oyewumi. Trenton, N.J.: Africa World Press, forthcoming.

Ansa, Tina McElroy. "Taboo Territory." Rev. of *Possessing the Secret of Joy*, by Alice Walker. *Los Angeles Times* 9 July 1992: BR 4+8.

Anshaw, Carol. "The Practice of Cruelty." Rev. of *Possessing the Secret of Joy*, by Alice Walker. *Chicago Tribune* 21 June 1992: sec.14,3.

Baker, Houston A., Jr. "Workings of the Spirit: Conjure and the Space of Black Women's Creativity." *Workings of the Spirit: The Poetics of Afro-American Women's Writings.* Chicago: University of Chicago Press, 1991.

Baker, Houston, and Charlotte Pierce-Baker. "Patches: Quilts and Community in Alice Walker's 'Everyday Use.'" *Alice Walker: Critical Perspectives Past and Present.* Ed. Henry Louis Gates and K.A. Appiah. New York: Amistad, 1993. 309–16.

Baraka, Imamu Amiri. "Other Aspects, Single Entity: Black Woman." *Black World* 19.9 (July 1970): 7–11.

Bates, Karen Grigsby. "Possessing The Secrets of $uccess: Toni Morrison is the Senior Member of a Triumphant Trio of Best-selling Writers." *Emerge: Black America's Newsmagazine* 4.1 (October 1992): 47–49.

Bauer, Margaret D. "Alice Walker: Another Southern Writer Criticizing Codes Not Put To 'Everyday Use.'" *Studies in Short Fiction* 29 (Spring 1992): 143–51.

Berry, Faith. "A Question of Publishers And A Question Of Audience." *The Black Scholar* 17.2 (March-April 1986): 41–49.

Bloom, Harold, ed. *Alice Walker.* New York: Chelsea House. 1989.

Bobo, Jacqueline "Sifting through the Controversy: Reading *The Color Purple.*" *Callaloo: An Afro-American and African Journal of Arts and Letters* 2.2 (Spring 1989): 332–42.

Brown, Joseph A. "'All Saints Should Walk Away':The Mystical Pilgrimage of Meridian." *Callaloo: An Afro-American and African Journal of Arts and Letters* 2.2 (Spring 1989): 310–20.

Butler, Cheryl B. "The Color Purple Controversy: Black Women Spectatorship." *Wide Angle: A Film Quarterly of Theory, Criticism, and Practice* 3.3&4 (1991): 62–69.

Butler, Robert James "Alice Walker's Vision of the South in *The Third life of Grange Copeland.*" *African American Review* 27.2 (Summer 1993): 195–204.

Byerman, Keith. *Fingering the Jagged Grain: Tradition and Form in Recent Black Fiction.* Athens, GA: University of Georgia Press, 1985.

_____. "Desire and Alice Walker: The Quest for a Womanist Narrative." *Callaloo: A Journal of Afro-American and African Arts and Letters* 12.2 (1989): 321–31.

Campbell, Jane. *Mythic Black Fiction: The Transformation of History.* Knoxville: University of Tennessee Press, 1986.

Campbell, Karlyn Kohrs. *Man Cannot Speak For Her.* Vol. 1. New York: Greenwood Press, 1989.

Christian, Barbara. *Black Feminist Criticism: Perspectives on Black Women Writers.* New York: Pergamon, 1985.

_____. "Alice Walker: The Black Woman Artist as Wayward." *Black Women Writers (1950-1980).* Ed. Mari Evans. New York: Anchor Books, 1984.

_____. *Black Women Novelists: The Development of a Tradition, 1892-1976.* Westport, CT: Greenwood Press, 1980.

Cixous, Hélène. "Sorties." *Modern Criticism and Theory.* Ed. David Lodge. Singapore: Longman, 1992. 293.

Cleage, Pearl. "A Stunning Journey for 'Joy.'" Rev. of *Possessing the Secret of Joy,* by Alice Walker. *Atlanta Journal* June 14, 1992: N8.

Coetzee, J.M. "The Beginnings of (Wo)man in Africa." Rev. of *The Temple of My Familiar,* by Alice Walker. *New York Times Book Review* 30 April 1990: 7.

Cooke, Michael G. *Afro-American Literature in the Twentieth Century: The Achievement of Intimacy.* New Haven: Yale University Press, 1984.

Courlander, Harold. *A Treasury of Afro-American Folklore.* New York: Crown, 1976.

Covino, William A. "Magic And/As Rhetoric: Outlines of a History of Phantasy." *Journal of Advanced Composition.* 12.2 (1992): 349–58.

_____. *Magic, Rhetoric, and Literacy: An Eccentric History of the Composing Imagination.* Albany: State University of New York Press, 1994.

Daly, Mary in Cahoots with Jane Caputi. *Webster's First New Intergalactic Wickedary of the English Language.* Boston: Beacon Press, 1987.

Davenport, Doris. "Afracentric Visions." Rev. of *The Temple of My Familiar,* by Alice Walker. *The Women's Review of Books* 6.12 (September 1989): 13–14.

Davis, Thadious. "Alice Walker's Celebration of Self in Southern Generations." *Women Writers of the Contemporary South.* Ed. Peggy Whitman Prenshaw. Jackson: University Press of Mississippi, 1984. 39–53.

Deleuze, Gilles, and Felix Guattari. *Kafka: Toward a Minor Literature.* Minneapolis: University of Minnesota Press, 1986.

Donahue, Deidre. "Walker's Disturbing 'Secret': Novelist Explores Trauma of the Mutilation of Women." Rev. of *Possessing the Secret of Joy,* by Alice Walker. *USA Today* 18 June 1992: D1.

Early, Gerald. "The Color Purple as Everybody's Protest Art." *The Antioch Review* 50.1&2 (Winter 1992): 399–412.

Ebony Book Shelf: The Color Purple. Rev. of *The Color Purple,* by Alice Walker. *Ebony* 37.12 (October 1982):26.

Evans, Mari, ed. *Black Women Writers (1950-1980): A Critical Evaluation.* Garden City, NY: Anchor-Doubleday. 1984. Section on Walker: 453–95.

Fontenot, Chester J. "Alice Walker: 'The Diary of an African Nun' and Dubois' Double Consciousness." *Journal of Afro-American Issues* 5 (1977): 192–96.

Gates, Henry Louis. *The Sygnifying Monkey: A Theory of Afro-American Literary Criticism.* New York: Oxford University Press, 1988.

Giddings, Paula. "Alice Walker's Appeal." Inter. with Alice Walker. *Essence* (July 1992): 58+

Gilbert, Sandra M., and Susan Gubar. *The Madwoman in the Attic: The Woman Writer and the Nineteenth Century Literary Imagination*. New Haven: Yale University Press, 1979.

_____. *No Man's Land: The Place of the Woman Writer in the Twentieth Century*. New Haven: Yale University Press, 1988.

Graham, Maryemma. "Skillful But Disturbing Novel." Rev of *The Color Purple*, by Alice Walker.. *Freedomways: A Quarterly Review of the Freedom Movement* 23.4 (1983): 278–80.

Harris, Trudier. "Folklore in the Fiction of Alice Walker: A Perpetuation of Historical and Literary Traditions." *Black American Literature Forum* 11 (Spring 1977): 3–8.

_____. "Three Black Women Writers and Humanism: A Folk Perspective." *Black American Literature and Humanism*. Ed. R. Baxter Miller. Lexington: The University Press of Kentucky, 1981. 50–74.

_____. "On *The Color Purple*, Stereotypes, And Silence." *Black American Literature Forum* 18.4 (1984): 155–61.

Henderson, Mae. "*The Color Purple*: Revisions and Redefinitions." *Alice Walker*. Ed. Harold Bloom. New York: Chelsea House, 1989. 67–80.

Hiers, John T. "Creation Theology in Alice Walker's *The Color Purple*." *Notes on Contemporary Literature* (September 1984): 2–3.

Hirsch, Marianne. "Clytemnestra's Anger: Writing (out) the Mother's Anger." *Alice Walker*. Ed. Harold Bloom. New York: Chelsea House, 1989. 195–213.

Hite, Molly. "Romance, Marginality, and Matrilineage: *The Color Purple*." *The Other Side of the Story: Structures and Strategies of Contemporary Feminist Narrative*. Ithaca: Cornell University Press, 1989. 103–126.

Hollister, Michael. "Tradition in Alice Walker's 'To Hell with Dying.'" *Studies in Short Fiction* 26.1 (Winter 1989): 90–94.

Holt, Sandra Waters, "A Rhetorical Analysis of Three Feminist Themes Found in the Novels of Toni Morrison, Alice Walker, and Gloria Naylor." *Dissertation Abstracts International*. 50.10 (Apr. 1990): 3224A.

hooks, bell. "Writing the Subject: Reading *The Color Purple*." *Alice Walker*. Ed. Harold Bloom. New York: Chelsea House, 1989. 215–228.

Hospital, Janette Turner. "What They Did to Tashi." Rev. of *Possessing the Secret of Joy*, by Alice Walker. *New York Times Book Review* 28 June 1992: 11–12.

Hurston, Zora Neale. *Mules and Men: Negro Folktales and Voodoo Practices in the South*. New York: Harper & Row, 1935.

Iannone, Carol. "A Turning of the Critical Tide?" *Commentary* (November 1989): 57–59.

Jackson, James E. "The Destructive Design of *The Color Purple*." *Political Affairs* (March 1986): 26–30.

Juncker, Clara. "Black Magic: Woman (ist) as Artist in Alice Walker's *The Temple of My Familiar*." *American Studies in Scandinavia* 24.1 (1992): 37–49.

Junega, Om P. "The Purple Colour of Walker's Women: Their Journey from Slavery to Liberation." *The Literary Criterion* 25.3 (1990): 66–76.

Kelly, Ernece B. "Walker Spins Moral Themes In Rich Tale." Rev. *The Temple of My Familiar*, by Alice Walker. *New Directions For Women* 18.3 (May-June 1989): 17.

Ladner, Joyce A. *Tomorrow's Tomorrow: The Black Woman*. Garden City, NY: Doubleday. 1971.

Laguerre, Michel S. *Voodoo and Politics in Haiti*. New York: St Martin's Press, 1989.

Larson, Charles R. "Against The Tyranny Of Tradition." Rev. of *Possessing the Secret of Joy*, by Alice Walker. *Washington Post* 5 July 1992: WBK 1+14.

LeGuin, Ursula K. "All Those at the Banquet." Rev. of *The Temple of My Familiar*, by Alice Walker. *San Francisco Review of Books* 14 (Summer 1989): 12–13.

Lenhart, Georgann. "Inspired Purple." *Notes on Contemporary Literature* (May 1984): 2–3.

Lenta, Margaret, "Comedy, Tragedy, and Feminism: The Novels of Richardson and Fielding." 26.1 *English Studies in Africa.* (1983): 13–26.

Lewis, T.W. III "Moral Mapping and Spiritual Guidance in *The Color Purple.*" *Soundings: An Interdisciplinary Journal* 73.2&3 (Summer-Fall 1990): 483–91.

Light, Alison "Fear of the Happy Ending: *The Color Purple*, Reading and Racism." *Essays and Studies* (1987): 103–17.

Mason, Theodore O., Jr. "Alice Walker's *The Third Life of Grange Copeland:* The Dynamics of Enclosure." *Callaloo: An Afro-American and African Journal of Arts and Letters* 12.2 (Spring 1989): 295–345.

Matthews, Anne. "Deciphering Victorian Underwear And Other Seminar; or How to be Profane, Profound and Scholarly—All the While Looking for a Job at the Modern Language Asociation's Annual Convention." *The New York Times Magazine.* February 10, 1991. 43+.

Mbiti, John S. *African Religions and Philosophy*. 2nd Edition. Oxford: Heinemann, 1990.

McHenry, Susan. "A Dialogue with Alice Walker." *Emerge: Black America's Newsmagazine* 3.10 (September 1992): 9–10.

Miller, Jane. *Women Writing About Men*. London: Virago, 1986.

Mitchell, Juliet, "Feminity, Narrative and Psychoanalysis." In *Modern Criticism and Theory*, Ed. David Lodge, Singapore: Longman, 1992. 430.

Murray, Pauli. "The Liberation of Black Women." *Voices of the New Feminism*. Ed. Mary Lou Thompson. Boston: Beacon Press. 1970. 87–102.

Nyabongo, V.S. "Rev. of *In Love & Trouble: Stories of Black Women*, by Alice Walker. *Books Abroad* 48.4 (Autumn 1974): 787.

O'Brien, John. Ed. *Interviews with Black Writers*. New York: Liveright, 1973. 186–211.

Ogunyemi, Chikwenye Okonjo. "Womanism: The Dynamics of the Contemporary Black Female Novel in English." *Signs: Journal of Women in Culture and Society* 11.1 (1985): 63–80.

O'Leary, Rev. Donald J. "On 'The Diary of an African Nun." *Freedomways* 9 (1969): 70–71.

Parker-Smith, Bettye J. "Alice Walker's Women: In Search of Some Peace of Mind." *Black Women Writers (1950-1980)*. Ed. Mari Evans. New York: Anchor Books, 1984. 478–493.

Perelman, Chaim. *The Realm of Rhetoric*. Trans. William Kluback. Notre Dame: University of Notre Dame Press, 1982.

Perry, Ruth, and Martine Watson Brownley, eds. *Mothering the Mind*. New York: Holmes and Meier, 1984.

Petry, Alice Hall. "Alice Walker: The Achievement of the Short Fiction." *Modern Language Studies* 19 (Winter 1989): 12–27.

Pinckney, Darryl. "Black Victims, Black Villains." Rev. of *The Color Purple*, by Alice Walker and "The Color Purple," by Steven Spielberg. *New York Review of Books* 29 Jan. 1987: 17–22.

Pratt, Louis H. "Alice Walker's Men: Profiles in the Quest for Love and Personal Values." *Studies in Popular Culture* 12.1 (November 1989): 42–57.

Prescott, Peter S. "A Long Road to Liberation." *Newsweek* 21 June 1982: 67–68.

Proudfit, Charles L. "Celie's Search for Identity: A Psychoanalytic Developmental Reading of Alice Walker's *The Color Purple.*" *Contemporary Literature* 32.1 (Spring 1991): 12–37.

Pullin, Faith. "Landscapes of Reality: The Fiction of Contemporary Afro-American Women." *Black Fiction: New Studies in the Afro-American Novel Since 1945.* Ed. A. Robert Lee. New York: Barnes and Noble, 1980. 173–203.

Rev. of *In Love & Trouble,* by Alice Walker. *Library Journal* 98.20. (15 November 1973): 3476.

Ridley, A. Chauncey "Animism and Testimony in Alice Walker's *The Color Purple.*" *MAWA Review* 4.2 (December 1989): 32–36.

Ross, Daniel W. "Celie in the Looking Glass: The Desire for Selfhood in *The Color Purple.*" *Modern Fiction Studies* 34.1 (Spring 1988): 69–84.

Royster, Philip M. "In Search of Our Fathers' Arms: Alice Walker's Persona of the Alienated Darling." *Black American Literature Forum* 20.4 (1986): 347–70.

Rubin, Merle. "Active Walker Reimagines the World." Rev. of *The Temple of My Familiar,* by Alice Walker. *Christian Science Monitor* 4 May 1989: 13.

Sadoff, Diane F. "Black Matrilineage: The Case of Alice Walker and Zora Neale Hurston." *Signs: Journal of Women in Culture and Society.* 11.1 (1985): 253–70.

Scholl, Diane Gabrielsen "With Ears to Hear and Eyes to See: Alice Walker's Parable *The Color Purple*" *Christianity and Literature* 40.3 (Spring 1991):255–66.

Showalter, Elaine, "Feminist Criticism in the Wilderness," in *Modern Criticism and Theory,* Ed. David Lodge. Singapore: Longman, 1992. 335.

_____. "Piercing and Writing." *The Poetics of Gender.* Ed. Nancy K. Miller. New York: Columbia University Press, 1986. 222–247.

Shapiro, Laura. Rev. of *Possessing the Secret of Joy,* by Alice Walker. *Newsweek* 8 June 1992: 56–57.

Siegel, Elaine V. *Female Homosexuality: Choice Without Volition.* Hillsdale, N.J.: The Analytic Press, 1988.

Smith, Barbara. "The Souls of Black Women." Rev. of *In Love & Trouble: Stories of Black Women,* by Alice Walker. *Ms* (February 1974): 42–43, 78.

Smith, Dinita. "'Celie, You a Tree.'" *Nation.* 4 Sept. 1982: 181–83.

Smith, Patricia A. "'Secret of Joy': Walker's Tender, Terrifying Tour de Force." Rev. of *Possessing the Secret of Joy,* by Alice Walker. *Boston Globe* 6 July 1992: 38.

Smith-Wright, Geraldine "Revision as Collaboration: Zora Neale Hurston's *Their Eyes Were Watching God* as Source for Alice Walker's *The Color Purple.*" *SAGE: A Scholarly Journal on Black Women* 4.2 (Fall 1987): 20–25.

Stade, George. "Womanist Fiction and Male Characters." *Partisan Review* 52.3 (1985): 264–70.

Tapahonso, Luci. "Learning to Love Through Storytelling." Rev. of *The Temple of My Familiar,* by Alice Walker. *Los AngelesTimes Book Review* 21 May 1989: 1, 13.

Tate, Claudia, ed. *Black Women Writers at Work.* New York: Continuum. 1983. 175–87, 193.

Teish, Luisah. *Jambalaya: The Natural Woman's Book of Personal Charms and Practical Rituals.* San Francisco: Harper, 1985.

Thomas, H Nigel "Walker's Grange Copeland as a Trickster Figure." *Obsidian II: Black Literature in Review* 6.1 (Spring 1991): 60–72.

_____. *From Folklore to Fiction: A Study of Folk Heroes and Rituals in the Black American Novel.* New York: Greenwood Press, 1988.

Towers, Robert. "Good Men are Hard to Find." Rev. of *The Terrible Two,* by Ishmael Reed and *The Color Purple,* by Alice Walker. *New York Review of Books* 12 August

1982: 35–36.

Turner, E. Daniel. "Cherokee and Afro-American Interbreeding in *The Color Purple.*" *Notes on Contemporary Literature* 21.5 (November 1991): 10–11.

Tuten, Nancy. "Alice Walker's 'Everyday Use.'" *Explicator* 51.2 (Winter 1993): 125–28.

Van Dyke, Annette. *The Search for a Woman-Centered Spirituality.* New York: New York University Press, 1992.

Walker, Alice. *The Color Purple.* New York: Washington Square Press, 1982.

_____. *In Search of Our Mothers' Gardens.* San Diego: Harcourt Brace Jovanovich, 1983.

_____. *In Love and Trouble: Stories of Black Women.* New York: Harcourt Brace Jovanovich, 1973.

_____. *Living By the Word: Selected Writings 1973-1987.* San Diego: Harcourt Brace Jovanovich, 1988.

_____. *Revolutionary Petunias and Other Poems.* New York: Harcourt Brace Jovanovich, 1973.

_____. "Finding Celie's Voice." *Ms.* December 1985.

_____. "Alice Walker's Reply." *Freedomways* 9 (1969): 71–73.

_____. "In the Closet of the Soul: A Letter to an African American Friend." *Ms.* November 1986: 32–33.

_____. *Meridian.* New York: Washington Square, 1976.

_____. *The Temple of My Familiar.* New York: Pocket Books, 1989.

_____. *The Third Life of Grange Copeland.* New York Pocket Books, 1970.

_____. *To Hell With Dying.* San Diego: Harcourt Brace Jovanovich, 1988.

Walker, Melissa. *Down From the Mountaintop: Black Women's Novels in the Wake of the Civil Rights Movement, 1966-1989.* New Haven: Yale University Press, 1991.

Wall, Wendy. "Lettered Bodies and Corporeal Texts in *The Color Purple.*" *Studies in American Fiction* 16.1 (Spring 1988): 83–97.

Washington, Mary Helen. "Black Women Myth and Image Makers." *Black World* August 1974: 10–18.

_____. "I Sign My Mother's Name: Alice Walker, Dorothy West, Paule Marshall." *Mothering the Mind.* Ed. Ruth Perry and Martine Watson Brownley. New York: Holmes and Meier, 1984.

_____. *Black-Eyed Susans: Classic Stories By and About Black Women.* Garden City, NY: Anchor Doubleday, 1979.

Watkins, Mel. "A Woman in Search of Her Past and Herself." Rev. of *Possessing the Secret of Joy,* by Alice Walker. *New York Times* 24 July 1992: C20.

Wesley, Richard. "Can Men Have It All? 'The Color Purple' Debate: Reading Between the Lines." *Ms.* (September 1986): 62, 90–92.

Whitaker, Charles. "Alice Walker: *The Color Purple* Author Confronts her Critics and Talks About Her Provocative New Book." *Ebony* (May 1992): 86–90.

Winchell, Donna Haisty. *Alice Walker.* Boston: Twayne, 1992.

Wolcott, James. "Party of Animals." Rev. of *The Temple of My Familiar,* by Alice Walker. *New Republic* 29 May 1989: 28–30.

Index

About the Contributors

DROR ABEND-DAVID is a doctoral candidate at New York University. A poet and short fiction writer, Abend-David's current research efforts are in Rhetoric and Cultural Studies with particular interest in media and poetry.

E. ELLEN BARKER is an Assistant Professor of English and Associate Chair of the Humanities Department at Dekalb College in Clarkston, Georgia. An ABD at Georgia State University, Prof. Barker is interested in the drama of Tennessee Williams.

MARGARET D. BAUER is an Assistant Professor of English at East Carolina University. A genuine comparatist, Prof. Bauer is deeply interested in intertextual reading of literature. Her book manuscript on Ellen Gilchrist is currently under reconsideration for publication by a university press.

MARC—A CHRISTOPHE is with the English Department at Howard University.

JEFFREY L. COLEMAN is an Assistant Professor of English at St. Mary's College of Maryland. Former poetry editor of the Arizona State University *Hayden's Ferry Review*, Coleman has published poetry in *Blue Mesa Review*. His research interest is the poetry of the Civil Rights Movement.

CATHERINE A. COLTON is a candidate for a Ph.D. in English at the University of Illinois at Chicago. Her current research efforts include feminist rhetoric and literacies as they are articulated in feminist reading and consciousness-raising sessions.

DAVID COWART is Professor and the Director of Graduate Studies in English at the University of South Carolina. He is the author of numerous essays and books, including, *Literary Symbiosis: The Reconfigured Text in Twentieth-Century Writing*; *History and the Contemporary Novel*; *Arches and Light: The Fiction of John Gardner*; and *Thomas Pynchon: The Art of Illusion*.

IKENNA DIEKE is an Associate Professor of Africana Studies at the University of Arizona. He is the author of *The Primordial Image: African, Afro-American, and Caribbean Mythopoetic Text*. He is presently completing two other books—*Inner Vision Incarnate: Self and Subjectivity in Alice Walker* and *African American Literature: Revision, Renewal, and the Politics of (Dis)Location*.

JUDY ELSLEY is an Associate Professor of English at Weber State University—Ogden, Utah.

ERNA KELLY is an Associate Professor of English at the University of Wisconsin—Eu Claire.

PRISCILLA LEDER is Professor of English at Southwest Texas State University at San Marcos.

FELIPE SMITH is an Associate Professor of English at Tulane University. He is the author of *American Body Politics: Race, Gender, and Black Literary Renaissance* (forthcoming from the University of Georgia Press).

PIA THIELMANN is an ABD in American Studies at the University of Kansas. Author of *Marge Piercy's Women: Visions Captured and Subdued*, Thielmann is completing her dissertation on the representation of interracial love in literature from the United States, Africa, and the Caribbean since WWII.

PRISCILLA L. WALTON teaches at the University of Lethbridge in Alberta, Canada. She is the author of numerous articles in journals such as the *North Dakota Quarterly* and *Comparative Literature in Canada*.

RUTH D. WESTON is an assistant poetry editor of *Nimrod International Journal*, which is published at the University of Tulsa.

ISBN 0-313-30012-7

90000>

EAN

9 780313 300127

HARDCOVER BAR CODE